Responsible Leadership

Since Enron, Worldcom and other high-profile cases of management and leadership misconduct, those involved in business leadership have become increasingly aware that one of the core challenges, if not *the* challenge, in business today is leading responsibly and with integrity. But what exactly is responsible leadership in an era of globalization? What makes a responsible leader? And how can responsible leadership be developed?

Responsible Leadership identifies the crucial dimensions of responsible leadership in business. The chapters focus on the capabilities, virtues and competences that individuals need to lead people and organizations in global, multicultural and complex business environments, and considers innovative initiatives and ways to further responsible leadership.

This exciting new text provides the reader with ideas, concepts and cases on responsible leadership. It is an essential purchase for all business students, academics and professionals concerned with leadership in 21st century business.

Thomas Maak is Research Director at the Institute for Business Ethics and Senior Lecturer in Corporate Responsibility at the University of St Gallen, Switzerland. His research and teaching focuses on business ethics, corporate citizenship, integrity management and responsible leadership.

Nicola M. Pless is Research Director at the Center for Public Leadership and Senior Lecturer in Responsible Leadership at the University of St Gallen, Switzerland. Her research, writing and teaching focuses on global leadership and talent development, diversity management and corporate social responsibility.

Dr Maak and Dr Pless are Visiting Senior Research Fellows at INSEAD, France, where they co-direct a research stream on Developing Responsible Leaders for Sustainable Business in the PwC-INSEAD initiative on high-performing organizations.

Responsible Leadership

Edited by
Thomas Maak and Nicola M. Pless

For Chuck,
a reflective, caring and responsible
Ulysses participant and partner
with our best wishes. We look
forward to our continuing
dialogue on responsible leadership!
Thomas & Nicola

Routledge
Taylor & Francis Group
LONDON AND NEW YORK

First published 2006
by Routledge
2 Park Square, Milton Park, Abingdon, Oxon OX14 4RN

Simultaneously published in the USA and Canada
by Routledge
270 Madison Ave, New York NY 10016

Routledge is an imprint of the Taylor & Francis Group

Typeset in Sabon
by Book Now Ltd
Printed and bound in Great Britain
by TJ International Ltd, Padstow, Cornwall

British Library Cataloguing in Publication Data
A catalogue record for this book is available from the British Library

Library of Congress Cataloging in Publication Data
A catalog record for this book has been requested

ISBN10: 0–415–35580–X (hbk)
ISBN10: 0–415–35581–8 (pbk)

ISBN13: 9–78–0–415–35580–3 (hbk)
ISBN13: 9–78–0–415–35581–0 (pbk)

Contents

List of illustrations		vii
Notes on contributors		x
Preface and acknowledgements		xvii
List of abbreviations		xix

1 Introduction: the quest for responsible leadership in business   1
   THOMAS MAAK AND NICOLA M. PLESS

PART I
What is responsible leadership?   15

2 Ethics: the heart of leadership   17
   JOANNE B. CIULLA

3 Responsible leadership: a relational approach   33
   THOMAS MAAK AND NICOLA M. PLESS

4 A compass for decision making   54
   LYNN SHARP PAINE

5 Spirituality as the basis of responsible leaders and
   responsible companies   68
   PETER PRUZAN AND WILLIAM C. MILLER

PART II
What makes a responsible leader?   93

6 Integrity, responsible leaders and accountability   95
   GEORGE G. BRENKERT

7 Leadership, character and virtues from an
   Aristotelian viewpoint   108
   ALEJO JOSÉ G. SISON

8   Leading responsibly across cultures   122
    SONJA A. SACKMANN

9   Towards responsible leadership through reconciling dilemmas   138
    TONG SCHRAA-LIU AND FONS TROMPENAARS

10 Leading in a world of competing values: a strategic
    perspective on corporate social responsibility   155
    DANIEL DIERMEIER

11 Responsible leadership at ABN AMRO Real: the case
    of Fabio Barbosa   170
    ERIK VAN DE LOO

PART III
How to develop responsible leadership in business?   **183**

12 Principle-based leadership: lessons from the
    Caux Round Table   185
    STEPHEN B. YOUNG

13 Leadership through social purpose partnering   202
    JAMES E. AUSTIN

14 Towards developing responsible global leaders: the Ulysses
    experience   213
    NICOLA M. PLESS AND RALF SCHNEIDER

15 Developing leaders for sustainable business   227
    MARK WADE

    Index   245

Illustrations

Figures

3.1 Core dimensions of responsible leadership   35
3.2 Values circles   38
4.1 The decision making compass   62
4.2 The zone of acceptability   65
7.1 The dynamics of virtue   116
8.1 A dynamic model of leading responsibly   126
8.2 A dynamic model of leading responsibly across cultures   129
9.1 Four basic organizational perspectives   143
9.2 Society versus internal goals dilemma   144
9.3 The long-term (LT) organizational and short-term (ST)
     shareholder dilemma   145
9.4 Sequential wealth creation   146
9.5 The shareholder versus society dilemma   147
10.1 Growth of corporate citizenship reports   156
10.2 Market segmentation and competitive advantage   159
10.3 Perception drivers   161
10.4 Reputation and the media   162
10.5 Strategy analysis framework   164
13.1 The collaboration continuum   204
15.1 The sustainable development learning framework   234
15.2 Looking through the sustainable development lens   235
15.3 Shell's commitment to contributing to sustainable
     development   236
15.4 Sustainable development makes good business sense   236

Tables

7.1 The means available to the Aristotelian rhetorician-leader   118
12.1 A cross-reference matrix: Caux Round Table principles and
     different religions   193
12.2 Examples of *concern for others* in different religious
     traditions   195

Foreword

Samuel A. DiPiazza Jr.
CEO, PricewaterhouseCoopers

The challenges that today's business leaders face are quite similar, regardless of the industry or profession in which they operate: delivering services and products of highest quality, creating and preserving value – and values – for multiple stakeholders, building and maintaining sustainable relationships, caring for the environment and for communities, and sustaining productive futures for the generations who follow. In short, our obligation as business leaders is to "leave it better than we found it".

Most businesses today operate in a global arena and must deliver on their commitments to a very diverse group of stakeholders – both internally and externally. We have witnessed many corporate responsibility initiatives in recent years, aimed at regaining the public trust that has been undermined or lost in the wake of scandals. All are important, whether they focus on Corporate Social Responsibility (CSR), governance, supply-chain integrity or sustainability. However, none of these will succeed if they are not embedded within the conceptual and practical foundation of responsible leadership that integrates people, planet, profit and principles. Corporate responsibility is first and foremost a challenge of responsible leadership.

But what is responsible leadership? What makes a responsible leader? And, how can it be developed? We at PricewaterhouseCoopers have a variety of leadership development programs and initiatives and you will read about one of them, Ulysses, in this book. Ulysses creates multicultural teams of partners and sends them to developing countries to work with NGO's, UN agencies and social entrepreneurs on social and environmental challenges. You will learn how this approach has impacted our partners and the world in which we live.

You will also learn about other approaches and answers in this much needed book on responsible leadership. And, you will find inspiring thoughts on how to cope with today's – and tomorrow's – leadership challenges: how to make responsible decisions, how to lead across cultures and reconcile dilemmas, how to put ethics at the heart of your leadership to become an authentic and trusted leader. We learn that responsible leadership is not about the grandiosity of a visionary leader but about his or her virtues and actions, based on humility and integrity; that we as leaders have to take all our relationships seriously and that leadership has many shapes and forms. Ultimately, however, it needs to rest on a firm values base. It is time to actively and passionately embrace ethics as a central component of leadership.

This book has been put together and edited by our "Ulysses" research team Nicola Pless and Thomas Maak from INSEAD & St. Gallen. It is a remarkable first step towards developing a theory for next generation leadership – leadership that is ethically sound, holistic in focusing on all stakeholders and sustainable – by inspiring people to join current and future leaders to build sustainable businesses that make this world a better place for many generations to come.

Contributors

James E. Austin holds the Snider Chair of Business Administration at the Harvard Business School, which is the third chaired professorship he has held at HBS where he has been on the faculty since 1972. He was the Co-Founder and Chairman of the HBS Social Enterprise Initiative. His doctorate and MBA degrees with distinction are from Harvard. His BBA with High Distinction is from the University of Michigan. He has authored and edited 16 books, including the award winning *The Collaboration Challenge: how nonprofits and businesses succeed through strategic alliances*. He is recognized internationally as an expert on cross-sector collaborations and has published dozens of articles and hundreds of case studies. He has been an adviser to corporations, non-profit organizations and governments throughout the world, including serving as a Special Adviser to the White House. He is also one of the founding leaders of the Social Enterprise Knowledge Network (SEKN) and co-author of *Social Partnering in Latin America* (Harvard University Press 2004).

George G. Brenkert is Professor of Business Ethics at the McDonough School of Business, at Georgetown University. He is Editor-in-Chief of *Business Ethics Quarterly* and a member of the Executive Committees of the Society for Business Ethics and the Association for Practical and Professional Ethics. He received his doctorate from the University of Michigan. He has published a book on *Political Freedom* (Routledge), as well as one on *Corporate Integrity and Accountability* (Sage) which draws on the papers from the Transatlantic Business Ethics Conference held at Georgetown University. In addition, he has published numerous articles in such journals as *Public Affairs Quarterly*, *Philosophy & Public Affairs*, *Public Policy & Marketing*, *Business Ethics Quarterly*, *Journal of Business Ethics* and *Business & Professional Ethics Journal*. He is currently working on a book on marketing ethics (Blackwell).

Joanne B. Ciulla is Professor and Coston Family Chair in Leadership and Ethics at the Jepson School of Leadership Studies, University of Richmond, USA, where she is one of the founding faculty members of the school. Ciulla has also held the UNESCO Chair in Leadership Studies at the United Nations International Leadership Academy and academic appointments at La Salle

University, the Harvard Business School and The Wharton School. She has a BA, MA and PhD in philosophy. She writes, lectures and consults on leadership ethics, business ethics and the philosophy of work. Her books include *The Ethics of Leadership*; *Ethics, The Heart of Leadership*; and *The Working Life: the promise and betrayal of modern work*. She recently co-authored a textbook entitled *Honest Work: a business ethics reader* and co-edited a collection called, *The Quest for Ethical Leaders: essays in leadership ethics*. Ciulla is on the editorial boards of *The Encyclopedia of Leadership Studies*, *The Leadership Quarterly*, *The Business Ethics Quarterly and Leadership*.

Daniel Diermeier is the IBM Distinguished Professor of Regulation and Competitive Practice and a Professor of Managerial Economics and Decision Sciences at the Kellogg Graduate School of Management and of Political Science at the Weinberg College of Arts and Sciences. He is the founding director of the Center for Business, Government and Society at Kellogg and the founding co-director of the Northwestern Institute on Complex Systems (NICO). He also served as the acting director of Kellogg's Ford Motor Company Center for Global Citizenship from 2001 to 2002. His teaching and research focuses on integrated strategy, the interaction of business and politics, crisis leadership, reputation management and strategic aspects of corporate social responsibility. He has received numerous teaching awards including the coveted L.G. Lavengood Professor of the Year Award (Kellogg 2001). Daniel Diermeier is the founder and managing partner of Diermeier Consulting LLC, based in Evanston, Illinois, providing clients with analysis and strategy advice in crisis leadership, reputation management, stakeholder management, regulatory and political strategy. Recent clients include Abbott Laboratories, Baker & McKenzie, BP, the City of Chicago, CIBC, Exelon, the FBI, Household International, Intercontinental Exchange, Johnson & Johnson, People's Energy, Scottsdale Bariatrics and Shell. He is also President of Evolve24, LLC, based in Ellisville, Montana, a reputation and issue analytics company. In December 2004 Professor Diermeier was appointed to the Management Board of the FBI.

Thomas Maak is Research Director at the Institute for Business Ethics and Senior Lecturer in Corporate Responsibility at the University of St Gallen, Switzerland. In the summer semester of 2004 he acted as the interim Chair in Business Ethics. He holds a BS and MS in Business Administration from the University of Bayreuth and a PhD in Business Ethics *summa cum laude* from the University of St Gallen, where he received the Amiticia best dissertation award in 2000. As visiting faculty, he co-directs a research stream on *Developing Responsible Leaders for Sustainable Business* within the PwC-INSEAD initiative on high-performing organizations at INSEAD, France. He has held visiting positions at the School for International and Public Affairs at Columbia University, New York and Georgetown University's McDonough School of Business in Washington, DC. His research and teaching focuses on business ethics, corporate citizenship, integrity management and responsible leadership. He is a member of the Executive Committee of the European Business Ethics Network EBEN.

William C. Miller is an internationally recognized expert on values-driven innovation. As president of the Global Creativity Corporation since 1987, he has explored with clients – which have included over one hundred corporations in more than a dozen countries worldwide – how creativity, business and spirituality are all facets of the same jewel. Two of his four books have been rated among the top thirty business books of the year in the USA. He has been a Guest Faculty member at the Sri Sathya Sai Institute of Higher Learning (India) and the Stanford University Graduate School of Business (USA). Throughout his career, William has maintained his devotion to his most deeply-held spiritual values, continually finding ways to create work as worship. Together with his wife Debra, he lives in India and, as a co-founder of the Global Dharma Center, now dedicates his work to the emerging practice of spiritual-based leadership.

Lynn Sharp Paine is a John G. McLean Professor at the Harvard Business School, where she is a member and former chair of the General Management unit and course head for the new required MBA course on Leadership and Corporate Accountability. Her research and writing, which include more than 150 case studies and numerous articles, focuses on issues of corporate ethics, governance and leadership. Lynn Paine's 2003 book *Value Shift: why companies must merge social and financial imperatives to achieve superior performance* (McGraw-Hill) was named a top ten business book by *Soundview Executive Book Summaries* and one of the year's best business books by *Library Journal*. She serves on the advisory board of Leadership Forum International (LFI) and the academic council of the Hills Program on Governance at the Center for Strategic & International Studies. She is also a member of The Conference Board's Commission on Public Trust and Private Enterprise. A member of Phi Beta Kappa and a *summa cum laude* graduate of Smith College, Lynn Paine holds a doctorate in moral philosophy from Oxford University and a law degree from Harvard Law School.

Nicola M. Pless is Research Director of Responsible Leadership at the Center for Public Leadership and Senior Lecturer in Organizational Behaviour at the University of St Gallen (HSG), in Switzerland. She is also a Visiting Senior Research Fellow at INSEAD, where she co-directs the research stream on *Developing Responsible Leaders for Sustainable Business* in the PwC-INSEAD research initiative on high-performing organizations. Her research, writing and teaching focuses on corporate social responsibility, global leadership and talent development and diversity management She also coaches executives and consults companies in leadership development and corporate social responsibility. Prior to joining the HSG and INSEAD faculty she worked for several years as an HR generalist, leadership development specialist and Vice President in the financial services industry. She holds a BS and an MS in Business

Administration from the University of Bayreuth, a PhD from the University of St Gallen and a Diploma in Clinical Organizational Psychology from INSEAD.

Peter Pruzan is Professor Emeritus at the Department of Management, Politics & Philosophy, Copenhagen Business School, Denmark. He is internationally known for his work on values-based leadership and corporate responsibility. He has degrees from Princeton (BSc), Harvard (MBA), Case- Western Reserve (PhD) and the University of Copenhagen (Dr Polit.). He was the president of a successful international business and has authored eleven books and over one hundred articles in international scientific journals. He has been an academic entrepreneur, initiating five national and two international institutes and associations focusing on corporate values and responsibility. His research goal is to integrate perspectives from management, philosophy and spirituality to develop values-based approaches to leadership and ethics. Together with his wife Kirsten, he lives in Denmark and spends several months each year in India, where he is a guest professor at leading Indian business schools.

Sonja A. Sackmann is Dean of the School of Management, Economics and Organization Science at the University Bw Munich, Germany. There she is also Director of the Institute of Human Resources & Organization Studies and Professor of Organizational Behaviour in the Department of Economics, Management and Organization Science. She conducts research, teaches and consults in the areas of leadership, culture, personal-, team and organizational development and change on an inter- and multinational basis. She has published several books and numerous articles on these topics. She received her BS and MS in Psychology from the Karl-Rupprecht University, Heidelberg and her PhD in Management from the Graduate School of Management, UCLA. She has taught at the Graduate Schools of Management at UCLA, USA, the Universities of St Gallen, Switzerland; Constance and EBS European Business School, Germany; Vienna, Austria and Jiao Tong University, Shanghai, China. Sonja Sackmann has held positions as Head of Research and Development, Partner and Managing Partner at the MZSG Management Zentrum St Gallen, Switzerland where she was responsible for consulting projects as well as developing and delivering innovative management development programmes and workshops for managers and executives of international, multinational and global companies such as BMW, Coca-Cola, DaimlerChrysler, Ford, Lufthansa and Volkswagen as well as for governmental organizations. Furthermore, she is active in several committees including the German Ministry for Education and Research (BMBF), the Bertelsmann Foundation and she is member of several organizations such as the World Corporate Ethics' Council, the Academy of Management, the European Academy of Management and the European Group of Organization Studies.

Ralf Schneider currently leads the PricewaterhouseCoopers (PwC) Eurofirm School of Business and is Chief Learning Officer for PwC within the Eurofirm. He is also Head of Global Talent Management. Prior to that he held different leadership positions within PwC at European and Global level including that of Chief Knowledge Officer, Head of Strategic Human Resource Management and in Human Resource Development. Before joining PwC, Ralf Schneider was Managing Director of an independent German training and HRD consultancy, specializing in international management development with a network in Europe, USA and Asia, where he has worked extensively. His work as a consultant and Senior Human Capital Executive has focused on the areas of human capital strategy, leadership development, organizational learning and change, corporate social responsibility, cultural diversity and knowledge management.

Tong Schraa-Liu obtained her Law degree in Shanghai, China and earned a second degree in Business Economics and an MBA in the Netherlands. She has extensive experience in cross-border alliances management and M&A integration, cross-cultural organizational development and global leadership development. At Trompenaars Hampden-Turner, she consults on cross-border alliances management, joint ventures, mergers and acquisition integrations and cross-cultural management. She has advised, among others, ABN-AMRO Bank, Dow Chemicals, DSM, General Motors, IBM, Masterfoods, PepsiCo and Shell. In addition, Tong has helped clients such as Boeing, ABB, PwC and Bombardier in their transcultural leadership development programmes. Since the early 1990s, Tong has run her own consultancy firm, advising European multinationals on their business expansion and M&A activities in China, Taiwan, South Korea and Japan, and Chinese organizations in establishing business cooperations with European counterparts. Tong is a faculty member of Duke Corporate Education/LSE and the Fuqua Business School, USA, teaching Global Leadership Development. She also teaches Cross-cultural Management at Nyenrode University – the Netherlands Business School and at the Amsterdam School of Business.

Alejo José G. Sison, PhD, is the Rafael Escolá Chair of Professional Ethics at the School of Engineering (TECNUN) of the University of Navarre. He is also the Academic Director of the Institute for Enterprise and Humanism. Previously, he worked at IESE (Barcelona) and at the University of Asia & the Pacific (Manila). In 1997, he was appointed Fulbright Senior Research Fellow and Visiting Scholar at Harvard University. Since then, he has received fellowships from the 21st Century Trust Foundation (London), the Academic Council on the United Nations System (Yale University), the American Society of International Law (Washington, DC) and the Salzburg Seminar. His research deals with the issues at the juncture of Ethics with Economics and Politics. His latest book is on *The Moral Capital of Leaders: why virtue matters* (Edward Elgar, 2003). He is currently working on a volume that brings Aristotle's ideas in the Politics to bear on issues of corporate governance.

Fons Trompenaars studied Economics in Amsterdam and later earned a PhD from the Wharton School, University of Pennsylvania. He wrote his dissertation on differences in conceptions of organizational structure in various cultures. He experienced cultural differences first-hand at home, where he grew up speaking both French and Dutch, and then later at work, with the Royal Dutch Shell Group in nine countries. He joined the Royal Dutch Shell Group in 1981. From 1985, he worked in job classification and management development at the Shell Research Laboratories in Amsterdam. In 1989 Fons Trompenaars became Managing Director of the Centre for International Business Studies, a consulting and training organization for international management that changed its trade name to Trompenaars Hampden-Turner in 1998. He has worked as a consultant for such companies as Shell, BP, Philips, IBM, Heineken, Applied Materials, AMD, VNU, TRW, Mars, Motorola, General Motors, Dow Chemical, CSM, Telfort, Wolters Kluwer, Gerling NCM, Merrill Lynch, Johnson & Johnson, Pfizer, ABN AMRO, ING, PepsiCo and Honeywell. Among his books are *Riding the Waves of Culture, Understanding Cultural Diversity in Business* (1993), which has been translated into French, German, Dutch, Korean, Danish, Turkish, Chinese, Hungarian, Polish and Portuguese. He also co-authored *Managing People Across Cultures, Managing Changes Across Corporate Cultures and Marketing Across Cultures*. In 1991 Fons Trompenaars was awarded the International Professional Practice Area Research Award by the American Society for Training and Development (ASTD). He was named one of the top five management consultants in a leading business magazine in August 1999.

Erik van de Loo is partner and co-founder of Phyleon, a centre for leadership and change in The Hague, The Netherlands. Phyleon specializes in interrelated change processes on individual, group and organizational level. As an adjunct clinical professor of management at INSEAD (Fontainebleau), he is programme co-director for the International Diploma Programme in Consulting and Coaching for Change as well as for Coaching for Leadership. He studied clinical psychology at Radboud University Nijmegen, obtained a doctoral degree in social sciences at Leiden University (1987) and holds a masters degree in Work and Organization in Occupational Health at SIOO (1997). He has a private psychoanalytic practice and is a member of the International Society for Psychoanalytic Study of Organizations and co-founder and programme director of European Psychodynamic Organizational Consulting (EPOC), a two-year training programme to bridge the world of psychoanalysis and organizational consulting. He was involved in management development and consulting work with national and multinational corporations such as ExxonMobil, DuPont de Nemours, Shell, Novo Nordisk, Nokia, ABN AMRO, Interpolis, Standard Bank (South Africa), KPMG and The Cabinet Office (London). He published several books, chapters and scientific articles on topics such as a clinical approach to consultation, irrational aspects of safety in industry, the organization in the mind, organizational stress and leadership.

Mark Wade currently leads the Sustainable Development Learning activity at Shell International in London, UK, and is charged with bringing about a step change in sustainable development awareness, understanding and capacity among people at Shell. He joined Shell in 1979 as a research biochemist in its Chemicals business. Since then he has served in a variety of posts, including Technical Graduate Recruitment manager for Shell International and Head of External Affairs for Shell Chemicals. In 1997 he moved to the Corporate Centre of Shell International as a founder member of the Sustainable Development Group. Mark relinquished his position as Head of Sustainable Development Policy, Strategy and Reporting early 2003 on moving to Shell Learning's Leadership Development group. He is Shell's Liaison Delegate to the World Business Council for Sustainable Development and Chairman of the Business Network of the European Academy of Business in Society. He is a regular contributor to conferences, seminars and publications on sustainable development.

Stephen B. Young is currently Global Executive Director of the Caux Round Table, an international network of senior business leaders seeking to promote corporate social responsibility and business ethics as an integral part of globalization. He is also President of his own firm, Winthrop Consulting, and founded the Minnesota Public Policy Forum. He has practised law for firms in New York City, St Paul and Minneapolis. Young was educated at the International School Bangkok, Harvard College and Harvard Law School and is a former Dean of the Hamline University School of Law and an Assistant Dean at Harvard Law School. Young has also taught at the University of Minnesota and Minnesota State University – Mankato. He has published articles on Chinese jurisprudence, the culture and politics of Vietnam and Thailand, legal education, law firm management, Native American law, the history of negligence, the law of war. He has written numerous opinion articles for the Pioneer Press and the Minnesota Journal on Law and Politics and has been published in the *Wall Street Journal*, the *New York Times*, the *Washington Post* and the *Minneapolis StarTribune*. He has served on the boards of the Citizens League, Resources for Child Caring, Vietnam's Women Memorial, Vietnam Social Service, Minnesota Sons of the Revolution and as Chair of United Arts in St Paul and the Minnesota Museum of Art. He is the founding board chair of the Center of the American Experiment. Currently, he serves on the board of Ready 4 K, a non-profit dedicated to better outcomes for families and young children in Minnesota.

Preface and acknowledgements

We first developed the idea to edit a book on responsible leadership in 2002 because we simply had trouble finding one. As we started to further engage in the topic that had interested us since the 1990s and talked to friends and colleagues about it, we received not only a lot of encouragement for the endeavour to map part of the territory ourselves, but also active support and participation from a group of distinguished academics and practitioners in the field of business and leadership ethics, decision sciences, multicultural management, non-profit management and leadership development. The result is a collection of chapters by wonderful colleagues, which we as editors have carefully tried to link together in this book.

As said before, the history of this book is linked to a number of people. We are indebted to Henri-Claude de Bettignies for his strong encouragement from the very beginning and to Karl Ruoss for his uncompromising support and guidance through rough times. We are very grateful to Joanne Ciulla for both her pioneering work on leadership and ethics and her strong support for this book project, and of course for the chapter she contributed. Heidi Hoivik was there when we needed her. Our dear friend Ed Lecomte would probably insist that he didn't contribute anything, but we know better.

The research that enabled this book would not have been possible without the generous support of several committed individuals – and leaders – in the PwC-INSEAD Initiative on High-Performing Organizations: Ralf Schneider, our mentor and friend; Paul Bachelor, Rich Baird and Frank Brown, as reflective practitioners and dialogue partners who saw the immediate relevance of this topic for the business world; as well as Jean-François Manzoni, who helped us by discussing and challenging our research approach, and Landis Gabel, who welcomed us warmly into the INSEAD community. As this book is part of an ongoing journey we look forward to working with them in the future. We are grateful to the *Ulysses family* – Ralf, Elena, Alina, Lisa, Hans Jürgen and Hermann – for creating a stimulating *holding environment*.

For more than insightful conversations we feel indebted to Anita Roddick, Fredy Lienhard, Manfred Kets de Vries, Barbara Kellerman, Ronald Heifetz and Bill George as well as Heike Bruch, Thomas Dyllick, Peter Gomez, Sascha Spoun, Johannes Rüegg-Stürm, Winfried Ruigrok, Günter Müller-Stewens, Chris Steyaert and Peter Ulrich.

It has been a pleasure to work with the ever optimistic editorial team at Routledge. Francesca Heslop, our editor, has been a source of support and shown enthusiastic commitment to the book project from the very beginning. Her assistant Emma Joyes was there when we needed her. The editing would have been impossible without the tireless efforts of our editorial assistant Lynette Tan. Last but not least we want to thank all the contributors of this volume who took time out of their busy schedules to prepare a chapter on what we hope will trigger your imagination as a reader and will eventually become a focus of leadership research, lifting the *veil of ignorance* of the norms and values on which all leadership is based.

Finally, we would like to thank our families for their uncompromising support and love. We dedicate this book to them – and to the responsible leaders who make this world a better place.

Abbreviations

AAFRC	American Association of Fundraising Counsel
AR	action research
ASEAN	Association of South East Asian Nations
BUPA	British United Provident Association
CEO	chief executive officer
CI	Conservation International
CPI	Cambridge Programme for Industry
CRT	Caux Round Table
CSR	corporate social responsibility
DVD	digital video disk
EABIS	European Academy of Business in Society
EFTA	European Free Trade Association
FDA	Federal Drug Administration
FDI	foreign direct investment
e.g.	exempli gratia, for example
et al.	et alii, and others
GP	Georgia-Pacific
HIV/AIDS	Human Immunodeficiency Virus/Acquired Immune Deficiency Syndrome
HQ	headquarters
HR	human resources
HSE	health, safety and environment
HTTP	hypertext transfer protocol
ibid.	ibidem, in the same place
i.e.	id est, that is
ILO	International Labor Organization
IMD	International Institute of Management Development
IMF	International Monetary Fund
IQ	intelligence quotient
J&J	Johnson & Johnson
Jr	junior
LT	long-term

MBA	Master of Business Administration
MPAA	Motion Picture Association of America
MPV	moral point of view
NAFTA	North American Free-Trade Area
NE	*Nicomachean Ethics*
NGO	non-governmental organization
NPV	net present value
OECD	Organization for Economic Cooperation and Development
PBW	Project Better World
PwC	PricewaterhouseCoopers
RAN	Rainforest Action Network
Rh	*Rhetoric*
SBU	strategic business unit
SD	sustainable development
SEKN	Social Enterprise Knowledge Network
SoL	Society for Organizational Learning
ST	short-term
TIAA-CREF	Teachers Insurance and Anuity Association – College Retirement Equities Fund
TNC	The Nature Conservancy
WBCSD	World Business Council for Sustainable Development
WTO	World Trade Organization
UK	United Kingdom
UNO	United Nations Organization
US	United States
VSO	Voluntary Service Overseas
WTO	World Trade Organization
WWW	World Wide Web

1 Introduction

The quest for responsible leadership in business

Thomas Maak and Nicola M. Pless

This book is about leadership and integrity in business. While most of us would probably consider one as inseparable from the other, the wave of corporate scandals in recent times suggests otherwise. Ever since Enron, WorldCom, Parmalat, and other high-profile cases of management failure and leadership misconduct, there has been a growing awareness that one of the core challenges, if not *the* challenge in business, is leading responsibly and with integrity. It is fair to say, then, that *responsible leadership* is one of the most pressing issues in the business world. However, it is most likely also one of the least understood. Given the hundreds and thousands of books and publications on leadership, this is a somewhat surprising fact.

As we look closer into possible causes for this discrepancy we find plausible explanations: one, there seems to be an implicit assumption that people who take on a leadership position have a heightened sense of responsibility, or will somehow act more responsibly once they are in a leadership position. Therefore, no explicit guidance is needed and not much thought must be given to the issue of leading with integrity. Two, leadership is far too often mistaken for *good management*, a leader being someone who motivates people to get things done efficiently. But that is management, not leadership. At best, leadership and management complement each other. At worst, we find only management but no leadership. Three, there is what Rost (1991) called the *industrial paradigm* in leadership research, imposing on researchers a leadership effectiveness focus – and a denial that leadership is a normative phenomenon. Leadership values might be important, but leadership research is supposed to be *value-free*, as if the ethics of leadership were something otherworldly. You ought to have it as a leader, but it is somehow a given, it comes with your upbringing and education, and therefore has no place in scientific research. As we browse through the myriad of publications on leadership we thus find a lot on good (as in effective) leadership, but next to nothing on *responsible* leadership.

The challenge, however, is not so much the lack of awareness but the need for normative transformation (Ghoshal 2005) to define what responsible leadership is. To begin with, responsible leadership is a specific frame of mind promoting a shift from a purely economistic, positivist and self-centred mindset to a frame of thinking that has all constituents and thus the common good in mind too. This normative transformation in leadership, the transition from one *attractor pattern* (Lorenz, in Morgan 1997) to another, is long overdue. More disturbing is the fact that we find almost as many definitions of leadership as we find authors, which has led Bennis and Nanus to the cynical observation:

> Never have so many labored so long to say so little. Multiple interpretations of leadership exist, each providing a sliver of insight but each remaining an incomplete and wholly inadequate explanation.
>
> (Bennis and Nanus 1997: 4)

Among those interpretations we find a continuous stream of *great man* theories, starting with Alexander the Great and Attila the Hun, both of whom are known for being effective leaders, neither of whom is known for being a particularly ethical leader. Of course, we also find the great moral leaders of the twentieth century: the Gandhis, the Kings and the Mandelas. The problem with concentrating on exceptional personalities, whether on bad or on good ones, is that we limit in a myopic way leadership and its capacity for influence and change to a small number of (mostly male) individuals who, in one way or another, by virtue of ability, destiny or time in history, became outstanding leaders.

A variation of these theories focuses on charisma. But the problem of charisma with respect to responsible leadership is that it has no guiding ethical value. We cannot pinpoint the emotional relationship between leader and followers that is constituted by charisma and derive guiding principles from it. Charisma, from a moral point of view, is a useless concept (Ciulla 2005). Besides, from a business perspective, 'if we select people principally for their charisma and their ability to drive up stock prices ... instead of their character, and we shower them with inordinate rewards, why should we be surprised when they turn out to lack integrity?' (George 2003: 5).

Other leadership theories have suggested that how leadership should be exercised depends on the situation. Some look at personal traits, some at the power structure or the exchange of goods and services, that is, the transactional side of leadership. And yet, even the most sophisticated theories fall short when it comes to explaining what a leader's and/or leadership responsibilities are, let alone considering the role of responsible leadership in a global stakeholder society with all its complexity in terms of values, interests and cultures.

What exactly is responsible leadership in such a complex environment? What makes a responsible leader? And what needs to be done to develop responsible leaders? Along the lines of these key questions, we intend to fill a void and initiate further discussion and research with this interdisciplinary collection of original articles. It was important to us to collect views on responsible leadership from a diverse group of experts to frame the topic from a broad perspective. Therefore, you find among our contributors philosophers, psychologists, psychoanalysts, business ethicists, economists and management and leadership scholars as well as practitioners like learning and development experts, consultants and executives, from Asia, Europe and North America. We are proud that nearly half of the contributions are authored or co-authored by women. This diverse group of distinguished leadership scholars and practitioners who share a profound interest in the moral dimension of leadership shed light on different aspects of one of today's most challenging tasks: leading responsibly and building a respected business *in* society. By this, we may better understand what business leaders should – and should *not* – do.

While leaders need certain capabilities and should have good character in order to be(come) responsible leaders, none are born that way. Nor is responsible leadership limited to individual traits. As we will see in what lies ahead, it is rather a balance of leaders' character, the leader's relationship with people and followers, the roles and tasks he or she fulfils and sound processes. Responsible leadership depends not only on principled individuals and their education and training, but also on a 'holding environment' (Kets de Vries 1999: xvii) – an organizational and environmental context where responsible leaders can flourish. Whatever it is, responsible leadership has to be authentic, as Bill George, former CEO of Medtronic, points out:

> We need ... people of the highest integrity, committed to building enduring organizations. We need leaders who have a deep sense of purpose and are true to their core values. We need leaders who have the courage ... to meet the needs of all their stakeholders, and who recognize the importance of their service to society.
>
> (George 2003: 5)

Obviously, leadership in a stakeholder society has to be looked at differently and reach beyond traditional leader–follower concepts to meet the needs of multiple stakeholders with multiple interests based on different, often conflicting values. There is no leadership without followership. But how will different stakeholders follow the lead? Leaders can lavish as much charisma on external stakeholders as they like – few, if any, will follow if they do not care about their values and wishes. Fortunately, leaders cannot force their will on others either, not even on employees, as leadership in a democratic society needs legitimation and cannot be built solely on status, pure seniority and power, let alone coercion. If business leaders behave in a selfish way, their actions will be considered illegitimate, too. Leaders therefore face multiple challenges and leadership needs legitimation, which in turn requires a morally sound values base. It is, for the most part, 'a complex moral relationship between people, based on trust, obligation, commitment, emotion, and a shared vision of the good' (Ciulla 1998: xv).

In what follows, we intend to shed light on this complexity and hopefully set the stage for further inquiry and research, both theoretical and practical, on what is one of the most challenging, intriguing and least researched areas of leadership and business ethics. In line with the above-mentioned key questions, there will be three main parts to this book. We start in the first part of the book with reflections on the notion of responsible leadership. The key question here is: *What is responsible leadership?* It aims to identify the crucial dimensions of responsible leadership in business, thus laying the groundwork for a better understanding of its roots, requirements and the relationships it is built on. In the second part of the book we ask the question: *What makes a responsible leader?* The contributions here focus on the capabilities, virtues and competences that individuals need to lead people and businesses in global, multicultural and complex business environments. Finally, the third part of the book seeks to illuminate the question of *how to develop responsible leadership in business*. In this part we look at innovative initiatives and ways to further responsible leadership through the means of transformative change via professional networks, cross-sector partnerships and learning and development programmes.

Part I: What is responsible leadership?

Joanne Ciulla, building on her pioneering work on ethical leadership, introduces us to the special character of leadership, emphasizing that ethics lies at the very heart of leadership. As morality magnified, the morality of a leader ripples through organizations, communities and societies. We know that leaders have the potential to inflict great harm or bestow great benefits on their constituents. When a leader errs many people suffer. Ciulla emphasizes that leadership is a specific type of human relationship and ethics about the way that we treat each other in various relationships. Her chapter begins with a critical look at the leadership literature, then goes on to examine some key issues in leadership ethics. These include the relationship between ethics and effectiveness, altruism and self-interest and the moral standards of leaders. The last part looks at two normative theories of leadership and suggests some directions for leadership ethics. As mentioned in the beginning, a hallmark of traditional leadership research is that it fails to reflect on its own normative side, let alone produce an ethic that leaders can refer to. There are, however, two significant exceptions: James MacGregor Burns' theory of *transforming leadership* (1978, 2003) and Robert Greenleaf's theory of *servant leadership* (1977/2002). Ciulla introduces both these explicitly normative theories and reflects on the question of to what extent these concepts may serve current and future leaders as a guiding force. She reminds us in her concluding remarks that we will find answers to the question of what *good* leadership is only if we first find ways to apply leadership ethics as critical theory to guide us. Responsible leadership needs a frame for reflection and introspection and a values base to build on. It is therefore unthinkable without leadership ethics.

Thomas Maak and *Nicola Pless* pick up on the importance of relationships and lay out a relational approach towards responsible leadership in business. They do so first by looking at some of today's key challenges for leaders and discuss a diversity challenge, an ethics challenge, as well as a trust, values and stakeholder challenge. Faced with these challenges, leadership is a demanding and complex task as leaders have to balance multiple and thus often conflicting values in a creative and ethically sound way. They define responsible leadership as the art of building and sustaining morally sound relationships with all relevant stakeholders of an organization. They then discuss the concept of the leader as a moral person, underscoring that character and virtues are an important element but that a leader also needs *ethical intelligence* by which they mean moral awareness, reflection skills, critical thinking and moral imagination. In the last part of the chapter they discuss the roles and responsibilities of a responsible leader and propose that he or she is at times servant to others, steward and therefore custodian of values and resources, architect of sound processes and shared systems of meaning, responsible change agent, coach to nurture and support others and, finally, storyteller who uses the means of storytelling to lead responsibly.

Lynn Sharp Paine then argues in her chapter that one of the key tasks of a responsible leader is to reconcile social and financial values in a truly integrative manner, thus shifting value-creation in an organization to a higher level of performance. Her model of *centre-driven leadership* calls for leadership to target its efforts on the area where ethics and economics meet each other. Lynn Paine introduces her *4P concept* as a framework for centre-driven leadership: *purpose, principles, people* and *power* are not only the cornerstones to guide leaders in shaping an organization's moral personality. They also serve them as a metaphorical compass for ethically sound decision making. Among the key questions leaders should therefore ask themselves are: Will this action serve a worthwhile purpose? Is this action consistent with relevant principles? Does this action respect the legitimate claims of the people likely to be affected? And do we have the power to take this action? Without a framework like Paine's decision making compass to inject the moral point of view into their deliberations, decision makers are vulnerable to the blind spots and biases inherent in many commonly used frameworks such as competitive analysis or cost–benefit analysis. Paine stresses that both are powerful aids, but they do not ask leaders to think about stakeholder impact, social contribution or conformity with legal and ethical norms. What's needed is thus an analytical model that takes the claims of others seriously in their own right and that reveals, rather than obscures, the moral texture of the relationships within which every company must operate.

Peter Pruzan and *William Miller* conclude the first part of the book by discussing spirituality as the basis for responsible leadership – and responsible companies. They have conducted in-depth interviews with corporate leaders around the world and demonstrate that *spiritual-based leadership* can be a powerful foundation for responsible leadership in business. It is typical of the managerial profession to emphasize measurable results and to operationalize these terms. This attitude has become ingrained in corporations' vocabulary, policies, stakeholder communications and reporting systems. However, something important is missing in this rush towards pragmatism by corporate leaders: a sincere, soul-searching inquiry into what they really mean when they speak of responsibility at the individual and organizational level. Pruzan and Miller's essay raises and responds to fundamental questions about the nature of responsibility and how explicit consideration of responsibility is vital for the well-being and success of leaders and their organizations. In particular, they explore four questions: What is responsibility? Can organizations be responsible? Why be responsible? And, what obstacles are there to being responsible? These inquiries pave the way for the thesis that true responsibility, both for leaders and their organizations, is grounded in a perspective that transcends the limitations of economic rationality. The interviews that Pruzan and Miller have conducted with leaders from Europe, the USA and Asia demonstrate that spirituality, however individual leaders define and understand it, can provide a powerful foundation for individual and organizational identity, responsibility and success. When leaders and their organizations operate from a spiritual-based perspective, they naturally behave responsibly on behalf of themselves, their communities, society, the environment and all of creation.

Part II: What makes a responsible leader?

The contributions in the second part of the book focus on the capabilities, virtues and competences that individuals need to lead people from different backgrounds, with different interests, and most likely faced with conflicting values, in a global stakeholder society. Among these are moral awareness, integrity, reflection and reasoning skills, ethical decision making skills, interpersonal and cross-cultural skills, as well as introspection and a sense of community. In the first chapter of this section, *George Brenkert* explores the notion of integrity. Such thorough investigation is crucial for our understanding of responsible leadership because many claims are made for and on behalf of integrity, and much of this is somehow over-blown and confused, as Brenkert points out. He discusses what is important about integrity by drawing our attention to four prominent features, the axiological, the temporal, the motivational and the social dimension of integrity. He then elaborates on the relationship between integrity and responsible leadership, and why the two exist in tension rather than in a harmonious relation. Brenkert reminds us that a person of integrity must make moral judgements of coherence, consistency and continuity with respect to the basic values he or she has. However, as we do not always know what our values and principles require we need to engage others. This social side of integrity is key as leadership integrity is attributed only if it stands the test of external evaluation. Thus, accountability is one of the important measures whereby a responsible leader may seek to ensure his or her integrity. Brenkert concludes his chapter by discussing some implications of such an understanding of integrity for businesses and educational institutions.

Alejo Sison discusses leadership, character and virtues from an Aristotelian viewpoint. We learn from Aristotle that virtue is that specific human excellence found in a person's actions, habits and character. Each of these levels of functioning has its own criteria of moral goodness, and a feedback loop or reinforcement mechanism, usually called *learning* or *habituation*, exists among them. Of special significance for a leader is the use of rhetoric means. Sison stresses that leadership is fundamentally the art of persuasion. Aristotle teaches that the means available to the speaker or potential leader are his speech or arguments (*logos*), the emotional disposition of his listeners (*pathos*), and the character (*ethos*) that he projects. The speaker's character, as in the case of the leader, is the controlling factor; and he would be convincing only to the extent that he displays practical wisdom (*phronesis*), good will (*eunoia*), and virtue (*arete*). Aristotle thus demands that technical competence in crafting speeches and capturing an audience's benevolence be inseparable from moral excellence. Aristotle reminds us that a true leader has to be authentic. Not only should his values match his words, but also his actions. Thus, leading with integrity requires that a leader's moral dispositions and intentions are matched by her words and actions.

Sonja Sackmann explores in the following chapter the issue of leading responsibly across cultures. In a global stakeholder society this endeavour is among the key challenges and requires not only an appropriate mindset but also certain leadership skills. Sackmann begins her chapter by discussing the concept of responsibility in leadership on the basis of different leadership models and concepts related to moral/ethical behaviour. She then proposes and discusses a dynamic model of leading responsibly, taking into account the cultural context that may influence interactions and leadership across cultures. The cultural context is discussed from a multiple cultures perspective that according to Sackmann is appropriate for today's and tomorrow's workplace realities. She stresses that leaders need to be aware of their own cultural identity (and the related biases with respect to what is considered responsible), and that they need to be aware of the identities of their interaction partners and the fact that many of them will have multiple cultural identities, thereby shifting expectations depending on the issues at stake. Responsible leaders are sensitive to cultural specifics, have good diagnostic skills as well as social skills, they are empathetic and tackle dilemmas (which occur frequently) openly and constructively. The latter topic is the focal point of the next chapter.

Tong Schraa-Liu and *Fons Trompenaars* argue in their chapter that in an increasingly interconnected global arena, responsible leadership is concerned with constantly reconciling and aligning the demands, needs, interest, values and opposites resulting from the intrinsic responsibility of leaders towards employees, customers, suppliers, communities, shareholders, NGOs, the environment and society at large. They contend that the propensity to reconcile these dilemmas is the most discriminating competence that differentiates successful from less successful leaders today. Leaders and their organizations improve and prosper not by choosing one end over the other, but by reconciling the opposites at both ends and achieving one value *through* its opposite. What sounds like a paradoxical approach towards leadership is according to Schraa-Liu and Trompenaars leadership reality in the global arena. Responsible global leaders are those who feel a responsibility towards the bottom-line and their shareholders, while at the same time, through reconciliation also take responsibility for integrating a diverse workforce, multicultural customers and suppliers, local and global communities, as well as all other relevant stakeholders. Responsible leaders recognize, respect and reconcile multiple values and demands, ultimately sustaining a successful business. Reconciling *outer* dilemmas starts, however, with the *inner* world of leaders, as Schraa-Liu and Trompenaars point out. Therefore, responsible leadership starts by leading from within, reconciling the leader's inner journey with her outer action, heart with mind, feeling with reason, embodying the true responsibility in one's own life before one is able to fulfil the responsibility with compassion towards the external stakeholders and society at large.

Daniel Diermeier tackles the challenge of leading in a world of competing values from a *strategic* perspective. He argues for a different look at CSR – one that goes beyond Friedman's assertation that *the social responsibility of business is to increase its profits* or the literature on *doing well by doing good* – and focuses on the leadership problem of what to do in an environment where companies are increasingly held accountable by standards other than shareholder value maximization. He points out that questions of whether managers like it or not and whether such demands are beneficial to society or not are largely beside the point: the multi-value environment is a fact – values are everywhere. Thus, firms and industry need to learn how to compete in an environment of moral values. Yet, existing scholarship has little to offer in this regard. He argues that both existing approaches, the normative and the empirical, miss the key problems that need to be addressed to provide guidance for leading responsibly in a world of competing values. Drawing on the empirical literature on value change as well as on modern competitive strategy, Diermeier stresses that corporate leadership needs a clear understanding of competitive positioning and reputation management. Applying a strategic orientation helps leaders to evaluate competing value-orientation of stakeholders and is therefore an essential step to responsible leadership.

Erik van de Loo explores responsible leadership from the angle of an individual leader – Fabio Barbosa, CEO of ABN AMRO Real in Brazil – who has managed to mobilize people and organizations along the path of corporate social responsibility. Based on observations and in-depth interviews, van de Loo applies a clinical approach to leadership (van de Loo 2000, Kets de Vries 2004), analyzing over the life of this particular leader the dynamic interplay between rational and non-rational, visible and non-visible, business and personal factors. Van de Loo presents his findings along the following questions: What is Fabio Barbosa's vision on banking and responsible leadership? How did he translate his vision into leadership strategies and behaviours in order to mobilize people and organization for corporate social responsibility? What are the origins of his vision and how has he himself developed as a leader? Finally, what are the lessons learned for developing responsible leadership in business? In answering these questions, van de Loo shows that firstly, an individual leader like Fabio Barbosa can indeed make a difference. Secondly, his impact is likely the result of a combination of factors: a configuration of values, competences and qualities which make him both quite unique and effective. He displays certain personal characteristics, such as persistence, discipline, respect, self-confidence, self-awareness as well as autonomy of thinking, which he combines with strong values and which he articulates and communicates as a leader. Thirdly, leadership qualities are not innate but developed by way of socialization and learning from role models over the span of a leader's life and career. Finally, although it may take a leader like Fabio Barbosa a long time to fully develop into the responsible person he is, the results are nonetheless rewarding, both for his followers as well as for himself.

Part III: How to develop responsible leadership in business

Finally, the third part of the book seeks to illuminate the question of *how to develop responsible leadership in business*. In this part we look at innovative initiatives and ways to further responsible leadership by means of transformative change through professional networks, cross-sector partnerships and learning and development programmes. These different approaches share the underlying idea that small but critical changes can create large effects (Morgan 1997), and that leaders as change agents can play an important role in this transformation. Leaders (need to) have the ability to reflect on the business and organizational context in which they are operating and to choose the points at which to intervene for social change. The texts of Young, Austin, Pless and Schneider, and Wade present examples of small-scale change initiatives in business that aim at triggering larger effects in business and society.

Stephen Young highlights the importance of leadership principles and presents key lessons from the *Caux Round Table*. The Caux Round Table (CRT) is an international network of senior business leaders working to promote moral capitalism and 'to facilitate change for the better in humanity's ablity to raise living standards, provide for social justice and realize the fullness of individual human dignity in all our days', as formulated by George J. Vojty, Chairman of the CRT. The approach of the network is based on four implicit assumptions: first and foremost, that business has a responsibility in society; secondly, that change needs committed and principled business leaders with, thirdly, an action orientation, and who, fourthly, lead by example. With respect to the responsibility in resolving socio-economic problems in the world members of the network maintain the standpoint that the business community should play an important role in improving economic and social conditions. They also believe that corporate responsibility arises from the actions of committed individuals. Therefore, the network develops recommendations from business leaders for business leaders. An example is the CRT *Principles for Business*, understood as a global standard against which business behaviour can be measured. In his chapter Young links these *Principles for Business* with the teachings in eleven spiritual and religious traditions (ranging from Christianity to Buddhism and African spiritual understandings), showing the universal applicability of the CRT *Principles for Business* in these traditions. The members of the CRT are also committed to act as living examples for principled business leadership. Based on nearly twenty years of experience with senior business leaders participating in the CRT network, Young derives five leadership lessons learnt: firstly, application of principles separates leadership from management (the *big picture*); secondly, principles must be implemented through management systems and benchmarks (the *little picture*); thirdly, leadership must address the interests and needs of people as well as their values and aspirations; fourthly, culture counts in defining how people will respond to principles; and fifthly, dysfunction in corporate cultures centres on the decision making of the most senior leaders and managers.

James Austin then tackles the question why and how business leaders and their companies are forging *social purpose partnerships*. With respect to the *why* question, he observes two motivation patterns for engaging in activities for social betterment – altruism and utilitarianism. From a practical point of view it seems that a values based commitment coupled with a benefit for the firm is more likely to produce a long-term and sustainable social engagement. One of the main drivers for companies to partner with institutions from other sectors (i.e. civic groups, governmental entities) is the realization that through partnering, one can bundle energy and realize synergies which allow to enhance performance and impact in the solution of many societal problems. Regarding the *how* question, Austin stresses that existing partnerships usually fall into the philanthropic, transactional or integrative relationship paradigm. On the basis of four case examples he shows that social engagement and strategic advantages do not necessarily contradict each other and that even an altruistic approach can ultimately lead to practical and strategic business advantages. However, he argues that an integrative approach towards collaboration can bring partners to a higher level of joint value creation and generate more sustainable value for partners as well as society. Creating such alliances comes with new challenges and places new demands on leaders. Austin understands cross-sector collaborations as a transformative force through which leaders can make a difference in the world. These alliances can create multiple transformations: on the individual level of partners who can learn and grow personally; on the level of the partnering organizations that are enriched in their institutional values and attitudes and ultimately strengthened in their capabilities to achieve their respective missions; and on the societal level where, through a multiplier effect (collaboration tends to breed more collaboration), society is transformed gradually through the positive impact and the additional social capital formed by cross-sector partnerships. Ultimately, leadership through cross-sector collaborations redraws the boundaries and creates new institutional configurations for achieving change.

A programme that links cross-sector collaboration and leadership development is the innovative Ulysses programme at *PricewaterhouseCoopers*. *Nicola Pless* and *Ralf Schneider* describe in their chapter how the programme provides an experiential learning frame for developing future global leaders at PwC through participation in cross-sector aid projects. The assumption is that through this learning intervention, firstly, an awareness and understanding for the responsibilities of business and leaders for the pressing problems in the world is raised; secondly, deeply rooted human values (like equality, care for other human beings, recognition, cooperation) are activated; thirdly, capabilities to build sustainable relationships are enhanced; and last but not least, motivation to initiate further social change inside and outside the organization is triggered. One of today's key challenges of talent development is to prepare future leaders for the social, cultural, environmental and strategic challenges of business in an uncertain and complex environment and to develop executives who lead business responsibly and sustainably in a global stakeholder society. Pless and Schneider present PwC's approach towards developing responsible global leaders by outlining the organizational context and the leadership challenges that call for a development programme like Ulysses. They then present the programme itself, its learning philosophy, objectives, phases and the developmental methods used. Finally, they discuss some of the success factors for developing future leaders through aid projects in cross-sector partnerships.

Mark Wade concludes the third part of the book with his chapter on *Shell's* approach to preparing leaders for sustainable business. In a global environment, where change is a constant, where corporate accountability is demanded, and where society is increasingly concerned about the long-term sustainability of the social and natural environment as well as economic development, companies are no longer expected to satisfy only investors on financial performance, but also a wide range of other parties on environmental and social performance. How can companies and their leaders live up to these expectations? Wade stresses that this is an essential question for organizational success and well-being. In the course of the events around Brent Spar and Nigeria, Shell learnt the hard way that being misaligned with society's expectations can create crisis. However, Wade sees such crisis situations as a true test of leadership: how well one copes with challenges of this scale and how leadership transfers the negative energy into the positive transformation of the organization. For Shell these events became a *catalyst for change* towards sustainable development (SD). The transformation started with the initiation of a large stakeholder dialogue in 1996, an update of Shell's General Business Principles in 1997, and continued in the proceeding years with the embedding of SD within the organization through both hardwiring (aligning systems and processes) and softwiring (winning the heart and minds of people and mobilizing them for SD). Like any transformation, this process is long and arduous with some hurdles and resistance to overcome. Wade underscores therefore the necessity to have a business case for SD, to translate SD into something that is tangible and relevant and accompanies people with a concerted learning approach. SD became both a value and a broad framework of thinking, encouraging an inclusive, outward-looking and values-based approach to business. As such, SD provides also a context in which the leadership competences that Shell has defined can be applied and organizational learning can take place. Wade provides insights into Shell's learning framework and provides examples of SD leadership at different levels in the corporation – approaches that not only bring value to Shell's businesses, but benefits to society at large.

The business *in* society perspective is at the core of *responsible leadership*. It requires a relational as well as a transitional perspective, capturing the complexity of leadership in both a moral and a practical sense, and 'living by sort of a rhythm that encourages a high level of intuitive insight about the whole gamut of events from the indefinite past, through the present moment, to the indefinite future', as Robert Greenleaf (1977: 38) put it in his reflections on servant leadership almost thirty years ago. Insight and foresight, empathy and listening skills, self-knowledge and a sense of community, moral imagination and a morally sound values base are among the hallmarks of a responsible leader. Mirroring this complexity, the book combines theoretical analysis and practical experience, individual and organizational aspects of leadership, strategic and normative perspectives, leadership ethics and a leader's morality. Responsible leadership involves complex, dynamic relationships based on values, emotions and mutual recognition. The reader will find insights on many of the challenges that come with it. However, the deeper we dig into 'the heart of leadership' (Ciulla 2006), the more questions we encounter. In this sense, too, the book is written to inspire and further the debate on responsible leadership in business. Because which ever way we look – backward or forward –

there is an explicit need for it, and the discussion on responsible leadership and the ethics of leadership has only just started.

Bibliography

Bennis, W. and Nanus, B. (1997) *Leaders: strategies for taking charge*, 2nd edn, New York, NY: Harper Business Essentials.

Burns, J.M. (1978) *Leadership*, New York: Perennial.

Burns, J.M. (2003) *Transforming Leadership: a new pursuit of happiness*, New York: Atlantic Monthly Press.

Ciulla, J.B. (ed.) (1998) *Ethics: the heart of leadership*, Westport, CT, London: Praeger.

Ciulla, J.B. (2006) 'Ethics: The heart of leadership', in Th. Maak and N.M. Pless (eds), *Responsible Leadership in Business*, London, New York: Routledge.

George, B. (2003) *Authentic Leadership: rediscovering the secrets to creating lasting value*, San Francisco, CA: Jossey-Bass.

Ghoshal, S. (2005) 'Bad management theories are destroying good management practices', *Academy of Management Learning and Education*, 4(1): 75–91.

Greenleaf , R.K. (1977/2002) *Servant Leadership: a journey into the nature of legitimate power and greatness*, 25th anniversary edn, New York, Mahwah, NJ: Paulist Press.

Kets de Vries, M.F.R. (1999) *The New Global Leaders*, San Francisco, CA: Jossey-Bass.

Kets de Vries, M.F.R. (2004) 'Organizations on the couch: a clinical perspective on organizational dynamics', *European Management Journal*, 22(2): 183–200.

Morgan, G. (1997) *Images of Organization*, Thousand Oaks, CA: Sage.

Rost, J.C. (1991) *Leadership for the 21st Century*, Westport, CT, London: Quorum.

Van de Loo, E. (2000) 'The clinical paradigm: Manfred Kets de Vries's reflections on organizational therapy', *European Management Journal*, 18(1): 2–22.

Part I

What is responsible leadership?

2 Ethics

The heart of leadership

Joanne B. Ciulla

Introduction

Leadership is morality magnified. Unlike individual morality, the morality of a leader ripples through organizations, communities and societies. We know that leaders have the potential to inflict great harm or bestow great benefits on their constituents. When a leader errs, many people suffer. Leadership is a specific type of human relationship and ethics is about the way that we treat each other in various relationships. This chapter will show why ethics lies at the very heart of leadership. It begins with a critical look at the leadership literature, then goes on to examine some key issues in leadership ethics. These include the relationship between ethics and effectiveness, altruism and self-interest, and the moral standards of leaders. The last part looks at two normative theories of leadership and suggests some directions for leadership ethics.

Treatment of ethics in leadership studies

Leadership ethics

Today people often wonder, 'Where have all the great leaders gone?' It is not clear that leaders are worse today then they were in the past, but we do know more about them than ever before. It is difficult to have heroes in a world where every wart and wrinkle of a person's life is made public. Ironically, the increase in information that we have about leaders has increased the confusion over the ethics of leadership. The more defective our leaders are, the greater our longing to have responsible leaders. Lately, the question of bad leadership has been on many scholars' minds. Barbara Kellerman (2004) has written on the question: What can we do about bad leaders? Jean Lipman-Blumen (2005) has done extensive research on the question: Why do people follow leaders who are *toxic*? The ethical issues of leadership are explicit in public debates, but have tended to lie simmering below the surface of the existing leadership literature.

Most scholars and practitioners who write about leadership genuflect at the altar of ethics and speak with hushed reverence about its importance to leadership. Somewhere in almost any book devoted to the subject, one finds a few sentences, paragraphs, or pages or even a chapter on how integrity and strong ethical values are crucial to leadership. Yet, given the central role of ethics in the practice of leadership, it is remarkable that, until recently, there has been little in the way of sustained and systematic treatment of the subject by scholars.

Throughout this chapter I will use the term *leadership ethics* to refer to the study of the ethical issues related to leadership and responsible or principled leadership. The study of ethics generally consists of the examination of right, wrong, good, evil, virtue, duty, obligation, rights, justice, fairness, and so on in human relationships with each other and other living things. Leadership studies, either directly or indirectly, tries to understand what leadership is and how and why the leader–follower relationship works: i.e. What is a leader and what does it mean to exercise leadership? How do leaders lead? What do leaders do? Why do people follow? Many areas of leadership literature from psychology focus on different types of relationships. For example, contingency theories focus on the relationship of the leader and the group in a given situation (Fiedler 1967; Vroom and Yeatton 1973). The vertical dyad linkage model focuses on dyads such as the relationship between leaders and managers (Dansereau, Jr *et al.* 1975). Since leadership is a distinctive kind of human relationship with a distinctive set of moral problems, it seems appropriate to refer to the subject as *leadership ethics*.

Ethics without effort

Ethics is one of those subjects that people rightfully feel they know about from experience. Most people think of ethics as practical knowledge, not theoretical knowledge. One problem in applied ethics is that scholars from other fields sometimes feel that their practical knowledge and common sense (and of course, their own exemplary moral character) are adequate for a discussion of ethics in their area of research. We all know something about psychology too, but few scholars would write a psychology paper without consulting the literature on the subject.

What is striking about leadership studies is not the absence of philosophic writings on ethics, but the fact that authors expend so little energy on researching ethics from any discipline. Scholars who reject or ignore writings on ethics usually end up either reinventing fairly standard philosophic distinctions and ethical theories or doing without them and proceeding higgledy-piggledy with their discussion.

An example of the paucity of research energy expended on ethics is *Bass & Stogdill's Handbook of Leadership* (Bass 1990). On the book jacket it is hailed by one reviewer as 'the most complete work on leadership' and 'encyclopaedic'. This is considered the source book on the study of leadership. The text is 914 pages long and contains a 162-page bibliography.

There are 37 chapters in this book, none of which treat the question of ethics in leadership. If you look ethics up in the index, five pages are listed. Page 569 contains a brief discussion of different work ethics; page 723 is a reference to the gender differences in values; and page 831 refers to a question raised about whether sensitivity training is unethical. The reader has to get to a sub-section in the last chapter of the book called, 'Leadership in the Twenty-First Century' to find a two-page exposition on ethics. There we are treated to a meagre grab bag of empirical studies and one fleeting reference to James MacGregor Burns's argument that transformational leaders foster moral virtue (Burns 1978). The second section on ethics, 'A Model for Ethical Analysis', sounds more promising. Bernard Bass (1990: 906), the author, defines ethics as a 'creative searching for human fulfilment and choosing it as good and beautiful'. He goes on to argue that professional ethics focuses too much on negative vices and not on the good things. Bass takes his definition of ethics from the sole reference to ethics in this section, *The Paradox of Poverty: a reappraisal of economic development policy* by Paul Steidlmeier (1987). Bass suggests a model for ethical analysis that 'determines the connection between moral reasoning and moral behaviour and how each depends on the issue involved' (1990: 906). After reading these two pages, one learns practically nothing about ethics and leadership. It is not surprising that the standard reference work on leadership does not carry much information on ethics, in part because there is not much research on it. Bass was very unhappy with my criticism of his handbook in 1995 and has promised a more extensive section on the subject in the 4th edition of the handbook, which will be out in 2006.

Leadership and the Rosetta stone

One of the problems with leadership studies is that most of the research has been done from one discipline. Research in the twentieth century mostly focused on traits, group facilitation, effectiveness or the skills that leaders needed. This is clearly the case if you look at the contents of Bass and Stogdill. The largest section in the book is on the personal attributes of leaders.

Marta Calas and Linda Smircich offer a post-modernist critique of the field that indirectly helps to explain why there has been little work on ethics in leadership studies. They point out the positivist slant in much of the leadership research (particularly by scholars in psychology and business). According to Calas and Smircich, the *saga* of leadership researchers is to find the Rosetta stone of leadership and break its codes. They argue that, since the research community believes that society puts a premium on science, researchers' attempts to break the Rosetta stone have to be *scientific*. Hence the *scientists* keep breaking leadership into smaller and smaller pieces until the main code has been lost and cannot be put together (Calas and Smircich 1988). This fragmentation accounts for one of the reasons

why there is so little work on ethics and leadership. Ethical analysis generally requires a broad perspective on a practice. For example, in business,
ethical considerations of a problem often go hand in hand with taking a
long-term view of a problem and the long-term interests of an organization.

Calas and Smircich also observe that the scholarly leadership literature
seems irrelevant to practitioners, whereas the scholars themselves do not
feel like they are getting anywhere – nobody seems happy. They believe
that leadership researchers are frustrated because they are trying to do
science but they know they are not doing good science. The researchers
are also trying to do narrative, but the narrative is more concerned with
sustaining the community of researchers than helping explicate leadership.
Calas and Smircich argue for a multidisciplinary approach to leadership
that emphasizes the use of narratives, such as case studies, mythology and
biography.

Locating ethics

What do the definitions really tell us?

Leadership scholars have spent large amounts of time and trouble worry-
ing about the definition of leadership. I have written extensively on why
debates over the definition of leadership are really debates about the values
related to leadership (Ciulla 1995). Joe Rost (1991) argued that leadership
studies could not progress without a common definition of leadership. He
collected 221 definitions of leadership, ranging from the 1920s to the
1990s. The following definitions are adapted from Rost (1991: 37–96) and
are representative of the literature in each era.

- 1920s [Leadership is] the ability to impress the will of the leader on
  those led and induce obedience, respect, loyalty and cooperation.
- 1930s Leadership is a process in which the activities of many are
  organized to move in a specific direction by one.
- 1940s Leadership is the result of an ability to persuade or direct men,
  apart from the prestige or power that comes from office or external
  circumstance.
- 1950s [Leadership is what leaders do in groups.] The leader's
  authority is spontaneously accorded him by his fellow group members.
- 1960s [Leadership is] acts by a person, which influence other persons
  in a shared direction.
- 1970s Leadership is defined in terms of discretionary influence.
  Discretionary influence refers to those leader behaviours under control
  of the leader, which he may vary from individual to individual.
- 1980s Regardless of the complexities involved in the study of
  leadership, its meaning is relatively simple. Leadership means to inspire
  others to undertake some form of purposeful action as determined by
  the leader.

- 1990s Leadership is an influence relationship between leaders and followers who intend real changes that reflects their mutual purposes.

If we look at the sample definitions from different periods, we see that the problem of definition is not that scholars have different meanings of leadership. Leadership does not denote radically different things to different people. One can detect a family resemblance between the definitions. All of them talk about leadership as some kind of process, act or influence that in some way gets people to do something. A roomful of people, each holding one of these definitions, would understand each other.

These definitions generally say the same thing: leadership is about a person or persons somehow moving other people to do something. Where the definitions differ is in their connotation, particularly in terms of their implications for the leader–follower relationship. In other words, *how* leaders get people to do things (impress, organize, persuade, influence and inspire) and *how* what is to be done is decided (forced obedience, voluntary consent, dictated by the leader or a reflection of mutual purposes) have normative implications. In other words, the very way that you define leadership contains in it normative assumptions about it as a relationship between leaders and followers (Ciulla 2004b).

Definitions of leadership are also social constructions that reflect the values and paradigms of leadership at a particular time and place. All of these definitions are from the United States, but they also reflect broader trends in other countries. In the 1920s and 1930s the model of leadership in the workplace was command and control over industrial labour. Under Frederick Winslow Taylor's scientific management, managers did the thinking and employees obeyed. It is interesting to note that on the world stage, this is an era of emerging fascism. Some of Taylor's biggest fans were Stalin and Mussolini (Ciulla 2002). In contrast with the 1920s and 1930s, leadership in the 1960s was about inspiration and shared goals. By the 1960s the paradigm of leadership was largely influenced by Martin Luther King and the social movements of the time in both the United States and Europe.

Leadership scholars who worry about constructing the ultimate definition of leadership are asking the wrong question but trying to answer the right one. The ultimate question about leadership is not, what is the definition of leadership? We are not confused about what leaders do, but we would like to know the best way to do it. The whole point of studying leadership is to answer the question, what is good leadership? The use of the word *good* here has two senses: ethical and effective.

Ethics/effectiveness continuum

A good leader is an ethical and effective leader. While this may seem like stating the obvious, the problem we face is that we do not always find ethics and effectiveness in the same leader. Some leaders are highly ethical but not very effective. Others are very effective at serving their constituents but not very ethical in what they do, why they do it and how they do it. This distinction between ethics and effectiveness is not always a crisp one. Sometimes being ethical is being effective and sometimes being effective is being ethical. In other words, ethics is effectiveness in certain instances. There are times when simply being regarded as ethical and trustworthy makes a leader effective and other times when being highly effective makes a leader trustworthy (Ciulla 2004a). On the flip side of the ethics/effectiveness continuum are situations where it is difficult to tell whether a leader is unethical, incompetent or stupid. As Terry Price has argued, the moral failures of leaders are not always intentional. Sometimes moral failures are cognitive and sometimes they are normative (Price 2005). Leaders may get their facts wrong and think that they are acting ethically when, in fact, they are not. In some situations leaders act with moral intentions, but because they are incompetent, they create unethical outcomes. As the old saying goes, 'the road to hell is paved with good intentions'.

History only confuses the ethics-and-effectiveness question. Historians do not write about the leader who was very ethical but did not do anything of significance. They rarely write about a general who was a great human being but never won a battle. History defines successful leaders largely in terms of their ability to bring about change for better or worse. As a result of this, great leaders in history include everyone from Gandhi to Hitler. Machiavelli was disgusted by Cesare Borgia the man, but impressed by Borgia as the resolute, ferocious, cunning and highly effective Prince. While leaders usually bring about change or are successful at doing something, the ethical questions waiting in the wings are the ones found in the various definitions mentioned earlier. What were the leader's intentions? How did the leader go about bringing change? And was the change itself good?

Effectiveness

Most of the time, leaders must be effective to be ethical, but they do not always have to be ethical to be effective. The problem with the existing leadership research is that few studies investigate both senses of good and, when they do, they usually do not fully explore the moral implications of their research questions or their results. The research on leadership effectiveness touches indirectly on the problem of explicitly articulating the normative implications of descriptive research. The Ohio studies and the Michigan studies both measured leadership effectiveness in terms of how leaders treated subordinates and how they got the job done. The Ohio studies measured leadership effectiveness in terms of consideration, the degree to which leaders act in friendly and supportive manner, and initiating structure, or the way that leaders structure their own role and the role of subordinates in order to achieve group goals (Fleishman 1953). The Michigan studies measured leaders on the basis of task orientation and relationship orientation

(Likert 1961). These two studies generated a number of other research programmes and theories, including the situational leadership theory of Hersey
and Blanchard (1977), which looks at effectiveness in terms of how leaders
adapt their leadership style to the requirements of a situation. Some
situations require a task orientation, others a relationship orientation.

Implicit in all of these theories and research programmes is an ethical
question. Are leaders more effective when they are nice to people, or are
leaders more effective when they use certain techniques for structuring and
ordering tasks? One would hope that the answer is both, but that answer is
not conclusive in the studies that have taken place over the least three
decades. According to Gary Yukl (1989), the only consistent finding from
this research is that considerate leaders usually have more satisfied followers. The interesting question is, what if this sort of research showed that you
did not have to be kind and considerate of other people to run a country or
a profitable organization? Would scholars and practitioners draw an *ought*
from the *is* of this research? It is difficult to say when researchers are not
explicit about their ethical commitments. The point is that no matter how
much empirical information we get from the *scientific* study of leadership, it
will always be inadequate if we neglect the moral implications.

Deontology and teleology

The ethics-and-effectiveness question about leadership parallels deontological and teleological perspectives in ethics. From the deontological point of
view, intentions are the morally relevant aspects of an act. As long as the
leader acts according to his or her duty or moral principles, the leader acts
ethically, regardless of the consequences. From the teleological perspective,
what really matters is that the leader's actions result in bringing about something morally good or *the greatest good*. Deontological theories locate the
ethics of an action in the moral intent of the leader and his or her moral jus-
tification for the action, while teleological theories locate the ethics of the
action in its results. We need both deontological and teleological theories to
account for the ethics of leaders. Just as a good leader has to be ethical and
effective, he or she also has to act according to duty and with some notion of
the greatest good in mind. In modernity we often separate the inner person
(intentions) from the outer person (behaviour). Ancient Greek theories of
ethics based on virtue do not have this problem. In virtue ethics you basically
are what you do.

John Stuart Mill saw this split between the ethics of the person and the
ethics of his or her actions clearly. He said the intentions or reasons for an
act tell us something about the morality of the person, but the ends of an
act tell us about the morality of the action (Mill 1987). This solution does
not really solve the ethics-and-effectiveness problem. It simply reinforces
the split between the personal morality of a leader and what he or she does
as a leader.

Should leaders have a higher moral standard?

People often say that 'leaders should be held to a higher moral standard', but does that make sense? If true, would it then be acceptable for everyone else to live by lower moral standards? The curious thing about morality is that, if you set the moral standards for leaders too high, requiring something close to moral perfection, then few people will be qualified to be leaders or will want to be leaders. For example, how many of us could live up to the standard of having never lied, said an unkind word or reneged on a promise? Ironically, when we set moral standards for leaders too high, we become even more dissatisfied with them because few can live up to our expectations. We set moral standards for leaders too low, however, when we reduce them to nothing more than following the law or, worse, simply not being as unethical as their predecessors. A business leader may follow all laws and yet be highly immoral in the way he or she runs a business. Laws are moral minimums that do not and cannot capture the scope and complexity of morality.

History is littered with leaders who did not think they were subject to the same moral standards of honesty, propriety and so on as the rest of society. One explanation for this is so obvious that it has become a cliché: power corrupts. David G. Winter's (2002) and David McClelland's (1975) work on power motives and on socialized and personalized charisma offer psychological accounts of this kind of leader behaviour. Michael Maccoby (2000) and a host of others have talked about narcissistic leaders who, on the bright side, are exceptional and, on the dark side, consider themselves exceptions to the rules. Ludwig and Longenecker (1993) have written about the way success corrupts leaders and causes them to lose strategic focus. Leaders then often abuse their power to get what they want and cover up their bad behaviour when they get caught.

E.P. Hollander's (1964) work on social exchange demonstrates how emerging leaders who are loyal to and competent at attaining group goals gain *idiosyncrasy credits* that allow them to deviate from the group's norms to suit common goals. As Price (2000) has argued, given the fact that we often grant leaders permission to deviate or be an exception to the rules, it is not difficult to see why leaders sometimes make themselves exceptions to moral constraints. This is why I do not think we should hold leaders to different or higher moral standards than ourselves. If anything, we have to make sure that we hold them to the same standards as the rest of society. What we should expect and hope is that our leaders will fail less than most people at meeting ethical standards, while pursuing and achieving the goals of their constituents. So when we say leaders should be held to a higher moral standard what we really mean is that leaders must be more successful at living up to moral standards, because the price of their failure is greater than that of an ordinary person. The really interesting question for leadership development and organizational and political theory is: What can we do to keep leaders from the moral failures that stem from being in a leadership role? The checks and balances of a democracy and corporate boards and auditors are some of the formal structures we use to prevent the moral failure of leaders. We also need to develop self-discipline in aspiring leaders.

Altruism and self-interest

Some leadership scholars use altruism as the moral standard for ethical leadership. In their book, *Ethical Dimensions of Leadership*, Rabindra Kanungo and Manuel Mendonca (1996) write, 'Our thesis is that organizational leaders are truly effective only when they are motivated by a concern for others, when their actions are invariably guided primarily by the criteria of the benefit to others even if it results in some cost to oneself'(1996: 35). When people talk about altruism, they usually contrast altruism with selfishness, or behaviour that benefits oneself at a cost to others. Altruism is a very high personal standard and, as such, is problematic for a number of reasons. Both selfishness and altruism refer to extreme types of motivation and behaviour. Edwin Locke brings out this extreme side of altruism in a dialogue with Bruce Avolio (Avolio and Locke 2002). Locke argues that, if altruism is about self-sacrifice, then leaders who want to be truly altruistic will pick a job that they do not like or value, expect no rewards or pleasure from their job or achievements, and give themselves over totally to serving the wants of others. He then asks if anyone would want to be a leader under such circumstances. One might also ask, would we even want such a person as a leader? While I do not agree with Locke's argument that leaders should act according to their self-interest, he does articulate the practical problem of using altruism as a standard of moral behaviour for leaders.

Avolio's argument against Locke is based on equally extreme cases. He draws on his work at West Point, where a central moral principle in the military is willingness to make the ultimate sacrifice for the good of the group. Avolio also uses Mother Teresa as one of his examples of altruistic behaviour. In these cases, self-sacrifice may be less about the ethics of leaders in general and more about the jobs of soldiers and missionaries. The Locke and Avolio debate pits the extreme aspects of altruism against its heroic side. Here, as in the extensive philosophic literature on self-interest and altruism, the debate spins round and round and does not get us very far. Ethics is about the relationship of individuals to others, so, in a sense, both sides are right and wrong.

Altruism is a motive for acting, but it is not in and of itself a normative principle (Nagel 1970). Requiring leaders to act altruistically is not only a tall order, but it does not guarantee that leaders or their actions will be moral. For example, a terrorist leader who becomes a suicide bomber might have purely altruistic intentions, but the means that he uses to carry out his mission – killing innocent people – is not considered ethical even if his cause is a just one. One might also argue, that it is unethical for a person to sacrifice his or her life for any reason besides self-defence because of the impact that it has on family, and so on. Great leaders such as Martin Luther King, Jr and Gandhi behaved altruistically, but their leadership was ethical because of the means that they used to achieve their ends and the morality of their causes. We have a particular respect for leaders who are martyred for a cause, but the morality of King and Gandhi goes beyond self-sacrifice. Achieving their objectives for social justice while empowering and disciplining followers to use non-violent resistance is not only morally good but difficult to do.

It is interesting to note that Confucius explicitly calls the golden rule altruism. When asked by Tzu-Kung what the guiding principle of life is, Confucius answers, 'It is the word altruism [shu]. Do not do unto others what you do not want them to do to you' (1963: 44). The golden rule crops up as a fundamental moral principle in most major cultures (Wattles 1996). The golden rule tells us how to transform knowledge of one's own self-interest into concern for the interests of others. In other words, it provides the bridge between altruism and self-interest (others and the self) and allows for enlightened self-interest. This highlights another reason why altruism is not a useful standard for the moral behaviour of leaders. The minute we start to modify altruism, it not only loses its initial meaning, it starts to sound like a wide variety of other ethical terms, which makes it very confusing.

Plato believed that leadership required a person to sacrifice his or her immediate self-interests, but this did not amount to altruism. In Book II of the *Republic*, Plato writes:

> In a city of good men, if it came into being, the citizens would fight in order not to rule ... There it would be clear that anyone who is really a true ruler doesn't by nature seek his own advantage but that of his subjects. And everyone, knowing this, would rather be benefited by others than take the trouble to benefit them.
>
> (1992: 347d)

Rather than requiring altruistic motives, Plato is referring to the stress, hard work and (sometimes) thankless task of being a morally good leader. He is saying that, if you are a just person, leadership will take a toll on you and your life. He goes on to say that the only reason a just person accepts a leadership role is out of fear of punishment. He tells us, 'Now the greatest punishment, if one isn't willing to rule, is to be ruled by someone worse than oneself. And I think it is fear of this that makes decent people rule when they do' (1992: 347c). Leadership here is not motivated by altruism but by enlightened self-interest. Plato's comment sheds light on why we sometimes feel more comfortable with people who are reluctant to lead than with those who really want to do so. We sometimes worry that people who are too eager to lead want the power and position for themselves, or that they do not fully understand the responsibilities of leadership.

Morality sometimes calls upon leaders to do things that are against their self-interest. This is less about altruism than it is about the nature of both morality and leadership. One reason why we have leaders is to guide and look after the interests of groups, organizations, communities or countries. When leaders do this, they are doing their job; when they do not do this, they are not doing their job. Implicit in the idea of leadership effectiveness is the notion that leaders do their job. When a mayor does not look after the interests of a city, she is not only ineffective, she is unethical for not keeping the promise that she made when sworn in as mayor. When she does look after the interests of the city, it is not because she is altruistic, but because she is doing her job. In this way, altruism is built into the way we describe what leaders do. While altruism is not the best concept for characterizing the ethics of leadership, scholars' interest in altruism reflects a desire to capture, either implicitly or explicitly, the ethics-and-effectiveness notion of good leadership.

The normative theories

Transforming leadership

James MacGregor Burns's (1978) theory of transforming leadership is compelling because it rests on a set of moral assumptions about the relationship between leaders and followers. Burns uses the terms *transforming* and *transformational* in his book. However, in his more recent work (Burns 2003), he prefers to refer to his theory as *transforming* leadership. Burns's theory is clearly a prescriptive one about the nature of morally good leadership. Drawing from Abraham Maslow's work on needs, Milton Rokeach's research on values development and research on moral development from Lawrence Kohlberg, Jean Piaget, Erik Erickson and Alfred Adler, Burns argues that leaders have to operate at higher need and value levels than those of followers. A leader's role is to exploit tension and conflict within people's value systems and play the role of raising people's consciousness.

On Burns's account, transforming leaders have very strong values. They do not water down their values and moral ideals by consensus, but rather they elevate people by using conflict to engage followers and help them reassess their own values and needs. The moral questions that drive Burns's theory of transforming leadership come from his work as a biographer and a historian. When biographers or historians study a leader, they struggle with how to judge or keep from judging their subject. Throughout his book, Burns uses examples of a number of incidents where questionable means, such as lying and deception are used to achieve honourable ends or where the private life of a politician is morally questionable. For example, see Burns's discussion of Roosevelt's treatment of Joe Kennedy (1978: 32–3). If you analyze the numerous historical examples in Burns's book you find two pressing moral questions shape his theory. The first is the morality of means and ends (and this also includes the moral use of power) and the second is the tension between the public and private morality of a leader. His theory of transforming leadership is an attempt to characterize good leadership by accounting for both of these questions.

Burns's distinction between transforming and transactional leadership and modal and end-values offers a way to think about the question, 'What is a good leader?' in terms of the relationship to followers and the means and ends of actions. Transactional leadership rests on the values found in the means of an act. These are called modal values, which are things like responsibility, fairness, honesty and promise keeping. Transactional leadership helps leaders and followers reach their own goals by supplying lower level wants and needs so that they can move up to higher needs. Transforming leadership is concerned with end-values, such as liberty, justice and equality. Transforming leaders raise their followers up through various stages of morality and need. They turn their followers into leaders and the leader becomes a moral agent. Leaders need to use both kinds of leadership and, according to Burns, both kinds of leadership have moral aspects to them.

As a historian, Burns focuses on the ends of actions and the changes that leaders initiate. In terms of his ethical theory, at times he appears to be a consequentialist, despite, his acknowledgement that, 'insufficient attention to means can corrupt the ends' (1978: 426). However, because Burns does not really offer a systematic theory of ethics in the way that a philosopher might, he is difficult to categorize. Consider, for example, Burns's two answers to the Hitler problem (Ciulla 1995): Was Hitler a good leader? In the first part of the book, he says quite simply that once Hitler gained power and crushed all opposition, he was no longer a leader. He was a tyrant. Later in the book, he offers three criteria for judging how Hitler would fare before *the bar of history*. Burns says that Hitler would probably argue that he was a transforming leader who spoke for the true values of the German people and elevated them to a higher destiny. First, he would be tested by modal values of honour and integrity or the extent to which he advanced or thwarted the standards of good conduct in mankind. Second, he would be judged by the end-values of equality and justice. Lastly, he would be judged on the impact that he had on the well-being of the people that he touched. According to Burns, Hitler would fail all three tests. Burns does not consider Hitler a leader or a transforming leader because of the means that he used, the ends that he achieved and the impact of Hitler as a moral agent on his followers during the process of his leadership. By looking at leadership as a process and not a set of individual acts, Burns's theory of good leadership is difficult to pigeonhole into one ethical theory.

Burns's theory is frequently misunderstood and misused by scholars. His transformational leader is not an all-knowing guru who morally elevates followers. Bass believes that charismatic leadership is a necessary ingredient of transformational leadership (1985: 31), charisma is not as central to Burns. Rather a transforming leader is engaged in a dialogue about values that elevates the leader and the followers. A really good leader makes followers into leaders. This process is more like discourse ethics than a purely emotional bonding process. Near the end of his book, Burns reintroduces this idea with an anecdote about why President Johnson did not run in 1968. Burns tells us, 'Perhaps he did not comprehend that the people he had led – as a result in part of the impact of his leadership – had created their own fresh leadership, which was now outrunning his'. All of the people that Johnson helped – the sick, the blacks and the poor – now had their own leadership. Burns says, 'Leadership begat leadership and hardly recognized its offspring'. 'Followers had become leaders' (1978: 424). Burns criticizes the leadership literature for bifurcating literature on leadership and followership. He says that the leadership literature is elitist, projecting heroic leaders against the drab mass of powerless followers. The followership literature, according to Burns, tends to be populist in its approach, linking the masses with small overlapping circles of politicians, military officers and business people (1978: 3).

Servant leadership

The second example of a normative theory of leadership is servant leadership. Robert K. Greenleaf's book *Servant Leadership: a journey into the nature of legitimate power and greatness* (1977) presents a view of how leaders ought to be. However, the best way to understand servant leadership is to read *Journey to the East* (1956), by Hermann Hesse. Hesse's story is about a spiritual journey to the East. On the journey a servant named Leo carries the bags and does the travellers' chores. There is something special about Leo. He keeps the group together with his presence and songs. When Leo mysteriously disappears, the group loses their way. Later in the book the main character HH discovers that the servant Leo was actually the leader. The simple, but radical shift in emphasis is from followers serving leaders to leaders serving followers. It comes from a normative view of leadership found in ancient Eastern and Western thought.

Servant leadership has not gotten as much attention as transformational leadership in the literature, but students and business people often find this a compelling characterization of leadership. According to Greenleaf, the servant leader leads because he or she wants to serve others. People follow servant leaders freely because they trust them. Like the transforming leader, the servant leader elevates people. Greenleaf says servant leadership must pass this test: 'Do those served grow as persons? Do they *while being served* become healthier, wiser, freer, more autonomous, more likely themselves to become servants?' He goes on and adds a Rawlsian proviso, '*And*, what is the effect on the least privileged in society?' (1977: 13–14). Servant leadership, like transforming leadership rests on moral principles.

Conclusion: the future of leadership ethics

The main question people ask about leadership is not, 'What is leadership?' It is, 'What is *good* leadership?' We want leaders who do things right and do the right thing. Scholars and practitioners need to fully explore the interface between the knowledge and skills of leadership and the moral capacities needed for responsible leadership. Leadership ethics should serve as a critical theory that opens up new dialogues between researchers from different disciplines and practitioners from a variety of contexts. Existing theories and the empirical literature have strong normative implications that have not been fully developed. Work in leadership ethics should generate different ways of thinking about leadership and new ways of asking research questions. Scholarship from history, philosophy and the arts, combined with social science research promise to enrich our understanding of good leadership.

The territory of ethics lies at the heart of leadership studies and has veins that run though all leadership research. As an area of applied ethics, leadership ethics should be responsive to the pressing ethical concerns of societies and organizations. Today the most important and most confusing public debate is over what ethical issues are relevant in judging whether a person *should* lead and whether a person is capable of leadership. Research into leadership ethics would not only help us with questions like, 'What sort of person should lead?' and 'What are the moral responsibilities of leaders and followers?' It should give us a better insight into what leadership is, what it ought to be and how to develop competent and morally responsible leaders.

Questions

1   How do our ideas about what makes a leader effective encourage or hinder the development of ethical leaders?
2   What social conditions shape the way that we think about leaders in business and government?
3   What can we do to keep leaders from failing to live up to moral standards?
4   Why are we uncomfortable with people who are too eager to be leaders?
5   How can followers improve their leaders?

Bibliography

Avolio, B.J. and Locke, E.E (2002) 'Contrasting different philosophies of leader motivation: altruism versus egoism', *The Leadership Quarterly*, 13(2): 169–91.

Bass, B.M. (1985) *Leadership and Performance Beyond Expectations*, New York: Free Press.

Bass, B.M. (1990) *Bass & Stogdill's Handbook of Leadership: theory, research, and managerial applications*, 3rd edn, New York: Free Press.

Bass, B.M. and Steidlmeier, P. (1999) 'Ethics, character, and authentic transformational leadership behavior', *The Leadership Quarterly*, 10(2): 181–217.

Burns, J.M. (1978) *Leadership*, New York: Harper Torchbooks.

Burns, J.M. (2003) *Transforming Leadership*, New York: Atlantic Monthly Press.

Calas, M.B. and Smircich, L. (1988) 'Reading leadership as a form of cultural analysis', in J.G. Hunt, B.R. Baliga, H.P. Dachler and C.A. Schriesheim (eds) *Emerging Leadership Vistas*, Lexington, MA: Lexington Books.

Ciulla, J.B. (1995) 'Leadership ethics: mapping the territory', *Business Ethics Quarterly*, 5(1): 5–28.

Ciulla, J.B. (2002) *The Working Life: the promise and betrayal of modern work*, Three Rivers Press.

Ciulla, J.B. (2004a) 'Ethics and leadership effectiveness', in J. Antonakis, A.T. Cianciolo and R.J. Sternberg (eds) *The Nature of Leadership*, Thousand Oaks, CA: Sage.

Ciulla, J.B. (ed.) (2004b) *Ethics: the heart of leadership*, 2nd edn, Westbury, CT: Quorum Books.

Confucius (1963), 'Selections from the Analects', trans. W.-T. Chan (ed.), *A Source Book in Chinese Philosophy*, Princeton, NJ: Princeton University Press.

Dansereau, Jr, F., Graen, G. and Haga, W.J. (1975) 'Vertical dyad linkage approach to leadership within formal organizations: a longitudinal investigation of the role making process', *Organizational Behaviour and Human Performance*, 13: 46–78.

Fiedler, F.E. (1967) *A Theory of Leadership Effectiveness*, New York: McGraw-Hill.

Fleishman, E.A. (1953) 'The description of supervisory behavior', *Journal of Applied Psychology*, 37: 1–6.

Greenleaf, R.K. (1977) *Servant Leadership: a journey into the nature of legitimate power and greatness*, New York: Paulist Press.

Hersey, P. and Blanchard, K.H. (1977) *Management of Organizational Behavior: utilizing human resources*, Englewood Cliffs, NJ: Prentice-Hall.

Hesse, H. (1956) *The Journey to the East*, New York: Picador.

Hollander, E.P. (1964) *Leaders, Groups and Influence*, New York: Oxford University Press.

Kanungo, R. and Mendonca, M. (1996) *Ethical Dimensions of Leadership*, Thousand Oaks, CA: Sage.

Kellerman, B. (2004) *Bad Leadership: what it is, how it happens, and why it matters*, Boston, MA: Harvard Business School Press.

Likert, R. (1961) *New Patterns of Management*, New York: McGraw-Hill.

Lipman-Blumen, J. (2005) *The Allure of Toxic Leaders: why we follow destructive bosses and corrupt politicians – and how we can survive them*, New York: Oxford University Press.

Ludwig, D.C. and Longenecker, C.O. (1993) 'The Bathsheba Syndrome: the ethical failure of successful leaders', *The Journal of Business Ethics*, 12(4): 265–73.

Maccoby, M. (2000) 'Narcissistic leaders', *The Harvard Business Review*, 78(1): 68–75.

McClelland, D. (1975) *Power: the inner experience*, New York: Irvington.

Mill, J.S. (1987) *Utilitarianism and Other Essays*, ed. Alan Ryan, New York: Penguin.

Nagel, T. (1970) *The Possibility of Altruism*, Oxford: Clarendon Press.

Plato (1992) *Republic*, trans. G.M.A. Grube, Indianapolis, IN: Hackett.

Price, T.L. (2000) 'Explaining ethical failures of leadership', *The Leadership and Organization Development Journal*, 21(4): 177–184.

Price, T.L. (2005) *Understanding Ethical Failures in Leadership*, New York: Cambridge University Press.

Rost, J.C. (1991) *Leadership for the Twenty-First Century*, New York: Praeger.

Steidlmeier, P. (1987) *The Paradox of Poverty: a reappraisal of economic development policy*, Cambridge, MA: Ballinger.

Wattles, J. (1996) *The Golden Rule*, New York: Oxford University Press.

Winter, D. (2002) 'The motivational dimensions of leadership: power, achievement, and affiliation', in R.E. Riggio, S.E. Murphy and F.J. Pirozzolo (eds) *Multiple Intelligences and Leadership*, Mahwah, NJ: Lawrence Erlbaum.

Vroom, V.H. and Yetton, P.W. (1973) *Leadership and Decision-Making*, Pittsburgh, PA: University of Pittsburgh Press.

Yukl, G.A. (1989) *Leadership in Organizations*, 2nd edn, Englewood Cliffs, NJ: Prentice-Hall.

3 Responsible leadership
A relational approach

Thomas Maak and Nicola M. Pless

Introduction

Based on a relational approach, we tackle in this chapter the question of responsible leadership in business. We start by outlining the main leadership challenges in a stakeholder society. Of the challenges leaders face in an interconnected world, most emerge from the interactions among a multitude of stakeholders. The ability to build sustainable relationships in a responsible and empathetic way becomes a key quality of current and future leaders. Consequently, the roles and responsibilities of leaders need to reflect the demands of leading businesses *in* society. After having defined the leader as a moral person, we present relational roles and responsibilities of leaders. We suggest that a responsible leader is at times servant, steward, architect, change agent, coach as well as storyteller. We conclude this chapter by briefly elaborating on the question if, and how, responsibility in business can be developed.

The challenge of responsible leadership

Much has been written and said in the aftermath of Enron and other recent cases of corporate misconduct on the lack of integrity and responsibility in executive leadership. The ethical fallout has been attributed to personal greed, grandiosity, and an *everything-is-possible* mentality. While this was obviously the case in Enron, one should not forget that leadership needs followers and a favourable environment. Not long before courageous employees blew the whistle on Enron, the company was hailed as one of the most inventive and best companies to work for. They even had a state-of-the-art ethics programme. To say, then, that it was a case of bad leadership by failed individuals would be too easy a way out. It certainly was to a large extent. However, the world is more complex than that. Jeffrey Skilling and Andrew Fastow were long considered to be *good leaders* not in a moral sense but in a business sense because they delivered results; in other words, they were effective (see Ciulla in this book for a discussion on the ethics-and-effectiveness question). And while it is true that greed, narcissism and a risk-taking and gambling mentality were main causes in the fall of Enron, there was also a context, both within the company as well as in the market where such (bad) leadership could flourish. In fact, it could be that, because the leaders of Enron showed drive, enthusiasm and optimism, others followed. In hindsight, we can conclude that Skilling and Fastow were irresponsible leaders; but we should not forget that during their time in charge, one might have judged them differently. Does this mean that responsible leadership is only relative and fluid? Of course not. But leadership is, and always has been, a complex phenomenon and this makes it difficult to pinpoint what *responsible* leadership is.

Indeed, given the significance of leadership in both business and society it is surprising to see how little we know about *responsible leadership*. What is it? How can it be developed? What makes a responsible leader? Very few authors have so far engaged in defining what responsible leadership is. Those who have (Greenleaf 1977/2002, Burns 1978, Ciulla 1995), have taken an explicitly normative stand or reflected from an ethical perspective on leadership in business. As the above example shows, being a responsible leader obviously requires more than being an effective, visionary and good manager. It also means having and adhering to the right values, having a good character. It furthermore requires that the relationships a leader engages in are based on sound values and principles. These relationships are manifold, as we will see below. Besides these characteristics of the leader, there is the framework of rules and regulations in the markets; the social expectations and embeddedness in society; in other words, the context of leadership. If we take into consideration these different elements then it becomes obvious that any approach towards responsible leadership should reflect this complexity. Thus, a holistic approach towards leadership, based on, and guided by, sound principles and incorporating the various elements just mentioned, would have to include and discuss the following: the *person* of a leader; the *relationships* she engages in; what she does as a leader and thus the *roles* she fulfils and the *responsibilities* she has; as well as the actual process of leading responsibly (see Figure 3.1).

Leadership challenges in a stakeholder society

Before we discuss the different dimensions in more detail, let us look at the *contextual challenges* leaders face as they impact our understanding of the demands of responsible leadership. Most new leadership challenges result from interdependence and interconnection of people and processes in the global business environment. Due to communication and economic globalization continents, cultures, countries and companies are getting much closer than they have ever been before, creating many market opportunities but also undeniable threats for business leaders: destruction of indigenous habitats, degradation of the environment, a rising number of ethnic con-

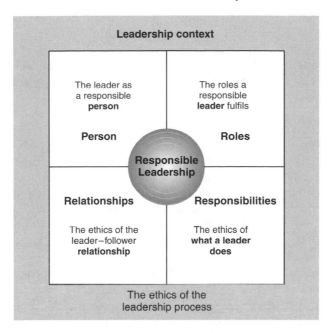

Figure 3.1 Core dimensions of responsible leadership

flicts and the omnipresent risk of (global) terrorism, as well as the risk of damage to their reputation or loss of public trust due to accidents and ethical misbehaviour, broadcasted in real-time by global media outlets. As Rosen *et al.* put it, 'business leaders ... must understand the seamless interaction of all these dimensions, the interconnectedness of which creates our twenty-first-century culture' (2000: 22).

The complexity of operating in an interconnected, intercultural environment places new demands on organizations and their leaders, namely to navigate successfully and responsibly in a constantly changing, interconnected business world, facing uncertainty, ambiguity and the diversity of interests, needs and demands of multiple stakeholders. To put it differently, today's and tomorrow's leaders have to meet the following interconnected challenges: a diversity challenge, an ethics challenge, a trust challenge, a stakeholder challenge and a values challenge.

The diversity challenge

Due to globalization of businesses and demographic changes organizations are becoming more and more diverse in terms of gender, culture, religion, age, etc. This places new demands on leadership: leading an increasingly diverse workforce across distance, businesses, countries and cultures;

selecting, developing and retaining people from different backgrounds; leveraging their potential; creating a multicultural and inclusive environment (Cox 2001, Gilbert and Ivancevich 2000, Pless and Maak 2004) in which people regardless of background and orientation feel valued and respected, and can contribute according to their highest potential.

The ethics challenge

The ethics challenge of creating common ethical standards while respecting moral differences extends beyond the organization, as leaders may face complex ethical issues or moral dilemmas such as human rights issues (working conditions, child labour, etc.), corruption, or differences in social and environmental standards where, due to cultural differences, quick solutions may not always be at hand. How should leaders deal with a multitude of stakeholder interests, which are based on different values and world views? How can one apply fundamental norms and values in an increasingly diverse and complex environment? The ethical challenge is multifaceted: it requires leading with integrity while respecting diverse, sometimes conflicting interests; it calls for leaders to be conscious about their own values and moral standards as well as those of their constituents; and it demands that leaders act ethically while building relationships inside and outside the organization.

The trust challenge

One of the biggest challenges leaders will face in the coming years is the rebuilding of public trust that the business world in general has lost over the years of scandals and disasters (Enron, WorldCom, Parmalat, Bhopal, etc.). If a vast majority of people believe, as various polls have indicated, that CEOs and business leaders have poor ethical standards, then there is a fundamental challenge ahead. Not only may businesses face public criticism or consumer boycotts and further undermining of their reputations, society may even revoke their licences to operate. In a (global) stakeholder society, commercial viability and long-term business success depend on the ability of a firm and their leadership to act responsibly with respect to business, society and the environment. The challenge at hand to leaders is to transform their businesses into responsible corporate citizens, create high-performing organizations from an ethical, social, environmental *and* business perspective and ultimately develop an appropriate mindset in themselves as well as among their employees and future leaders.

The stakeholder challenge

There is widespread awareness that trustful relationships with different stakeholders (employees, clients, suppliers, shareholders, communities,

NGOs, etc.) is and will be one of the most important determinants of organizational viability and business excellence (Freeman 1984, 1994, Donaldson and Preston 1995, Wheeler and Sillanpää 1997, Svendsen 1998, Phillips 2003). For a leader, this requires a mature interpersonal approach to building stakeholder relations, using emotional skills and showing integrity (Solomon and Flores 2001). This involves not only recognizing different stakeholders and their interests, but also including different voices into a stakeholder dialogue, ensuring fair and respectful treatment of people, dealing competently with conflicts of interests, and reconciling (moral) dilemmas. This can be especially challenging because balancing competing values and interests involves subjective judgements about rights, accountability, and responsiblities and the same actions that serve the interests of some stakeholders or followers may be contrary to those of others (Yukl 2002: 407).

The values challenge

An underlying dimension to the challenges discussed so far is that they are all triggered by differences in values and the assumptions, behaviour, expectations and moral standards rooted in them. To better understand the significance and dynamics of different values and their implications for a concept of responsible leadership, the following framework shows the different categories and their relation. We do not consider it exhaustive, but we believe that it is useful to distinguish some core individual from interpersonal, organizational and basic societal values (see Figure 3.2).

The *societal values* reflect the ideals that guide the act of living together in a society. These values are a result of men's *struggle for recognition* (Honneth 1996) throughout history and over time. We find here, as a result from the eighteenth-century revolutions, values such as *liberty* and *equality*. Other values that are important in Western societies and other *civilized cultures* are the *inviolability of human dignity* (as laid down in the United Nations Declaration of Human Rights, itself a reaction to the atrocities of and men's struggle for recognition and survival in the first half of the twentieth century), the *preservation of the natural environment* and thus the basis of life, as well as *social justice*. These ideals get their meaning with reference to the societal narrative or vision of a just, peaceful and sustainable society.

Second, there are *individual values* or character traits such as integrity, honesty, humility, courage, etc. that get their meaning in the wider context of society. They are developed through life, are usually deeply ingrained in a person's character and thus part of her identity. These character traits are evident in behaviour and can be experienced by other people. There is another category of individual values such as *happiness*, which is not so much a character trait as a general mood (Stein and Book 2003). As a desired emotional state, individuals value it. However, it is fluid: sometimes given,

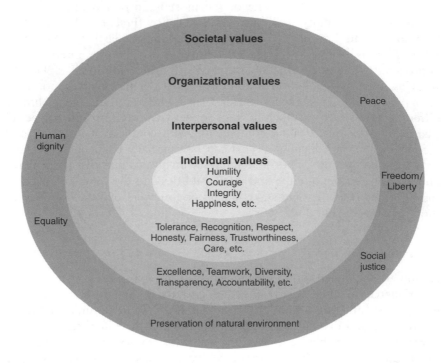

Figure 3.2 Values circles

sometimes absent and as such not ingrained in a person, but rather an ideal that people long for in search of the individual notion of a *good life*.

And third, there are relational values like tolerance, recognition and respect for others, fairness, caring for others, trustworthiness. These values determine the *interpersonal* context, shown in interpersonal relationships, and determine the quality of a relationship. They are the essence of a civilized society that is based on mutual recognition of human rights, civil rights and a person's dignity. In an *organizational* context, if cooperation and teamwork are the desired form of working together, then it is crucial that people share these values, translate them into behaviour and live them. Take for instance *mutual respect*: being open to different standpoints, understanding a different standpoint by articulating it in own words and accepting other standpoints as different but equal are examples of how relational values can be translated into observable behaviour.

One of the most demanding challenges for a responsible leader is the alignment of corporate values with personal, interpersonal and societal values across the values' circles. This not only requires astute awareness of the different values, based on reflection and dialogue, but also moral imagination (Johnson 1993, Werhane 1999) to balance those sometimes conflicting values through creative and at the same time ethically sound solutions. It also means that leaders live and embody the core values. 'We must hope', notes John Gardner, 'that our leaders will help us keep alive values that are not so easy to embed in laws – our feeling about individual moral responsibility, about caring for others, about honor and integrity, about tolerance and mutual respect, and about fulfillment within a framework of values' (1990: 77). What else do leaders need to meet these profound challenges? What competences and capabilities are required to act both effectively and with integrity in a complex web of interests and demands by a multitude of stakeholders? What constitutes *connective leadership* (Lipman-Blumen 2000) in an interconnected world?

We believe that *the ability to build and sustain trustful relationships to all relevant stakeholders is key* in meeting these challenges and that organizational leaders in particular need to have a mindset and relational capabilities which correspond to the new reality of doing business based on a network of sound relationships.

Relationships are the centre of leadership

Bill George, former CEO of Medtronic, writes in his remarkable reflections on his time as a leader:

> The capacity to develop close and enduring relationships is one mark of a leader. ... Authentic leaders establish trusting relationships with people throughout the organization as well as in their personal lives. The rewards of these relationships, both tangible and intangible, are long lasting.
>
> (2003: 23, 24)

However, as we have seen above, the importance of establishing trusting relationships extends well beyond the organization and the personal life of a leader. Most of the challenges that leaders face in an interconnected world emerge from the interaction with a multitude of stakeholders, locally, regionally and globally; both inside and outside the organization. Thus, the greater the need to engage with different stakeholders with different interests and different values, the more important it becomes for leaders to be able to connect with them and to act both interpersonally and ethically competent in these contexts.

There is, in fact, growing awareness that the development of sustainable relationships with clients, employees, shareholders and other stakeholders, is one of the most important determinants of current and future organizational viability and business excellence (Wheeler and Sillanpää 1997). If organizational success hinges on the ability to create sustainable stakeholder relations then it becomes a leadership task to create a context of meaning for quality stakeholder relations and a context of action, in the sense of initiating change towards a more inclusive relationship culture. Leadership, then, could be described as the art of building and sustaining morally sound relationships with all relevant stakeholders of an organization.

As obvious as the relational aspect of leadership may seem, scholars who have put the crucial leadership dimensions in the centre of their inquiries have either narrowed it down to a classic leader–follower relationship or treated it in a rather abstract way. No one that we know of has yet tried to apply a relational approach to the full range of relationships a leader has to engage in. We believe however that this makes a crucial difference because it helps to overcome some limitations. Burns, for example, a political scientist, who introduced transforming leadership (2003), one of the few explicitly normative leadership concepts, defines leadership as: 'when one or more persons engage with others in such a way that leaders and followers raise one another to higher levels of motivation and morality' (Burns 1978: 20). If we look at the complexity of relationships and the underlying, often conflicting, values a leader has to face then this seems to be a difficult task to achieve. At least, for the better part of the relationships she engages in.

Rost, who investigated most of what has been written on leadership in the twentieth century (1920–90), introduced the following definition: 'Leadership is an influence relationship among leaders and followers who intend real changes that reflect their mutual purposes' (Rost 1991: 102). Again, given the complexity of today's leadership environment, a relationship where all sides want to achieve change and agree on the purposes seems to be an ambitious goal; even if one agrees that this is how leadership ought to be. Can this definition really be applied to all leadership relationships?

What both Burns and Rost agree on is that leadership is grounded in the leader–follower relationship and that it cannot and should not be controlled by the leader in irresponsible ways by use of power, force, etc. It is a relationship where both sides exercise influence. However, in Burns's case, the leader should apply conflict techniques to enable the elevation to a higher moral level for leader and follower. Rost's approach on the other hand calls for a participatory, not necessarily morally uplifting, process and thus has strong democratic connotations. What we find in both definitions are core dimensions of the leadership relationship which have normative implications and thus call for ethical reflection: Who leads whom (influence relationship), by what means (power or mutual consent), to achieve which goal (compatibility/desirability)?

A different stream of research, which emphasizes the relational dimension by way of focusing on the impact of leaders on their followers and has gained widespread attention in the business world, evolves around the idea of charismatic leadership. The problem with charismatic leadership is however as Ciulla (2004) has pointed out, that it raises many, if not more, questions about ethics since it can refer to the best and the worst kinds of leadership depending on whether you look at a Ghandi or a Hitler. That is, whether you have a charismatic moral leader or an evil manipulator. Solomon therefore stated, 'Charisma ... is a generalized way of pointing to and emptily explaining an emotional relationship that is too readily characterized as fascination' (1998: 95). Because as a concept it has no ethical value, Solomon argues, we should rather focus on trust, on the importance of building trustful relationships. It is neither important, nor desirable that followers are emotionally attracted to leaders (by way of charisma); it is however important that they can trust a leader on the merits of her values, actions and integrity. More so, it is very likely that while employees or shareholders, for example, may think of a CEO as charismatic, his style and performance may even offend other stakeholders. Being charismatic in a certain narrow context 'does not mean that you are ethical when judged against moral concepts that apply in larger contexts' (Ciulla 2004: 320).

Responsible leadership as the art of building and sustaining relationships to all relevant stakeholders requires *socialized*, not *personalized* leaders (Howell and Aviolo 1992). Leaders, who can relate in different ways, who are able to align different values into a common vision, to listen to others, care for others and ultimately serve others. The main relationship task for a leader is to weave a web of inclusion where the leader engages himself among equals. This is not the *great man*, the detached charismatic or even morally superior person whom we find in many leadership theories. Plato saw this quite clearly in the *Statesman*, a later work, where he noted that people are not sheep, and leaders are not shepherds; Plato regarded the leader as a weaver whose main task was to weave together different kinds of people into the fabric of society (Plato 1971, cit. in Ciulla 2004: 322).

A responsible leader in business, then, can be understood as a weaver of trusting relationships, as a facilitator of stakeholder engagement, and one who balances power by aligning different values to serve both business success and the common good. Executive responsibility is multidimensional; as Chester Barnard pointed out in 1938, it is:

> that capacity of leaders by which, reflecting attitudes, ideals, hopes, derived largely from without themselves, they are compelled to bind the wills of men to the accomplishment of purposes beyond their immediate ends, beyond their times ... For the morality that underlies enduring cooperation is multidimensional. It comes from and may expand to all the world; it is rooted deeply in the past, it faces toward the endless future ... the quality of leadership, the persistence of its influence, the durability of its related organizations, the power of coordination it incites, all express the height of moral aspirations, the breadth of moral foundations.
>
> (Barnard 1938: 483–4)

What are these *aspirations*, what traits should a leader possess to relate and succeed responsibly?

The leader as a (moral) person

Responsible leadership does not depend on a *great man*, as we indicated earlier. On the one hand, what might be considered a good leader in a limited business context might not be considered an equally good leader in the broader context of a stakeholder society, due to different values and expectations. On the other hand, the obsession with great (visionary, charismatic, etc.) leaders that we frequently encounter may even hinder the development of responsible leadership in many areas as the focus is limited to traits and transactions, while different forms of leadership, e.g. the silent, serving, and caring ones, not to mention the context and relationships, are neglected.

That does not mean that a leader should not possess desirable moral qualities and a good character. The opposite is true. One should instead ask the question, as Joanne Ciulla does, 'Should leaders have a higher moral standard?'. If we think along the *great man* theory's claim of exceptional persons, the answer would clearly be yes. But this also means, on the dark side, that some leaders consider themselves an exception from the rule, as in the case of Enron, thus possibly engaging in narcissistic and/or bad leadership (Maccoby 2000, Kellerman 2004). Ciulla therefore convincingly argues in this book that we should not hold leaders to higher moral standards but to the same standards as the rest of society: 'So when we say leaders should be held to a higher moral standard what we really mean is that leaders must be more successful in living up to moral standards, because the price of failure is greater' (Ciulla 2006). Then we have to ask ourselves what dispositions leaders need to achieve this goal, and what can be done to keep leaders from moral failures that their position and the possible power that comes with it may hold for them. What do we need to keep us, as leaders and citizens, from giving in to the temptations we encounter in our daily lives? How do we balance our moral duties and our actions we pursue?

George writes that a leader has to be authentic and that leaders are defined by their values and character: 'The values of the authentic leader are shaped by personal beliefs, developed through study and introspection, and consultation with others – and a lifetime of experience. These values define the holder's moral compass' (George 2003: 20). George notes that these values have to be challenged from time to time but that a leader has to stay true to her values. Staying true, being authentic, *leading with integrity*, is only possible if principles and practice match. Thus, moral *experience* helps not only to refine a person's values, but practised morality is also the showcase for a person's integrity: if followers perceive that a leader's values and principles are in line with her actions – and that she walks the talk – then they will attribute her integrity.

What helps to transmit these values into action? With reference to Aristotle we can say that we need certain virtues, seasoned by experience to succeed and excel from a moral point of view. The virtues help us in *leading* a good and meaningful life; and thus ourself as well as others. Aristotle also reminds us that doing the right thing is not sufficient, that our character and virtues have to match and that we have to *live* what is good and desirable: 'First, he must know [that he is doing virtuous actions]; second, he must decide on them, and decide on them for themselves; and, third, he must also do them from a firm and unchanging state' (Aristotle 1999: 1105a). What we find, then, is that a leader does not have to be a moral hero but has to be a moral person (like everyone else). She should have certain moral qualities that make her a good person and show her integrity. Trust by followers is what follows. We note, thus, that a responsible leader should have *character* (having the right values and showing a firm – but not unchangeable – moral personality); be led by desirable *virtues* and principles such as respect, care, service, honesty, accountability, humility, trust, citizenship, respectful communication; and should practise *introspection* (George 2003). There are some hidden moral qualities or core dimensions of *ethical intelligence* (Pless and Maak 2005) that enable character building and living morality: *moral awareness, reflection skills and critical thinking* and *moral imagination*.

By *moral awareness* we mean that we should expect from leaders a certain stage of moral maturity, being able to apply advanced moral reasoning and being aware of and understanding one's own values, norms and interests as well as the ability to recognize them in others. The pioneering work of Dewey (1909, 1916, 1938), Piaget (1932/1973), Erikson (1963), Winnicott (1971), Kohlberg (1981) and Gilligan (1983), and its subsequent interpretation, offers helpful insights regarding the development of moral awareness. *Reflection skills and critical thinking* is what makes a *reflective practitioner* (Schon 1983). It provides leaders with a critical perspective on themselves as well as the organization, but also on the claims and interests of others (e.g. stakeholders) to generate an orienting perspective for informed, balanced and morally sound decision making. Finally, *moral imagination* (Johnson 1993, Ciulla 1995, Werhane 1999), is an often overlooked aspect of *ethical intelligence*. Moral imagination is a crucial capacity because it helps a leader to solve moral dilemmas in new ways without compromising the integrity of moral principles at hand. Consider the example of a Levi Strauss operations manager who found that two of the jeansmaker's suppliers in Bangladesh employed children under 14 years of age. While this was not forbidden under local law, it was a violation of both ILO and Levi Strauss norms. In order to adhere to the universal norm of preventing child labour, he could have forced the suppliers to terminate the contracts with the children. Having lived in the region for some years he knew however that such termination would have forced the children into other, most likely, worse jobs as families in

Bangladesh for socio-economic reasons depend on these incomes. After some reflection he therefore decided to propose to the suppliers that these would continue to pay the children's salaries until they reached the age of 14; Levi Strauss would in turn finance the children's education up to that point. The suppliers agreed to this solution.

What this case shows is that the local Levi Strauss leader applied moral imagination in a case that would have otherwise had a linear moral solution (child labour is bad, therefore it is not allowed to happen). Instead, a creative moral solution was developed to the benefits of all parties, especially the children. Responsible leadership needs moral imagination because the problems and ethical challenges that leaders may encounter are multifold and complex in a global stakeholder society. Doing the right thing in a traditional way might not always be the right thing to do – norms and principles may collide with local conditions and customs, requiring a different, more imaginative approach.

To be a good person and to have a virtuous character requires a healthy relationship of a leader to herself. Self-discipline and self-knowledge are cornerstones in that. *Self-discipline* can best be described as an overarching virtue including a firm value base; staying true to that base of values and principles no matter how tempting or challenging a situation might be; self-binding to certain moral principles (beyond the code of law); as well as humility with respect to oneself as a person and to the perks and privileges of professional life. *Self-knowledge* refers to the fact that leaders should not lead if they cannot lead themselves (Gardner 1990.) Self-leadership requires self-knowledge; one has to know oneself to be authentic and reliable as a leader. As obvious as this may seem, the many cases of bad or deluded *leadership* we come across tell a different story. Ciulla cites Confucius, who saw this quite clearly: 'If a man (the ruler) can for one day master himself and return to propriety, all under heaven will return to humanity. To practice humanity depends on oneself' (Confucius 1963: 38, cited by Ciulla 2004).

A leader's roles and responsibilities

In the beginning, we hinted at the fact that responsible leaders have different roles in fulfilling their task of leadership. These roles, to which we now turn, will provide us with a more detailed picture of what *responsible leadership* as a relational and normative phenomenon means. These roles overlap and do not reflect different persons, but one integrative person. That is, the responsible leader who is at various times a *servant* to others, a *steward* and as such a custodian of values and resources, an *architect* of inclusive systems and processes and a moral infrastructure, a *change agent* by being a transforming leader, a *coach* by supporting and nurturing followers, and a *storyteller* and creator and communicator of moral experience and shared systems of meaning.

The leader as servant

Greenleaf's idea of servant leadership (1977/2002) has been the second most influential, explicitly normative concept of leadership aside from Burns's idea of transforming leadership (1978, 2003). What makes it so appealing for many scholars and, particulary, practitioners, is the striking idea that leadership is not about the grandiosity of a leader but about those he or she serves. If *serving others* is the core of leadership then this has profound implications for both the dynamics and the responsibilities of leadership. First, it obviously implies attentiveness, responsibility and competence to serve others, to *care* for the needs of others (Tronto 1993). We thus find a strong element of an *ethics of care* (Gilligan 1983) in servant leadership. Second, to serve others and to care for their well-being (e.g. through meaningful work, fair pay and a healthy and safe work environment) requires listening skills (often leaders are good speakers but rather bad listeners), empathy, and the desire to support others – specifically, to support their development and nurture their growth. By being an active servant leaders can contribute to the greater good of others and thereby enable the 'release of human possiblities' (Gardner 1990: 74). And thirdly, the idea of the leader as servant is not limited to employees or internal stakeholders. With it comes a strong sense of community and accordingly a much broader focus on other stakeholders (including the environment and future generations). A servant leader pursues goals that are compatible with the needs and interests of all relevant stakeholders. Being good at building relationships towards these stakeholders, she initiates and engages in stakeholder dialogue; has a deep interest in and is well informed about the social and environmental context; tries to understand, respect and recognize their needs; integrates multiple perspectives. As listener and facilitator the servant leader prefers a thriving community to individual stardom; her true achievements may come to attention only if her leadership is absent as Hermann Hesse reminds us in *The Journey to the East*, by which Greenleaf was inspired to develop the concept of servant leadership:

> It was the absence of the servant Leo which revealed to us, suddenly and terribly, the extent of the dissention and the perplexities which shattered our hitherto apparent complex unity. ... Hardly had Leo left us, when faith and concord amongst us was at an end; it was as if the life-blood of our group flowed away from an invisible wound.
>
> (Hesse 1956: 112–13)

The true merits of a leader's service may not always be obvious. But things may fall apart if a community does not receive it.

The leader as steward

Navigating in a world of complexity, uncertainty, and conflicting interests and values is a challenging task, especially when business is done across countries and cultures (Bartlett and Ghoshal 1998, Hollenbeck 2001, Deresky 2003). It requires from leaders a global perspective on the business challenges (Black *et al.* 1999) as well as a social and moral radar to scan and assess the social, environmental and cultural environment as well as potentially conflicting stakeholder expectations and ethical dilemmas (Donaldson 1989, DeGeorge 1993, Donaldson 1996). The metaphor of the leader as *steward* strikes us as particulary appropriate against this background. It makes reference to both being a guardian of values, a stronghold to protect personal and professional integrity, and steering a business responsibly and respectfully even through troubled waters, thus protecting and preserving what one is entrusted with. A steward used to be someone who was entrusted with leading (and managing) a kingdom while the king or those rightfully in charge were away, or while the heir of a throne was still underage (Block 1993). Stewardship is to hold something in trust. If we connect this idea to the social, moral and environmental values and resources at stake, then we suggest thinking of a responsible leader as someone who is a *custodian of social, moral and environmental values and resources*. A leader should protect and hopefully enrich what she is entrusted with – with both business goals and the common good in mind. Thus, the core question she has to ask herself is: What am I passing on to the next (and future) generations?

The leader as coach

In a complex business environment, the role of the leader as coach cannot be underestimated. In general, it involves facilitating development, enabling learning and supporting individuals, teams and ultimately the organization to create an inclusive integrity culture. Of particular importance are: integrating and motivating people from multiple backgrounds to work together; fostering collaborative interaction, open communication and constructive conflicts (Kets de Vries 1999); giving and receiving feedback; mobilizing people to act responsibly by providing direction to followers (including providing direction about ethical standards and good and desirable business behaviour), by adressing ethical dilemmas and by acting as a role model to show that ethics and integrity matter (Trevino *et al.* 1998, Weaver *et al.* 1999). Other important roles of the coach include: coaching and training people to develop required business, interpersonal, intercultural and ethical skills, e.g. for dealing with dilemmas or moral ambiguity in areas of *moral free space* (Donaldson 1996, Donaldson and Dunfee 1999). This requires leaders to have strong reflection skills and a sound value base; to use advanced moral reasoning (Dalton 1998); to be aware of and able to control their own emotions (Wills and Barham 1994); to understand and cope with cultural differences and apply cross-cultural empathy (Kets de Vries 1999); and last but not least, to show respectful behaviour and to give constructive feedback so as to encourage desired behaviour in followers.

The leader as architect

The metaphor of leader as architect refers to the challenge of building an inclusive *integrity culture* (Pless and Maak 2004). Leaders need to create and cultivate an inspiring and supportive work environment where people find meaning, feel respected, recognized and included (thus, not being discriminated against or harassed); where they have fun and feel mobilized and are thus enabled to contribute according to their highest potential, both in a business and a moral sense. As architects, leaders should initiate a values-based HR-system. They should design management processes, structures as well as a moral infrastructure (policies, guidelines, business principles) to align business systems to the demands of building and supporting an inclusive integrity culture. With respect to external stakeholders, a leader should look at herself as an architect of dialogue, enabling and nurturing the dialogue with all relevant stakeholders. Drawing on the work of Smircich and Morgan (1982), we can look at leaders as creators of shared systems of meaning; as leading through vision, sensemaking and dialogue; as guiding both internal and external stakeholders in sustainable partnerships to an integrative view of business success and the common good.

The leader as storyteller

A very useful tool to support the creation of meaning and sensemaking is the use of stories. As creator and communicator of moral experience and shared systems of meaning, a leader has the task of breathing life into both individual and organizational responsibility. Because some of the issues at hand are of rather abstract nature, the use of stories to picture what, for example, the protection of human rights in practice means can be quite an efficient method. Anita Roddick, founder of The Body Shop, used stories widely to spread her mission and communicate her vision of a socially, culturally and environmentally friendly business that has made a difference in the world through ongoing commitment, fair trade and active citizenship behaviour:

> The people I work with ... also want to learn and find meaning in their life. They are open to leadership that has a vision, but this vision has to be communicated clearly and persuasively, and always, always with passion ... I believe that one of the most effective means of communication is storytelling ... within The Body Shop, [we use] both stories about products and stories about the organization. Stories about how and where we find ingredients bring meaning to our

essentially meaningless products, while stories about the company bind
and preserve our history and our sense of common purpose.

(Roddick 2000: 79–80)

Or consider the stories which are told by successors of responsible leaders
like James Burke of Johnson & Johnson (J&J) or Roy Vagelos of Merck,
who took on and succeeded in the fight against riverblindness. The story of
James Burke, who decided in the famous Tylenol case to pull all bottles off
the shelves because someone had tampered with Tylenol bottles in the
Chicago area, still serves as a culture building instrument at J&J. Stories
can illustrate and transport core values; they can help in building a moral
community; and they can trigger our moral imagination.

The leader as change agent

Finally, drawing on the work of Burns and Bass and Steidlmeier we understand leaders also as change agents, who are responsible for initiating change
towards a value-conscious and sustainable business in a stakeholder society.
While we cannot discuss here the pros and cons of Burns's concept of *transforming leadership* (1978, 2003) or Bass (1997) and Bass and Steidlmeier's
(1999) take on *transformational leadership*, we would like to stress the idea
of *responsible change*. It seems important to note that in times of constant
change, any transformation should be conducted and facilitated in a caring
and responsible manner and that it is, first and foremost, a leadership task.
It implies creating an appropriate (values-based) vision, mobilizing people,
building and sustaining commitment through ongoing sensemaking activities, and finally keeping momentum in times when change causes complexity, insecurity and disorientation. Responsible leaders have to be flexible,
tolerant, and should be able to simplify complexity, reduce uncertainty and
anxieties among followers by creating a 'holding environment' (Kets de Vries
1999: xvii), by supporting the search for meaning (Smircich and Morgan
1982, Weick 1995), and by upholding a clear vision and purpose.

It should be said again that all these roles and responsibilities are distinctive features of a responsible leader but come at best together as one, integrative personality. Are we, then again, looking for exceptional persons?
Not at all – some of it will come naturally, as it comes with being a mature
moral person, articulate citizen and caring member of a community. Other
aspects can be learned at any stage in life. Before we conclude, we want to
briefly touch on the question: How can responsible leadership be learned?

Can responsible leadership be learned?

Are leaders born or made? Responsible leaders, as most leaders, are
made in the sense that nobody is born with the qualities necessary to

cope with complex and demanding challenges of leading a business in a stakeholder society. However, Kant reminded us that, as human beings, we are capable of reason. We have the capacity for self-reflection, learning and development. As different thinkers in the fields of developmental psychology, psychoanalysis and moral development – Piaget, Dewey, Freud, Jung, Erikson, Kohlberg, Gilligan – have shown, human beings are able to learn and to develop through different stages to reach a certain level of psychological and moral maturity. Human development is a lifelong process; so is the development of leadership capacity in current and future leaders. We assume therefore that responsible leadership can be developed. Still, some people are more talented than others to become leaders. A certain degree of cognitive, emotional and relational intelligence (Pless and Maak 2005) and the ability and willingness to learn is required (Spreitzer *et al.* 1997). Developing responsible leaders, then, is on the one hand a question of identifying the *right* people and on the other hand a question of educating and developing them through the appropriate means.

While we cannot go into detail here explaining different ways to do this, we want to shed light on a particular promising way. There is agreement among many experts that experiential learning methods like challenging field assignments are the most powerful method to develop leadership capabilities (McCall and Hollenbeck 2002, Black *et al.* 1999, Wilson and Dalton 1998). However, little is known about how to develop responsible leadership vis-à-vis the challenge of building a truly sustainable business. The literature on service learning suggests that, through service learning projects, an awareness of social issues and citizenship responsibilities can be developed (e.g. Fleckenstein 1997). Given these insights, we suggest that responsible leadership can be developed through experiential learning. In particular, we have found in our own research that cross-sector partnership projects open up a learning space for multifold reflection regarding the role of a leader in stakeholder society and the role of the organization as a caring corporate citizen. In fact, successful co-learning and development projects with NGOs or social entrepreneurs can teach leaders how to partner and how to build sustainable relationships – these projects thus serve as a *business-in-society incubator*. Obviously, a lot more research needs to be done on what constitutes successful learning projects, on how this affects the stakeholder engagement, what effects it has on developing leaders and their followers, and how it affects the long-term performance of a business. Nevertheless, the future of developing responsible leadership in business is to be found in experiential learning programmes, not in classroom teaching (see e.g. Pless and Schneider, Chapter 14, this volume). And one cannot be sure what to find because, as George notes: 'The medium for developing into an authentic leader is not the destination but the journey itself – a journey to find your true self and the purpose of your life's work' (2003: 27).

Conclusion: a relational approach towards responsible leadership

In this chapter, we have outlined a *relational approach towards responsible leadership*. Leadership is all about relationships. Responsible leadership is about building and sustaining trustful relationships to all relevant stakeholders by being servant, steward, architect, change agent, coach and storyteller – by serving, supporting and caring for followers, by making them partners on a leadership journey towards building a truly sustainable business, contributing to the development of others, and to the common good. It 'entails the ability of leaders to sustain fundamental notions of morality such as care and respect for persons, justice and honesty, in changing organizational, social and global contexts' (Ciulla 2004: 326). Leadership authority, then, comes with relationship work, service, care and commitment. Responsible leaders contribute to the flourishing of followers – persons, teams, stakeholders and communities. Leaders in turn flourish in their relations to others and to themselves as they receive trust and recognition for being a good *weaver* in the web of humanity.

Questions

1   How do you explain the lack of focus on relationships and responsibilities in leadership studies?
2   Try to map your relationships as a leader – or as a follower – and describe the responsibilities they imply.
3   What are in your opinon the main leadership roles? How are they connected among each other and how do they serve an executive in leading responsibly?
4   Why is charismatic leadership a double-edged sword?
5   How can responsible leadership be developed?

Bibliography

Aristotle (1999) *Nicomachean Ethics;* trans. T. Irwin, Indianapolis, IN, Cambridge: Hackett.
Barnard, C. (1938) *The Functions of the Executive*, Cambridge, MA, London: Harvard University Press.
Bartlett, C.A. and Ghoshal, S. (1998) *Managing Across Borders*, Boston, MA: Harvard Business School Press.
Bass, B.M. (1997) *Transformational Leadership*, Mahwah, NJ: Lawrence Earlbaum.
Bass, B.M. and Steidlmeier, P. (1999) 'Ethics, character and authentic tranformational leadership behavior', *Leadership Quarterly*, 10(2): 181–218.
Black, J.S., Morrison, A.J. and Gregersen, H.B. (1999) *Global Explorers: the next generation of leaders*, New York, London: Routledge.
Block, P. (1993) *Stewardship: choosing service over self-interest*, San Francisco, CA: Berrett-Koehler.

Burns, J.M. (1978) *Leadership*, New York: Perennial.

Burns, J.M. (2003) *Transforming Leadership: a new pursuit of happiness*, New York: Atlantic Monthly Press.

Ciulla, J. (1995) 'Leadership ethics: mapping the territory', *Business Ethics Quarterly*, 5(1): 5–28.

Ciulla, J. (2004) 'Ethics and leadership effectiveness', in J. Antonakis, A.T. Cianciolo and R.J. Sternberg (eds) *The Nature of Leadership*, Thousand Oaks, CA, London, New Dehli: Sage, 302–27.

Ciulla, J. (2006) 'Ethics: the heart of leadership', in T. Maak and N.M. Pless (eds) *Responsible Leadership*, London, New York: Routledge.

Confucius (1963) 'The humanism of Confucius', in W.T. Chan (ed.) *A Source Book in Chinese Philosophy*, Princeton, NJ: Princeton University Press.

Cox Jr, T. (2001) *Creating the Multicultural Organization*, San Francisco, CA: Jossey-Bass.

Dalton, M.A. (1998) 'Developing leaders for global roles', in C.D. McCauley, R.S. Moxley and E. Van Velsor (eds) *The Center for Creative Leadership Handbook of Leadership Development*, San Francisco, CA: Jossey-Bass, 379–402.

DeGeorge, R.T. (1993) *Competing with Integrity in International Business*, Oxford, New York: Oxford University Press.

Deresky, H. (2003) *International Management: managing across borders and cultures*, Upper Saddle River, NJ: Prentice-Hall.

Dewey, J. (1909) *Moral Principles in Education*, Boston, MA: Houghton Mifflin.

Dewey, J. (1916) *Democracy and Education*, New York: Macmillan.

Dewey, J. (1938) *Experience and Education*, New York: Macmillan.

Donaldson, T. (1989) *The Ethics of International Business*, New York, Oxford: Oxford University Press.

Donaldson, T. (1996) 'Values in tension: ethics away from home', *Harvard Business Review*, 74(5): 48–56.

Donaldson, T. and Dunfee, T. (1999) *Ties That Bind*, Boston, MA: Harvard Business School Press.

Donaldson, T. and Preston, L.E. (1995) 'The stakeholder theory of the corporation: concepts, evidence and implications', *Academy of Management Review*, 20(1): 65–91.

Erikson, E.H. (1963) *Childhood and Society*, New York: W.W. Norton.

Fleckenstein, M.P. (1997) 'Service learning in business ethics', *Journal of Business Ethics*, 16(12/13): 1347–51.

Freeman, R.E. (1984) *Strategic Management: a stakeholder approach*, Boston, MA: Pitman.

Freeman, R.E. (1994) 'The politics of stakeholder theory: some future directions', *Business Ethics Quarterly*, 4(4): 409–22.

Gardner, J. (1990) *On Leadership*, New York: Free Press.

George, B. (2003) *Authentic Leadership: rediscovering the secrets to creating lasting value*, San Francisco, CA: Jossey-Bass.

Gilbert, J.A. and Ivancevich, J.M. (2000) 'Valuing diversity: a tale of two organizations', *Academy of Management Executive*, 14(1): 93–105.

Gilligan, C. (1983) *In a Different Voice*, Cambridge, MA: Harvard University Press.

Greenleaf, R.K. (1977/2002) *Servant Leadership: a journey into the nature of legitimate power and greatness*, 25th anniversary edn, New York, Mahwah, NJ: Paulist Press.

Hesse, H. (1956) *The Journey to the East*, New York: Picador.

Hollenbeck, G.P. (2001) 'A serendipitous sojourn through the global leadership literature', in W.H. Mobley and M.W. McCall, Jr (eds) *Advances in Global Leadership*, Amsterdam: JAI Press, vol. 2: 15–47.

Honneth, A. (1996) *The Struggle of Recognition: the moral grammar of social conflicts*, Cambridge, MA, London: MIT Press.

Howell, J.M. and Aviolo, B.J. (1992) 'The ethics of charismatic leadership: submission or liberation', *Academy of Management Executive*, 6(2): 43–54.

Johnson, M. (1993) *Moral Imagination: implications of cognitive science for ethics*, Chicago, IL, London: The University of Chicago Press.

Kellerman, B. (2004) *Bad Leadership: what it is, how it happens, why it matters*, Boston, MA: Harvard Business School Press.

Kets de Vries, M. (1999) *The New Global Leaders*, San Francisco, CA: Jossey-Bass.

Kohlberg, L. (1981) *The Philosophy of Moral Development*, New York: Harper & Row.

Lipman-Blumen, J. (2000) *Connective Leadership*, New York, Oxford: Oxford University Press.

Maccoby, M. (2000) 'Narcissistic leaders: the incredible pros, the incredible cons', *Harvard Business Review*, 78(1): 69–77.

McCall, M.W. and Hollenbeck, G.P. (2002) *Developing Global Experience: the lessons of international experience*, Boston, MA: Harvard Business School Press.

Phillips, R. (2003) *Stakeholder Theory and Organizational Ethics*, San Francisco, CA: Berrett-Koehler.

Piaget, J. (1932/1973) *Das moralische Urteil beim Kinde*, Frankfurt am Main: Suhrkamp.

Pless, N.M. and Maak, T. (2004) 'Building an inclusive diversity culture: principles, processes and practice', *Journal of Business Ethics*, 54: 129–47.

Pless, N.M. and Maak, T. (2005) 'Relational intelligence for leading responsibly in a connected world', in K.M. Weaver (ed.) *Proceedings of the Sixty-fifth Annual Meeting of the Academy of Management*.

Roddick, A. (2000) *Business as Unusual*, London: Thorsons.

Rosen, R., Digh, P., Singer, M. and Phillips, C. (2000) *Global Literacies: lessons on business leadership and national cultures*, New York: Simon and Schuster.

Rost, J.C. (1991) *Leadership for the 21st Century*, Westport, CT, London: Quorum.

Schon, D.A. (1983) *The Reflective Practitioner: how professionals think in action*, New York: Basic Books.

Smircich, L. and Morgan, G. (1982) 'Leadership: the management of meaning', *Journal of Applied Behavioral Science*, 18: 257–73.

Solomon, R.C. (1998) 'Ethical leadership, emotions, and trust: beyond "charisma"', in J. Ciulla (ed.) *Ethics: the heart of leadership*, Westport, CT, London: Praeger, 87–107.

Solomon, R.C. and Flores, F. (2001) *Building Trust in Business, Politics, Relationships, and Life*, Oxford, New York: Oxford University Press.

Spreitzer, G.M., McCall, M.W. and Mahoney, J.D. (1997) 'Early identification of international executive potential', *Journal of Applied Psychology*, 82(1): 6–29.

Stein, S.J. and Book, H.E. (2003) *The EQ Edge: emotional intelligence and your success*, Toronto: Multi-Health Systems.

Svendsen, A. (1998) *The Stakeholder Strategy*, San Francisco, CA: Berrett-Koehler.

Trevino, L.K., Butterfield, K.B. and McCabe, D.L. (1998) 'The ethical context in organizations: influences on employee atttitudes and behaviors', *Business Ethics Quarterly*, 8(3), 447–76.

Tronto, J.C. (1993) *Moral Boundaries: a political argument for an ethic of care*, New York, London: Routledge.

Weaver, G., Trevino, L.K. and Cochran, P. (1999) 'Corporate ethics programs as control systems: influences of executive commitment and environmental factors', *Academy of Management Journal*, 42(1): 41–57.

Weick, K.E. (1995) *Sensemaking in Organizations*, Thousand Oaks, CA: Sage.

Werhane, P. (1999) *Moral Imagination and Management Decision Making*, New York, Oxford: Oxford University Press.

Wheeler, S. and Sillanpää M. (1997) *The Stakeholder Corporation*, London: Pitman.

Wilson, M.S. and Dalton, M.A. (1998) *International Success: selecting, developing, and supporting expatriate managers*, Greensboro, NC: Center for Creative Leadership.

Wills, S. and Barham, K. (1994) 'Being an international manager', *European Management Journal*, 12(1): 49–58.

Winnicott, D.W. (1971) *Playing and Reality*, London, New York: Routledge.

Yukl, G. (2002) *Leadership in Organizations*, 5th edn, Upper Saddle River, NJ: Prentice-Hall.

4　A compass for decision making[1]

Lynn Sharp Paine

Introduction

The corporation is one of mankind's great inventions. It has enabled human beings to establish cooperative endeavours that overcome barriers of time and space while also reducing the costs that individuals acting alone would incur in organizing such efforts. Without the corporation or some such comparable structure, complex enterprises of the scale and scope seen in the world today would be unimaginable. The corporation has been equally crucial in fostering entrepreneurial activity, technological innovation and new businesses. It has created wealth and economic prosperity for many. In fact, the corporation's utility has made it the organizational form of choice for more and more people and purposes over time.

As its role has changed and expanded, however, the corporation itself has had to evolve. At various points in history, it has taken on new attributes that reflect society's changing ideas about what companies should do and how they should be managed. Some of these societal changes have necessitated only incremental modifications. Others, like the shift from corporate chartering to general incorporation statutes in the nineteenth century, have been revolutionary in their impact.

Today, the corporation is undergoing another revolutionary change. The moralization of the corporation represents a radical departure from the amoral, mechanistic conception that has dominated previous thinking. Like the legal changes that prompted the shift from charter-driven to finance-driven companies, the attribution of moral personality to the corporation necessitates fundamental changes in its internal structure and management.

This shift, in turn, has implications for corporate leadership. To build the organizational capabilities needed for success in the new era, companies will need leaders with the skills and commitments required to meld high ethical standards with outstanding financial results. One essential skill will be ethically-informed decision making.

A missing ingredient

As things now stand, ethical analysis is rarely a defined part of business decision making, and ethical issues are generally managed by exception. To the

This chapter comprises excerpts from Lynn Sharp Paine, *Value Shift: why companies must merge social and financial imperatives to achieve superior perforance.* © 2003, The McGraw-Hill companies. Reproduced with permission.

extent that moral concerns have come into managers' decision processes, they have generally taken the form of *smell tests*, *sleep tests* and *newspaper tests*: Does it smell okay? Will it keep me awake at night? How would it look on the front page of the newspaper? Like corporate strategy before the days of competitive analysis, ethical assessment has been more a matter of instinct or gut feeling than a considered and informed thought process.

Although instinct is an important guide to moral judgement – I would rarely advise anyone to ignore it – it is often incomplete, certainly inarticulate and sometimes mistaken. Few people, even experienced executives of impeccable personal character, have such well-honed instincts that they can intuitively and single-handedly grasp the moral questions raised by a new product proposal or a financial restructuring plan, let alone form a sound judgement about them or a plan for addressing them. Furthermore, the moral questions at the frontiers of technology, where leading companies must increasingly operate, are dauntingly complex. Although instinct may work well enough for simple questions of right and wrong that arise in familiar situations, its reliability diminishes rapidly in novel or complex situations. Nor is instinct much help when it comes to moral dilemmas – conflicts among values or competing responsibilities – or when members of a group have different moral instincts.

What's more, moral concerns are outside the purview of most common frameworks for management decision making. Just as a doctor using diagnostics for detecting cardiac problems might fail to see symptoms of breast cancer, a manager using the tools of competitive or financial analysis might easily fail to see important moral issues. Thus, a proposal may pass rate-of-return hurdles and competitive analysis screens while at the same time failing even basic moral tests. In fact, crucial issues may not even come to management's attention until after a moral challenge has been issued – and at that point it may be too late for an effective response.

What is needed is a method for integrating ethical considerations into the organization's decision-making processes. A structured process for identifying and evaluating ethical concerns can correct for the blind spots inherent in many conventional frameworks and help decision makers more effectively link the values they espouse with the choices they actually make. This chapter suggests such a process. This framework, which has grown out of my teaching and research, is not a moral algorithm or a theory of right action so much as a prompt to focus managers' attention on the moral aspects of their decision making.[2]

Ask, don't tell

This framework exploits the power of questions to engage people's moral faculties. For many, the idea of ethics is strongly associated with codes of conduct, values statements or lists of moral imperatives. Certainly, history has given us a long tradition of such *to do* and *not to do* lists as sources of moral guidance. However, another classic approach to moral insight has less to do with answers and more to do with the kinds of questioning and discussion used by two of the great practical moralists of all times – Socrates in ancient Greece and Confucius in ancient China. These thinkers sought to guide behaviour not by issuing directives but by engaging their listeners in a collaborative process of discussion and deliberation. Socrates, in particular, relied on an incisive process of questioning and probing that came to bear his name – the 'Socratic method'. Confucius depended more on illustrative examples and stories to bring out important points, but again in the context of discussion and mutual exploration.

These masters knew that moral insight is more apt to come from live interchange among informed and inquiring minds than from lists of abstract principles. Or put differently, principles and codes are nothing until brought to life in the context of human activity. Anyone who has looked at a typical code of conduct or statement of business principles knows how hard such documents are to read, let alone understand and retain. It is only when they are connected with actual concerns in the context of real situations that they engage the mind and the will. Codes and principles are neither self-applying nor self-interpreting. In the end, they derive whatever force they have from people's decisions to follow them, and they must be interpreted in light of facts and circumstances that themselves may be open to interpretation.

Few decisions of substance have only one moral aspect. More often, two or more important values conflict, as when a duty of confidentiality to one party conflicts with a duty of candor to another. Often a course of action that meets the needs of one group will create hardship for another. Codes, values statements and the like help to identify and frame the issues in such cases, but they cannot resolve moral conflicts or create a practical path of action. For that, the only answer is informed judgement based on thoughtful consideration of competing claims and differing perspectives. Working through a situation to arrive at a reasonable course of action calls for imagination as much as analysis and may even require in-depth research. Given the inherent variability of circumstances, a set of questions is likely to prove far more useful than a set of prepackaged answers.

The power of questions can be seen in many management activities. Consider strategy formulation. A company's strategy is not dictated by a set of abstract principles, useful though such principles may be. Formulating a sound strategy requires a careful process of analysis that takes into account a number of potentially competing considerations. Reasonable people can and do disagree; they bring to the process different facts, different interpretations of the facts and different beliefs about the likely future, as well as different aims and priorities. It is by sifting through the relevant considerations, deliberating about the merits of available alternatives, and imagining likely futures that decision makers arrive at what looks to be the most promising course. Of course, solutions sometimes come in a flash, but they more typically emerge through a shared process of thought that can be aided with a structured set of questions and analytic techniques: What opportunities are presented? What are our capabilities? Who are our existing and potential competitors? And so on.

Another example: When managers evaluate a potential investment or proposed new product from an economic point of view, they do so with certain characteristic questions in mind. How big is the market? How attractive are the profit margins? How much investment is required? What is the likely return on this investment? How long will it take to realize this return? And so on. Any serious project proposal will address such questions even before they are asked because the proponent knows that sooner or later they will be. Only by answering the whole set of such questions is it possible to determine whether the proposal makes any economic sense. Even so, it may be difficult to form a sound judgement without some experience base.

Business neophytes usually have to learn these questions – through the experience of being asked and perhaps not having answers or through formal training, although formal training will decay quickly unless put to use on the job. At first, learners may have to work through the questions somewhat laboriously by following a detailed checklist of important considerations. But eventually the questions become internalized as 'second nature', the need to answer them becomes ingrained, and answers are sought more or less by instinct. In simple, recurrent situations, even the answers themselves may be instinctual, but more complex cases that involve high stakes will usually require thorough analysis based on in-depth research. Here, again, a structured process can be helpful.

What questions, then, might help to inject the moral point of view into decision making?

The four modes of ethical analysis

The core question of ethics, the question at the root of the discipline, is the classic, 'How should we live?'[3] Although this overarching question – perhaps mankind's most fundamental – might seem a bit unwieldy for our purposes, it quickly unfolds into several subsidiary questions that look and feel more manageable: What should we aim for? How should we conduct ourselves? What do we owe others? What rights do we have?

Such subsidiary questions, each of which can be broken down further into subcomponents, suggest four modes of moral analysis that can be quite useful in making decisions. Each mode is associated with a distinctive form of practical reasoning and a tradition of ethical thought. Let me provide a thumbnail sketch of the four modes.

Purpose – will this action serve a worthwhile purpose?

This mode of analysis has to do with the ethics of ends and means or *pragmatic analysis*. *Pragmatic* is sometimes used to mean *expedient rather than moral*, but I am using the term in its more general sense to mean *goal-directed* or *purposeful*. Pragmatic analysis examines the quality of our goals and the suitability of the means we choose for attaining them.

This mode of analysis thus calls for clarity about both ends and means, but the ends must be judged worthwhile and the means found to be effective as well as efficient.[4] The central question is whether a proposed course of action will serve a worthwhile purpose. But an answer to this question will normally require answers to a cluster of subsidiary questions calling for facts as well as judgment:

- What are we trying to accomplish? What are our short- and long-term goals?
- Are these goals worthwhile? How do they contribute to people's lives?
- Will the course of action we're considering contribute to achieving these goals?
- Compared to the possible alternatives, how effectively and efficiently will it do so?
- If this is not the most effective and efficient course, do we have a sound basis for pursuing the proposed path?

Principle – Is this action consistent with relevant principles?

A second mode of analysis examines actions from the standpoint of applicable principles and standards. Its roots lie in the ethics of duty and ideals. Let's call it *normative analysis* since it references various norms of behaviour, those entailed by self-imposed ideals and aspirations as well as those found in bodies of standards such as law, industry codes, company codes and the emerging body of generally accepted ethical principles for business. In contrast to pragmatic analysis, which uses instrumental or means–end reasoning, normative analysis relies on reasoning from general principles to specific instances – what has sometimes been called *formal reasoning*.

The central question is whether a proposed course of action is consistent with the relevant principles. Among these may be principles that express duties or obligations whose fulfilment is required as well as principles that express ideals or voluntary standards associated with good practice. Normative analysis involves subsidiary questions such as:

- What norms of conduct are relevant to this situation – including those found in law, customary practice, industry codes, company guidelines or the emerging body of generally accepted ethical principles?
- What are our duties under these standards?
- What are best practices under these standards?
- Does the proposed action honor the applicable standards?
- If not, do we have a sound basis for departing from those standards?

- Is the proposed action consistent with our own espoused standards and ideals?

People – Does this action respect the legitimate claims of the people likely to be affected?

A third mode of analysis focuses on the expected consequences of a proposed course of action for the people likely to be affected by it. Will they be injured? Will they benefit? Will their rights be violated or infringed? This mode of analysis is sometimes called *stakeholder analysis* or *stakeholder impact analysis* because it takes the vantage point of those with a stake in the outcome. The central question is whether a proposed course of action respects the legitimate claims of the parties affected by it.[5]

Stakeholder analysis is useful for identifying opportunities to mitigate harms as well as to pursue mutual gains. Skill in social reasoning is essential for carrying out this kind of analysis, since understanding others' perspectives and circumstances is the starting point for evaluating their concerns, interests and expectations. However, formal reasoning is also involved insofar as norms play a role in assessing the claims presented. Key questions in stakeholder analysis include:

- Who is likely to be affected, both directly and indirectly, by the proposed action?
- How will these parties be affected?
- What are these parties' rights, interests, expectations and concerns as derived from law, agreement, custom, past practice, explicit norms or other sources?
- Does our plan respect the legitimate claims of the affected parties?
- If not, what are we doing to compensate for this infringement?
- Have we mitigated unnecessary harms?
- Are there alternatives that would be less harmful or more beneficial on balance?
- Have we taken full advantage of opportunities for mutual benefit?

Power – Do we have the power to take this action?

A fourth mode of analysis stems from the ethics of power. In a sense, this is the most fundamental question because it concerns the actor's authority and ability to act. Unless a proposed action is within the scope of the actor's legitimate authority and unless the actor actually has the ability – the skills, resources, clout, energy – to carry out the proposed plan, all the previous questions are moot. Following the dictum that ought implies can, this analysis might be termed an agency analysis. It examines the actor's moral right and material resources to act. From this perspective, then, the central question is whether the proposed action is within the actor's legitimate power. This question leads to the following subsidiary inquiries:

- What is the scope of our legitimate authority in view of relevant laws, agreements, understandings and stakeholder expectations?
- Are we within our rights to pursue the proposed course of action?
- If not, have we secured the necessary approvals or consent from the relevant authorities?
- Do we have the resources, including knowledge and skills as well as tangible resources, required to carry out the proposed action?
- If not, do we have the ability to marshal the needed resources?

These questions are not a set of moral precepts or standards of behaviour in any conventional sense but rather a set of analytical frames or moral *lenses*. Each lens is associated with a characteristic cluster of questions that can help managers *see* more clearly ethical issues that an economic perspective might obscure or relegate to the background. Like the varied lenses used by a photographer, each one brings into focus different features of the situation so that they can be more readily inspected and compared with other features. Of course, the aim here is not just to identify these features but also to evaluate their importance and then to address them, perhaps by modifying a plan or taking further action if that's what the situation calls for.

The importance of *merely* recognizing an issue, however, should not be underestimated. The long tradition of corporate amorality has meant that many managers are habituated to a kind of moral disengagement at work and can find themselves in an ethical minefield without even realizing it. Many leaders of corporate ethics programmes say that the vast majority of the problems they must deal with originate with decision makers who simply didn't see the issues or didn't see them early enough. Researchers have documented among managers a phenomenon they have called *moral muteness*, or the inability to engage with or speak about moral questions in the workplace (Bird and Waters 1989, Jackall 1988).

From time to time I have experienced the symptoms of this phenomenon. A few years back, in connection with an ethics seminar I agreed to present for a company's leadership development programme, I was to spend a day at corporate headquarters interviewing key executives to identify any special issues or concerns the seminar should cover. I was stunned when my agenda for the day indicated that each interview was set for only 20 minutes. When I asked about the time slots, the coordinating manager explained that he'd set up short meetings because he couldn't imagine what people would talk about in a longer period. (In the end, the company decided to forgo the background interviews and instead asked me to present a general seminar addressing issues in the industry.)

On the other hand, I have also found it quite easy to engage executives in discussing moral concerns. If asked the right questions in the right way, most of them have plenty to say on the topic, and many welcome an opportunity for thoughtful discussion of issues they don't normally talk about at work. In the classroom, I have found that the course of discussion can be radically altered by asking a simple question such as, 'What would be the most responsible thing to do here?' or 'Are there any ethical issues here?' or 'We've got a pretty good plan of action. Do you think this would be the right thing to do?' Even such broad general questions can open up a field of exploration that otherwise might never come up.

The lenses in this framework, however, go beyond simply identifying issues. Each lens suggests an overarching criterion of evaluation – contribution to a worthwhile purpose, consistency with governing principles, respect for the claims of others and consistency with legitimate authority. While leaving much to interpretation, these lenses nonetheless highlight the central ethical questions that company leaders and managers are likely to encounter and provide a basis for robust consideration of these issues in a decision-making context.

Notice that the lenses are not independent of one another. Rather than offering mutually exclusive and unique perspectives, they present a series of related but different angles for viewing and sizing up issues. Take, for instance, a simple question such as whether to disclose a workplace hazard to employees. A normative analysis might reveal an obligation to disclose, based perhaps on law or company standards. A stakeholder analysis would focus on employees' right to know. Because rights and duties often mirror one another, we are in effect looking at two sides of the same coin in this case. In a sense, the lenses provide a 360-degree moral assessment tool.

These four lenses, taken together, create the metaphorical *decision making compass* shown in Figure 4.1. Unlike a code of conduct that offers specific directives, the decision making compass is more of a navigational device designed to help chart a reasonable course through what can sometimes be a sea of conflicting demands. Unlike a magnetic compass or gyrocompass, this metaphorical compass is not oriented to any one direction, nor does it function independently of its user. Rather, it can be thought of as an orienting device or a tool for determining an appropriate direction.

The process of working through the questions associated with each cardinal point can do more than simply help decision makers to avoid gaffes and missteps. Whether applied to the traditional tasks of management or the decisions uniquely faced by leaders, it can also spark creative thinking and help to refine and strengthen proposed plans of action. The sequence in which the perspectives are considered is unimportant. In some cases, it will be necessary to revisit each one several times to forge a satisfactory proposal. In others, the analysis may elicit only one or two main issues. What's important is that the thought process should include each perspective. Ideally, a chosen course of action will in the end satisfy all four criteria.

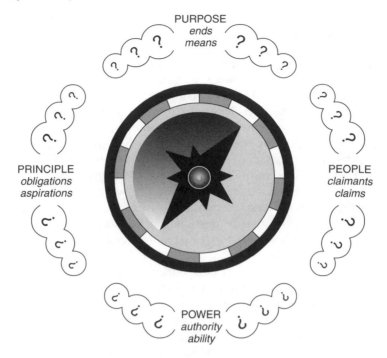

Figure 4.1 The decision making compass

Correcting for blind spots

Without a framework like the decision making compass to inject the moral point of view into their deliberations, decision makers are vulnerable to the blind spots and biases inherent in many commonly used frameworks. Competitive analysis, for instance, is a powerful aid in strategy formulation, but it does not ask decision makers to think about stakeholder impact, social contribution or conformity with legal and ethical norms. Cost–benefit analysis is another such ubiquitous framework. Based on the sensible and obvious idea that the benefits of an action should exceed its costs, this methodology has many valid uses. But what is a benefit? And what is a cost? And for whom? Here difficulties can arise unless we are careful.

Although cost–benefit analysis might in theory do a reasonable job of accommodating ethical considerations, in practice it frequently fails to do so. Because the method tends to focus on *monetary* costs and benefits, gains and losses that are not readily priced can be easily overlooked. And because the emphasis is generally on costs and benefits *for the decision maker*, effects on other parties are not taken as seriously as they should be.

Part of the difficulty lies in the method's insistence on monetizing all costs and benefits. For example, standard valuation and accounting techniques help little when it comes to costing out the loss of privacy associated with the unfettered gathering and exchange of consumer information. And by what logic can we place a monetary value on moral injuries such as the loss of trust caused by dishonesty, the degradation of the personality caused by abusive work practices, or the heightened risk of cancer associated with a new product? These are just a few examples where cost–benefit analysis comes up wanting.

Economists and lawyers have tried to develop monetary equivalents for such injuries, particularly in the area of health and safety risks. To the non-economist, however, these efforts are less than convincing. From a moral point of view, for example, it is problematic to value the health of a male executive more than that of a young mother just because the executive has greater earning potential or would be willing to pay more to avoid injury. Yet, that is the effect when such measures are used to monetize injuries and risks to safety. The exercise is no more convincing on the benefit side. Heightened trust, personal growth, strengthened community – these have no obvious or convincing monetary equivalents to plug into the analysis.

An equally vexing problem is deciding what to count as a *cost* and what as a *benefit*. In the absence of a moral framework, this simple categorization is not always so clear as one might think. An earthquake, for instance, produces human tragedy on a grand scale. At the same time, it can be a financial boon to engineers, builders and construction finance companies.

In the summer of 2001, Philip Morris, the US-based tobacco, beer and food giant, was taken to task for a cost–benefit analysis in which cost savings to society from smokers' early deaths were counted as a *positive effect* of tobacco usage. The analysis, commissioned by company officials in the Czech Republic, was done in an attempt to counter claims that cigarette sales were a drain on the country's economy and to make the case against proposed excise tax increases. The study concluded that smoking yielded the Czech government a net gain of $147.1 million in 1999, largely because of savings on health care, pensions and housing due to smokers' premature deaths (Fairclough 2001).

Public reaction was swift and to the moral point. Although the analysis apparently neglected to consider the costs and benefits of alternatives to tobacco usage, this technical limitation attracted little notice. What captured attention was the bizarre and seemingly callous decision to treat cost savings from premature deaths as a 'benefit' of tobacco usage. If a government's first duty is to protect and promote the welfare of its citizens, then surely anything that brings about their premature death should be counted as a cost, not a benefit. In the wake of the outcry, Philip Morris's CEO acknowledged that funding the study 'exhibited terrible judgment as well as a complete and unacceptable disregard of basic human values' (cited in Fairclough 2001).

He might have also noted that disregard for basic human values has been a recurrent problem with the cost–benefit method. Like many other decision guides used in business, cost–benefit analysis tends to blur distinctions that from a moral point of view are highly material. There's a world of difference, morally speaking, between cost savings that result from product-related deaths versus savings that result from product-related gains in efficiency. But this difference is easily lost if the focus is only on the amount of the savings. A similar point applies to other morally significant distinctions – between harms and wrongs, rights and interests, duties and desires.

Compare a company that harms competitors by improving its product with one that harms them with false claims of improvement. Even if the monetary loss to rivals is the same in the two cases, they merit very different moral assessments. The first company has caused harm but done nothing wrong. In fact, it has done just what it is supposed to do within a competitive system. The second, on the other hand, has both harmed its rivals and wronged them. It has also wronged its customers and society at large by offending against a basic principle of justice. The distinction between harms and wrongs is morally elemental. As former US Supreme Court justice Oliver Wendell Holmes, Jr, once pointed out (1881: 3), even a dog knows the difference between being kicked and being tripped over.

Equally basic is the distinction between rights and interests. Morally speaking, rights-based claims generally take priority over claims based only on interests or desires. Rights, it is sometimes said, *trump* interests. So, in a case of conflict, a consumer's right to the truth about a product's contents trumps a sales representative's interest in making more sales. An employee's right to the minimum wage trumps on employer's desire to lower costs. And, to take another example, if consumers have rights over certain types of personal information, then these rights trump companies' interests in unfettered access. Such priorities, however, are difficult to capture in a simple monetary calculus of costs and benefits (see Dworkin 1978).

For all its aura of objectivity and precision, cost–benefit analysis is highly vulnerable to distortions and biases that cloud the moral issues. Results can vary dramatically depending on what perspective is taken, what effects are included and what economic values are attached to the components of the analysis. Much of the clouding is due to the illusion of precision that comes from monetizing expected outcomes. That we can *objectify* such moral goods as trust, community or life itself by attaching monetary values to them is self-delusion of the highest order. We only compound the error by then calling ourselves rational for, say, trading off *consumer trust worth $500 million* for an increase of $800 million in shareholder value. What's needed is an analytical model that takes the claims of others seriously in their own right and that reveals, rather than obscures, the moral texture of the relationships within which every company must operate.

Centre-driven decision making

In a world that expects companies to create wealth while conducting themselves as moral actors, decision makers will need to practise what might be termed *centre-driven* decision making. This term refers to the area of overlap between ethics and economics shown in the diagram depicted here in Figure 4.2. If decision makers are to target this area, which might be termed the *zone of acceptability*, they will need skill in making decisions that stand up to the various forms of ethical analysis discussed here as well as the more familiar tests of financial attractiveness. Put simply, they will need to marry NPV (net present value) with MPV (moral point of view) analyses.

To locate this zone, executives cannot rely only on the tools and concepts of economic analysis. For all the reasons we have discussed, they will need a repertoire of ethical concepts and moral reasoning skills as well. This is where the decision making compass comes into play. Through the questions it poses, the compass provides a structured process for bringing the moral point of view to bear in making decisions and linking espoused values to actual choices.

Although the compass framework has grown out of my research and teaching, its deeper roots are found in various traditions of moral thought. Anyone familiar with these traditions will see traces of such philosophies as pragmatism, utilitarianism, liberalism, Confucianism, virtue ethics and so on. To academic experts in these different schools of thought, this mixing of traditions and doctrines is heresy, but for practitioners this mixing of traditions is a plus. By harnessing key insights from contending schools of thought, the compass provides a more powerful framework – one with diverse perspectives and built-in checks and balances.

The process of working through the different lenses is useful not only for identifying crucial issues but also for mapping areas of disagreement, generating new options, and, perhaps most important, evaluating possible choices. Sometimes a judgement emerges quickly and easily. The analyses converge, and a course of action meets, or fails, all the implicit criteria. At other times, the process will raise more questions than it answers. It may elicit conflicting principles or contested claims of right. In those cases, further analysis or in-depth research may be required. When existing standards conflict or fail to cover the case at hand, extended deliberations may be needed to formulate a new principle or determine the best trade-off between competing values.

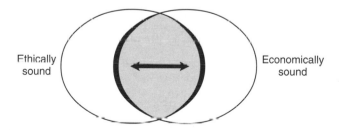

Figure 4.2 The zone of acceptability

Of course, time does not always allow for in-depth analysis, and some cases *are* simple. We come back to the *newspaper tests*, *smell tests* and *sleep tests*, with which the chapter began. These and other moral rules of thumb – *reciprocity tests*, *generality tests*, *legacy tests*, *mirror tests* and *trusted friend tests* – may be likened to the *quick ratios* and *acid tests* of financial analysis. They are no substitute for thorough assessment in complex cases, but they do serve a very useful function. Sometimes, they may be all one has to go on.

In a restless sea of moral and financial expectations, leaders cannot navigate with financial perspectives alone. To meet the new financial, legal and ethical accountabilities, companies will need to integrate the moral point of view into their decision making. The decision making compass is one framework for doing this. Undoubtedly there are others that could work just as well, or perhaps even better, so long as they raise the core questions highlighted in this chapter. Just as important as the framework is the care and rigor with which it is applied. What's essential is to have some way of engaging the moral perspective at the moment of decision. Otherwise, companies will find it very difficult to meet the new standard of performance on a sustained basis.

Questions

1   Describe the key steps in your individual decision-making process. Does this process give explicit attention to ethical considerations?

2   How does your company's leadership group ensure that ethical considerations are included in its decision making? Does it rely more on an analytic framework, a defined process or specifically designated individuals to identify and address these considerations?

3   Among the decision models and analytic frameworks used in different parts of your company, how many of them give explicit attention to ethical considerations?

4   Which of the four forms of ethical analysis are you most familiar with? Which would be easiest to use in the context of your company's existing culture and decision processes?

5   To what extent does your company's leadership development programme seek to build competency in ethics-informed decision making?

Notes

1   This chapter comprises several excerpts from the author's book *Value Shift: why companies must merge social and financial imperatives to achieve superior performance* (2003). The introduction is taken from *Value Shift*, pp. 227–8. Sections 2, 3 and 4 are adapted from *Value Shift*, pp. 200–08. Section 5 is taken from *Value Shift*, pp. 217–20, 222. The concluding section is adapted from *Value Shift*, pp. 223–6. Reprinted with permission from The McGraw-Hill Companies.

2 The following discussion of decision making draws on two of my previous publications. See Paine (1996) and (1997: 223–35).
3 'After all, our discussion is not about something incidenal, but about how we ought to live our lives.' Plato, *The Republic*, Book 1:352d, p. 34.
4 This usage follows the American philosopher William James, who described the pragmatic mentality as one oriented to 'last things, fruits, consequences', as opposed to 'first things, principles, "categories"' (see James 1948: 146).
5 Contemporary approaches to stakeholder analysis vary widely. For a recent roundup, see Donaldson and Preston (1995). For stakeholder analysis as it was envisioned by an early proponent, see Freeman (1984). Although some have criticized stakeholder theory, the typical criticisms do not apply to the type of stakeholder analysis recommended here (see, e.g., Sternberg 1996: 4).

Bibliography

Bird, F.B. and Waters, J.A. (1989) 'The moral muteness of managers', *California Management Review*, 32(1): 16.
Donaldson, T. and Preston, L.E. (1995) 'The stakeholder theory of the corporation: concepts, evidence, and implications', *Academy of Management Review*, 20(1): 65–91.
Dworkin, R. (1978) *Taking Rights Seriously*, Cambridge, MA: Harvard University Press.
Fairclough, G. (2001) 'Philip Morris says it's sorry for death report', *Wall Street Journal*, July 26: B1.
Freeman, R.E. (1984) *Strategic Management: a stakeholder approach*, Boston, MA: Pitman.
Holmes, Jr, O.W. (1881) *The Common Law*, Boston, MA: Little, Brown.
Jackall, R. (1988) *Moral Mazes: the world of corporate managers*, New York, NY: Oxford University Press.
James, W. (1948) 'What pragmatism means', *Essays in Pragmatism*, New York: Hafner.
Paine, L.S. (1996) 'Moral thinking in management: an essential capability', *Business Ethics Quarterly*, 6(4): 477–82.
Paine, L.S. (1997) *Cases in Leadership, Ethics, and Organizational Integrity: a strategic perspective*, Burr Ridge, IL: Richard D. Irwin.
Paine, L.S. (2003) *Value Shift: why companies must merge social and financial imperatives to achieve superior performance*, New York: McGraw-Hill.
Plato (2000) *The Republic*, ed. G.R.F. Ferrari, trans. T. Griffith, Cambridge: Cambridge University Press.
Sternberg, E. (1996) 'Stakeholder theory exposed,' *Corporate Governance Quarterly*, 2(1): 4–18.

5 Spirituality as the basis of responsible leaders and responsible companies

Peter Pruzan and William C. Miller

Introduction

Corporate Social Responsibility (CSR), *Responsible Leadership*, *Socially Responsible Investing* ... Such terms are rapidly becoming part and parcel of the modern management idiom. Some people unreservedly applaud what appears to be an increased focus on and awareness of responsibility in business. Others take a more cynical view. Still others say, 'Before we plunge ahead, let's pause and reflect on what we're really talking about here.'

We fall into this third category, even after having contributed to the theoretical and practical development of the concept of CSR for many years. We have observed that, typical of the managerial profession and its emphasis on measurable results, the focus is primarily on how to operationalize these terms – integrating them into the corporation's vocabulary, policies, stakeholder communications and reporting systems. But something important is missing in this rush towards pragmatism by corporate leaders: a sincere, soul-searching inquiry into what they really mean when they speak of responsibility at the individual and organizational level.

This essay raises and responds to fundamental questions about the nature of responsibility and how explicit consideration of responsibility is vital for the well-being and success of leaders and their organizations. In particular, we explore four questions: What is responsibility? Can organizations be responsible? Why be responsible? What obstacles are there to being responsible?

These inquiries pave the way for a thesis that true responsibility, for both leaders and their organizations, is grounded in a perspective that transcends the limitations of economic rationality. We present responsible leadership within a framework of what we call *spiritual-based leadership* and present excerpts from research interviews we have conducted with leaders from Europe, the United States and Asia that exemplify its relevance for the practical, day-to-day business world (information on this research programme can be obtained at http://www.globaldharma.org/sbl-home.htm).

The interviews clearly demonstrate that spirituality, however individual leaders define and understand it, can provide a powerful foundation for individual and organizational identity, responsibility and success. When leaders and their organizations operate from a spiritual-based perspective, they naturally behave responsibly on behalf of themselves, their communities, society, the environment and all of creation.

Setting the scene

To set the scene, consider the following two examples of responsible leadership and corporate responsibility: Grundfos (Denmark) and Excel Industries (India).

Grundfos

This Danish enterprise has approximately 50 companies, including 15 production companies around the world, and more than 11,000 employees. In 2004 its sales were 11.5 billion Danish Crowns (US$2.1 billion). Its Group Chairman and former CEO, Niels Due Jensen, has for a number of years been the leader of the Danish National Network of Business Leaders from over 700 companies dedicated to corporate social responsibility. According to him:

> Grundfos is probably the most successful pump company in the world. It is clearly with high pride that we in Grundfos are manufacturing pumps and pump systems, because these products really are helping society to grow, helping millions of people all over the world to fulfil certain very basic needs.

Grundfos is highly respected internationally, not only for its success in traditional economic terms, but also for its expanded concept of success that includes the aim of being helpful to others without doing harm.

> In Grundfos it has always been a part of our policies that profit is not a target in itself. Money and a good profitability are necessary for us to maintain a successful growing company, which is a good place for people to work in. Money is simply a means for being able to do things and for achieving various goals in life.
> We are in a business which does not do damage to others, but which is really helpful for human beings all over the world. It may be for people in Africa with simple needs for clean water, or it may be for people in highly developed societies where they need a lot of pumps in order for everything to be functioning.

Leading by values is at the core of their management philosophy, which reaches down to every employee, new and old:

We try to develop an organization of people who take responsibility not only for their job, but also for the company. Of course it takes a long time to get this perspective in the backbone of every employee, and for new employees it takes several years to understand the real meaning of these basic values. Living up to the values is an exercise on a daily basis.

Excel Industries

Excel Industries Ltd in India is an agricultural chemical company whose aim is to 'provide solutions through contributing to the photosynthesis cycle from soil health to plant health to crop productivity to nutrition'. It started as a small kitchen laboratory in 1941 with a capital of Rs.10,000 (approximately US$230 at 2005 exchange rates). Its revenues in 2004 were Rs.4.75 billion (approximately US$110 million) with 3,000 employees.

Excel has pioneered work in rain farming and watershed management. It is actively pursuing the use of alternative energy sources, conducts research to minimize the effect of chemical fertilizers and has introduced eco-friendly measures such as integrated crop and pest management systems. Recently, Excel has also developed processes for using organic compounds and enzymes to deal with environmental problems resulting from municipal solid waste, sewage sludge, industrial waste streams and contamination of soils and waters. This is all based on the values of the company, as K.C. Shroff, one of the three brother-founders of Excel, states: 'The 21st century will see the rise of a new culture, one that is based on holistic principles, harmony and sustainable development. Only those who follow its principles will survive.' A telling story of the culture of responsibility in this organization is a time when a particular division was not growing well, Shroff scolded his colleagues saying: 'You're focusing too much on making money; that's the problem. Focus totally on serving the farmers. Then the money will take care of itself.'

In 1995, *The Week* magazine in India recognized K.C. Shroff as 'Man of the Year' for his work on sustainable development in arid rural areas. In 2000, the Indian Environmental Association gave an Award of Excellence to Mr Shroff in recognition of his pioneering service for the protection and preservation of the environment over five decades.

The underlying similarity between Grundfos and Excel Industries: a spiritual basis for responsibility

Certainly, both of these companies have leaders strongly committed to promoting responsible behaviour throughout their organizations. But the questions arise: What lies behind their stories? What are their motives? What is their rationale? Niels Due Jensen speaks for himself and Grundfos:

Spirituality gives me a deeper meaning of life, and therefore also regulates the way I behave on a regular daily basis in my private life as well as in my job-life.

My principle of *love your neighbour* has guided me in the direction of also developing what we call *social responsibility* at Grundfos. ... Because of my spiritual background I have always had this activity within Grundfos high on my agenda.

As one practice of corporate responsibility, Grundfos employs 150 mentally and physically handicapped persons among its 4,500 employees in Denmark. Mr Jensen comments:

Having employees with a mental or physical handicap working for Grundfos has become a natural part of the company's life and behaviour. We in the management have made it clear that this is our responsibility. You may call it the need to love your neighbour, and this means your neighbour in this local society, but first of all your employees in the company. It is my strong belief that my example has been of importance to many business leaders in Denmark.

K.C. Shroff has this to say in the *Life Positive* magazine about Excel Industries and his passionate concern for nature and the earth:

Our Mother Earth has been badly hurt by greed. She must heal. We are working for God. We are his means. The whole cosmic creativity is through that [working for God]. If we can become a part of that, what a joy it is! Productive action is spirituality. Profit is a by-product of services rendered. At Excel, service is the motivation.

(Varughese 2004: 34)

Excel's 50-year mission statement ends with:

We have a responsibility towards industry and community. Rural community is the heart of India. We will be friends and contributors to the well being of both the industrial and the rural community. Company is family. We will work and contribute, learn and grow together. This is our resolution and we resolve so. We pray to the Almighty that we be granted the strength to fulfil our mission

And in 2004 in Zurich, Switzerland, Excel received the prestigious 'International Spirit at Work' award for its explicit policies and practices of spirituality in its workplace.

Grundfos and Excel Industries are vanguards of an emerging phenomenon of deeply committed leaders who have tapped into a profound and sustainable source of commitment for corporate responsibility: their spirituality.

How can we understand this emerging phenomenon of spirituality as the basis of responsibility, especially in relation to other perspectives that have preceded it? Let us proceed by first considering the four fundamental questions regarding the notion of *responsibility* that we referred to earlier.

What is responsibility?

Most of us have an intuitive feeling or understanding of what it means to be responsible – or to be irresponsible. Perhaps we can recall having the satisfaction of knowing we listened to the voice of our conscience and did the right thing in the right way when faced with a moral dilemma. Or perhaps we have experienced remorse when we behaved in a way we felt was *irresponsible*. And perhaps we have even felt anger or frustration when witnessing what we felt was irresponsible behaviour of others, including corporations.

According to *Webster's Deluxe Unabridged Dictionary*, (responsibility) is derived from the late Latin *responsabilis* – requiring an answer. The word can be seen as having two parts: response + able, i.e. the ability to respond, to be able to answer for one's conduct and obligations. Ultimately it means: 'expected or obligated to account (for something, to someone) ... involving duties ... able to distinguish between right and wrong ... trustworthy, dependable, reliable'. But this definition raises substantive questions, such as why be accountable, for what and to whom?

Before we begin to consider possible answers to such questions, it is necessary to consider whether only individual human beings, characterized as we are by consciousness, can be responsible. Or can groups of humans, such as organizations, also be responsible?

Can organizations be responsible?

Increasingly, management rhetoric speaks of a company's vision, values and virtues. But is it meaningful to ascribe qualities that are ordinarily attributed to individuals – including the ability and obligation to behave responsibly – to organizations? For example, a *hot* item in modern management terminology is Corporate Social Responsibility. What does it mean if we say that a corporation has a responsibility for something? Individuals are conscious beings with a conscience, with feelings, and with the ability to analyze, reflect, and to make rational choices, and therefore with the ability to *act responsibly*. Does an organization also have this ability?

This line of questioning is not just an academic exercise. Rather, it is a fundamental precursor for being able to deal with the remaining two questions of this chapter: Why should organizations be responsible? What obstacles are there to being responsible?

We can provide two possible affirmations to the idea that organizations can be responsible (Pruzan 2001a). The first, a rather weak response, argues that organizations are *judicial persons* with legal responsibilities, and that this responsibility is borne by the leadership of the organization. Building on this legal perspective, the response also contends that companies can also have obligations that arise from more-or-less explicit norms other than strictly legal rules, including expectations from owners, guidelines from branch organizations and company codes of conduct.

The second affirmative answer is a stronger but more complex response, based on the view that organizations are social systems – created not just by means of legal documents and financial transactions but also by an ongoing, identity-creating dialogue among its members. In such a participative corporate culture, employees speak of *we* when they refer to the company, with shared points of view, stories and values. As such, the organization has the characteristic of being a community. Just as an *I*, a sense of personal identity, is a pre-condition for an individual to feel a sense of responsibility, so is the existence of a *we*, a sense of identity as a community, a pre-condition for an organization as a whole to *feel* that it has responsibilities.

Although we speak here of a self-referential capability, the identity-creating *dialogue* we refer to need not be explicitly in words. We can also experience implicit norms that, although tacit, provide guideposts for responsible behaviour as well as sanctions for behaviour that is considered to be irresponsible. These will typically be embedded in the corporate culture, in its special vocabulary, traditions, rituals and its reward and recognition systems.

So there is a broad spectrum of possible viewpoints on corporate responsibility. At one end is a narrow, static definition in the form of legal requirements, where responsibility is impersonal and defined by formal, structural relationships. When viewed only from a legal framework, responsibility means following the letter of the law, but not necessarily the full spirit and intention of the law.

At the opposite end of the spectrum, the organization's members have a collective identity, a *we-ness* that defines the essence of the organization. From this more inclusive viewpoint, the organization and its members have the ability, just as an individual does, for experiencing that it has responsibilities and for living up to them.

Why be responsible?

Only infrequently is this question brought to the level of conscious reflection in organizations, even among leaders in major corporations. Presumably most of them feel that the answers are obvious – while we believe they are not. Even the increasing number of social/ethical/*triple-bottom-line*/sustainability reports being issued by major corporations almost never include an explicit statement about such a primary question. But an explicit inquiry, both by individual leaders and a company's leadership group, is a pre-condition for successfully integrating *responsibility* into their own and the organization's self-awareness – and therefore into the policies, processes and practices that promote responsible behaviour.

We have observed four overarching and progressively more inclusive perspectives on the question of 'Why be responsible?', each with its own history, logic and language: the rational perspective, the humanist perspective, the holistic perspective and the spiritual-based perspective (Miller and Miller 2002).

The rational perspective

Essentially, this perspective on 'Why be responsible?' is instrumental. It answers that a leader or a company should only be responsible if this serves some other, higher priority goals – typically the classical business goals of growth, market capitalization and shareholder value. In other words, the responsibility of business and its leadership is wealth creation on behalf of owners/shareholders.

This instrumental perspective on business and leadership responsibility originally emerged at the beginning of the twentieth century. For example, according to Frederick Taylor, the acknowledged progenitor of *scientific management*:

> The principle object of management should be to secure the maximum prosperity for the owners coupled with the maximum prosperity for each employé ... maximum prosperity for the employee means not only higher wages than are usually received by men of his class, but of more importance still, it also means the development of each man to his state of maximum efficiency ... maximum prosperity can exist only as the result of maximum productivity.
>
> (Taylor 1911/1998: 1, 2)

This perspective dominated leadership thinking well into the 1960's. Perhaps its clearest and most referred to expression from that period is the (in)famous statement by Nobel Laureate Milton Friedman:

> Few trends could so thoroughly undermine the foundations of our free society as the acceptance by corporate officials of a social responsibility other than to make as much money for their shareholders as possible.
>
> (Friedman 1962: 133)

Friedman's basic argument, that companies only have two responsibilities – to live up to the law and to maximize shareholder wealth – is readily accepted by most leaders in major corporations today. It is therefore not surprising that such a utilitarian perspective is the foundation for the so-called *business case* that has dominated recent debates about corporate responsibility. The fundamental answer provided by the business case to the question as to why companies should be responsible is straightforward: to protect the company's licence to operate and its earnings.

The humanist perspective

This perspective is based on the assumption that to be responsible is a natural consequence of being human – it is part of our human nature. A clear expression of this argument is provided by William Hewlett, co-founder of Hewlett-Packard: 'Men and women want to do a good, a creative job; and if they are provided with the proper environment they will do so' (Hewlett and Packard 1980: 3).

From this perspective, which first gained momentum in the 1950s and 1960s (MacGregor 1960) and became the norm of many major corporations by the 1980s, a leader's responsibility includes providing a working environment that motivates the employees to be responsible and helps them to become self-actualized.

There are two versions of this humanist perspective on 'Why be responsible?' One is the empathy argument, founded on the human capacity to sympathize and empathize, which is more fundamental than our competence for analysis and rational choice. It builds on our ability to experience feelings of endearment to others and to put ourselves in their shoes. According to Max De Pree, Chairman Emeritus of the world renowned furniture company Herman Miller, in his now classic exposition on leadership: 'We are emotional creatures, trying through the vehicles of product and knowledge and information and relationships to have an effect for good on one another' (De Pree 1987/2004: 87). In stark contrast to the rational perspective on responsibility, where thought precedes action, empathy can lead to intuitive, spontaneous, even heroically responsible leadership behaviour, where a leader only after the fact is able to *rationalize* and come up with logical arguments for why he or she acted as they did.

The humanist perspective on responsibility also finds expression in what we refer to as an integrity argument. Its essence is that we are responsible, first and foremost, to ourselves and therefore that we should perform our leadership so that we live up to our own values, so there is unity in our thoughts, words and deeds. Clearly, this focus on one's self as the ultimate object of responsibility can appear to be similar to the *what's in it for me?* rational perspective presented earlier. Nevertheless, there is a significant difference between the two. The rational perspective focuses on living up to demands by others to generate financial wealth. The humanist perspective focuses on living up to one's own values and humaneness.

The holistic perspective

The essence of the holistic response to 'Why be responsible?' is that we are all interdependent, and this implies a duty to respect the rights of others. Support for this perspective can be found in religious norms. For example, all major religions have some form of what has been called the *Golden Rule* – that you should 'do unto others what you want them to do to you'. Support can also be found in cultural norms such as the Universal Declaration of Human Rights approved by the General Assembly of the United Nations in 1948: 'Whereas recognition of the inherent dignity and of the equal and inalienable rights of all members of the human family is the foundation of freedom, justice and peace in the world' (United Nations 1948). While this perspective may be said to hold for all human beings, it is especially relevant for business leaders because they have the power, granted in hierarchical organizational contexts, to make decisions that affect others. This is one of the fundamental propositions underlying the recent focus on a *stakeholder theory of the firm* (Wheeler and Sillanpää 1997). From this viewpoint, the responsibility of business leadership evolves beyond wealth-creation for shareholders, as in the rationalist perspective, to wealth creation for the benefit of all stakeholders – including employees, customers, shareholders, suppliers, community, nature, society and even future generations.

This holistic perspective on responsible business behaviour was first voiced in the late 1960s and gained momentum in the 1980s and 1990s (Freeman 1984). At present, a growing minority of major international corporations are in the process of integrating this holistic perspective on identity, purpose and duty into their self-reference, and are employing it to supplement (not replace) more traditional viewpoints about success and responsibility. They are experimenting with new forms of reporting such as *triple bottom line reporting* in accord with international guidelines, such as those of the Global Reporting Initiative:

> Accountability, governance, and sustainability – three powerful ideas that are playing a pivotal role in shaping how business and other organizations operate in the 21st century. Together, they reflect the emergence of a new level of societal expectations that view business as a prime mover in determining economic, environmental and social well being. These three ideas also point to the reality that business responsibility extends well beyond the shareholders, to people and places both near and distant from a company's physical facilities.
>
> (Global Reporting Initiative 2002)

Although this holistic perspective to 'Why be responsible?' is more inclusive than the rational and humanist perspectives on responsibility, it still neglects the deeper, more fulfilling spiritual aspects of human and organizational life.

The spiritual-based perspective

The final perspective on 'Why be responsible?' holds that responsibility is grounded in our nature as spiritual beings who have an inherent longing (whether or not we are aware of it) to realize who we truly are, individually and collectively. Thus, our most intrinsic motivation is to realize our essential spiritual nature and purpose, not to fill an ever-present set of *need-based* desires (Chakraborty 1991). Although this perspective first emerged in writings on leadership from the 1990s (Harman and Porter 1997), its basis is wisdom handed down over the ages by those who have been recognized for their spiritual accomplishments (Huxley 1946/1990).

A basic tenet of this perspective is that once leaders have developed their own spiritual self-awareness, they naturally exercise it in some form of service beyond self-interest (Greenleaf 1998). The dualistic distinction between one's self and others becomes replaced by a deeply felt connectivity – and the ordinary distinction between responsibility to one's self and to others attenuates.

Thus, when responsibility becomes more inclusive, traditional concepts of managerial *power* expand from controlling others to serving them (Pruzan 2001b). It follows from this perspective that the nature of business itself is transformed. Wealth creation is no longer the goal; it becomes a means for enabling and sustaining spiritual fulfilment and service to society. Business leaders become responsible for promoting the well-being and spiritual fulfilment of everyone touched by the business: employees, customers, suppliers, competitors, shareholders and society.

In one of our interviews for the Spiritual-Based Leadership research programme, Andre Delbecq, former dean of Santa Clara University's graduate school of business in the United States, spoke about how spirituality shifts our view of business and organizational leadership:

> I think a business exists to provide an innovative and compelling answer to a societal need in the form of a needed service or product. When this purpose is approached through a spiritual lens, it will be shaped differently in many ways. The needs you pay attention to shift. The system you create to receive inputs and transform outputs will also shift, allowing greater inclusiveness of the concerns of all stakeholders. The character of the organization's culture will shift. Your tolerance regarding the discipline of having to meet Wall Street's expectations about profitability will shift. You will see all the elements of business challenges as part of a calling to service. All of the struggles of business leadership as a form of societal service take on a very different coloration when they are seen from a spiritual perspective.

This brings us to the question, 'What is spirituality?' – at least according to business leaders. As part of our research programme, we posed this question to each of the executives we interviewed around the world. Here is a selection of their replies:

Spirituality is inspired responsibility towards people, other living beings and the world ... seeing and relating with Divinity in every aspect. Self-improvement plus world service equals spirituality.

I would say that spirituality is man's quest into his innate Divinity. It's more like a road than a state of affairs ... a quest more than an arrival.

Spirituality is attunement with a universal spirit. It is being so in tune with that spirit that you are not acting from a place of ego or desire or greed, but you are acting from a place that is on behalf of the welfare of the totality.

Spirituality is our deep connection with a force greater than ourselves; it is a very individual, lived experience that includes longing and belonging, for which the fruits are love and compassion.

Spirituality is taking the principles that are taught in most religions and living them as a natural way of life.

Spirituality for me is the essence of being. It is a place where the heart resides; it is soul.

Thus, there is a rather wide range of understandings about spirituality – a range that was also matched when we asked them what they felt was the relationship between spirituality and religion:

To me spirituality and religion are the same thing.

While religion offers many beautiful things like rituals and ceremonies, to me it is not spirituality. Spirituality has no borders or restraints, it doesn't separate, it connects.

I think spiritually is how you live your entire life. I see religion as something that is handed down to you. It is something external to you, whereas spirituality is something that is within you.

How does a spiritual-based perspective on responsibility relate to the rational, humanist and holistic perspectives on responsibility? In these perspectives on responsibility, if *spirituality* is considered at all, it is only considered to be one of many aspects of life along with work, family, leisure time, health, etc. That is, if life were a pie, spirituality would be one slice of the pie. From the spiritual-based perspective, however, spirituality is the pie itself. Work, family, leisure and health are all *slices* of spirituality, they are all contexts for growing spiritually. In accord with this, Steven Covey states that 'Spirituality cannot be something a person toys with, a little compartment of their lives. It has to be at the core in a way that affects every other part of their lives' (Hendricks and Ludeman 1997: 9).

To see how the spiritual perspective of responsibility includes yet transcends the other three perspectives, consider the reflections of Ananth

Raman, Chairman of Graphtex Inc., an American manufacturing company that is part of the Swiss firm Catisa, which operates in 30 countries around the world. Ananth Raman started his work with Catisa in Nigeria and ended up overseeing the company's operations in nine African countries before transferring to the United States. He told us about his evolution to a spiritual perspective on responsibility:

> When I was in one of the West African countries, the country was full of corruption, and you couldn't do anything without bribing someone. The policy in my corporation was that you could not give bribes. At first, I wondered how I was going to get along without giving bribes. Ultimately, I chose to stay with the ethical values that the company ascribed to ... because this was what I was taught.
>
> Values such as justice, truth, respect for others, equanimity, ability to take decisions, honesty and integrity are the core values that became very strong for me. ... These are more on the ethical side, rather than on the spiritual side. Somewhere along the line however, these two kinds of values began to link.
>
> Now I think of ethical values as nothing but a reflection of my spiritual values. When we talk about self-respect in an ethical sense, we are talking about being respectful to your colleagues, shareholders and customers because it is a good business practice. But when you go a little deeper and look at it from a spiritual point of view, you realize that it is really about respecting the inner Self, the inner Divinity of each person. I think this brings about a whole new dimension. This is how I like to link spirituality with ethics and values in business.

What obstacles are there to being responsible?

We have thus far considered three major, overarching questions regarding responsible leadership and corporate responsibility: What do we mean by responsibility? Can organizations be responsible? Why be responsible? This has led us to consider a spiritual-based perspective for responsibility as the latest to emerge and the most inclusive among the variety of viewpoints prevalent today.

But for leaders and their companies to develop the capability for integrating responsibility into their mindsets regarding purpose, identity and success, it is not sufficient to reflect only on questions of *what*, *can* and *why*. Also the obstacles to experiencing and living up to responsibility must be considered.

In our experience, there are six key obstacles that can hinder leaders and their companies in their progress towards developing a mindset and culture of responsibility: time, distance, internal pressures, external pressures, ego and the desire to maximize personal wealth. As demonstrated below, spiritual-based leaders and their organizations have shown in practice how each of these obstacles can be transcended.

Time

Corporate leaders face increasing pressures from financial markets to maximize short-term gains. These demands represent a barrier to living up to longer-term responsibilities, for example, living up to the company's values and visions. How does a spiritual-based leader respond?

Bob Galvin, former Chairman and CEO of Motorola, once described during a development programme the primary job of leaders as: 'Inspiring acts of faith – things are do-able that are not necessarily provable – spreading hope, and building trust. Faith, hope, and trust ... Theology is very practical business' (Seminar at Motorola University, Chicago, IL, 1993). He relates that in the early 1950s, Motorola had the opportunity to get a contract with a South American country, installing a micro-wave radio system. The first part of the contract was for US$10 million, which was a sizeable amount in the context of overall revenues of roughly US$100 million. To some minds, the opportunity to achieve such instant growth would have the highest priority. But not for Galvin and his executives:

> One of the executives came in and told me that we had won the order but that he had decided not to take it. The reason: The general who ran the country wanted the contract to read $11 million so they could skim the difference off the top. I told him that I was sorry that this had happened, and to refuse the contract even if they dropped their demand for padding and wanted to do it at the original price.

And Bob Galvin didn't stop there: 'Further, I told him that we would do no further business with this country until there was a change of leadership' (Hendricks and Ludeman 1997: 30). Instead of succumbing to time pressures for immediate financial gain, he tapped into his spiritual theme of *faith, hope and trust* and kept his company's integrity intact. In the short term, they lost the new revenues. But in the long term, Motorola experienced substantial growth and became a model of corporate responsibility.

Another perspective on the relationship between time and responsibility is to consider to what extent leaders and organizations are responsible to the long-term beneficiaries of near-term efforts? In its perhaps most dramatic formulation, this question can be posed as, 'To what extent are leaders and corporations responsible to the not-yet-born?' This is in keeping with the increasingly popular notion of sustainability (as evidenced by the growing number of *sustainability reports* being produced by major corporations). Perhaps the most widely recognized definition of sustainability is that provided in the report, *Our Common Future* (Brundtland 1987) by the United Nations World Commission on Environment and Development. The commission was popularly called the Brundtland Commission after its chairman, the then Prime Minister of Norway and Director-General of the World Health Organization from 1998 to 2003, Gro Harlem Brundtland. In that report, sustainable development is defined as 'development that meets the needs of the present without compromising the ability of future generations to meet their needs' (Brundtland 1987: 8).

With respect to future generations, Ramon Ollé, CEO of the Japanese-owned Epson Europe provided us with his thoughts about the spiritual basis for his life and how it influences his leadership. His scope of leadership includes Europe, Africa and the Middle-East, roughly 3,000 employees, with a turnover of 2.2 billion Euros (approximately US$2 billion) in 2003:

> I understand spirituality as the inner part of a human. It is our inner force. The higher you are in a company, the more your decisions affect things over the long term. There are certain measures in a corporation that cannot be evaluated in a month, in half a year, or even in a year. Our responsibility as leaders is not about ensuring that the company survives for even the next few years. Our responsibility is to ensure that the company will survive and thrive for the next 120 years. We cannot just pay attention to the short term. When you begin to think this way, you are really entering into the spirit of family, into the spirit of a multi-cultural environment, and into the spirit of humanity as a whole.

Distance

How does *distance to others* affect our sense of responsibility to them? Or, put more bluntly, 'To what extent are leaders and corporations responsible to those who are out-of-sight and far-away?' In the Bible, Jesus was asked, 'Which commandment is first and most important of all?' Jesus' answer included: 'You shall love your neighbour as yourself' (Amplified Bible 1987, Mark 12: 31). But who are our neighbours?

One such definition of *neighbour* starts with one's employees and the local members of one's society. As Niels Due Jensen, Chairman of Grundfos states:

> My principle of *love your neighbour* has guided me in the direction of also developing what we call *social responsibility* at Grundfos. You may call it the need to love your neighbour, and this means your neighbour in this local society, but first of all your employees in the company.

But how *far away* can a person be before business leaders no longer consider him or her to be a *neighbour* that they should love as themselves? This consideration of *distance* is particularly relevant for leaders in corporations that aggressively pursue the growth syndrome and merger mania. The following are a few striking statistics. The combined sales of the world's top 200 corporations are far greater than a quarter of the world's economic activity and bigger than the combined economies of all countries minus the biggest nine; they have almost twice the economic clout of the poorest four-fifths of humanity yet have been net job destroyers in recent years (Anderson and Cavanagh 2000).

These statistics underscore a serious problem: *Quite often, when corporations grow, so does the distance between those who make decisions and those who are affected by them.* For leaders of major corporations, seeing, hearing and speaking to those they affect by their decisions is virtually impossible – making it very difficult for them to live up to an ethics of closeness based on personal experience. In such situations, leading often is reduced to reacting to quantitative analyses of key financial and productivity figures (market shares, contributions to profits, rates of return) and listening to the advice of consultants and experts. When decisions are dominated by an economic rationale, the propensity to develop an inclusive sense of responsibility often becomes replaced by an ideology of growth (Pruzan 1998).

In contrast to this, consider Amber Chand, who long ago envisaged fulfilling a responsibility to 'contribute to the well-being of artisan communities worldwide by stimulating demand for their products'. With that mission in mind, she co-founded Eziba Inc., a USA-based, international retail marketing firm. During an interview, she described the spiritual basis of her sincere sense of *distance* responsibility to the suppliers as well as the customers:

> Spirituality for me is the essence of being. Spirituality is a place where the heart resides; it is soul. ... Compassion, balance, grace and friendliness are words that ring as a spiritual theme for me.
>
> We are more committed than ever to supporting talented artisans around the world and are now perceived as a leading retailer with a socially responsible mission. I head up Eziba's non-profit *Partnership Program* and *Gifts That Give Back* marketing campaign. The Partnership Program is a key initiative at Eziba where we forge alliances with other non-profit organizations that have a resonant mission to support the well-being of communities around the world. In our four years of growth our revenues have increased from US$200 thousand in the first year to US$10 million in our fourth year. And we've grown our customer base to 180,000 customers.

Internal pressures

The management of change is receiving ever-increasing attention. In a world of dramatically intense competition, company survival is never guaranteed no matter how well established a company may be. Pressures from within an organization can manifest as demands for: survival; ethical behaviour; good working conditions; job security and satisfaction; and living up to the organization's values and its commitment to product quality and customer service.

These pressures present significant challenges to corporate leadership in relation to the question, 'To what extent are leaders responsible to the organization's employees in living up to the organization's core values, particularly during times of business stress and struggle?' A poignant example of how such pressures might responsibly be addressed from a spiritual-based perspective is that of Lars Kolind, former Chairman and CEO of Oticon in Denmark. Today, this Danish firm is one of the world's premier makers of aids for the hearing impaired, but it wasn't always so. In the 1980s the company was failing financially when they hired Lars Kolind to be the new CEO to turn it around. Regarding his spiritual view of life, Lars Kolind told us:

> (Making a difference) is fundamentally why we exist and that has something to do with our relation to a higher being. I personally have no doubt that being in contact with a higher power increases the quality of one's life in the broadest sense. This applies to everyone. I have never felt satisfaction in just making money. I am only happy because I started by making a difference, whether it was for the family, or the environment, or the hearing-impaired or whatever it was, that is what gives me satisfaction.

When he took over, things were far worse than he anticipated. He was compelled to make a drastic reduction in staff if the company was to survive. How did he apply his spiritual view of life to this downsizing and the impact that it would have on the lives of Oticon's employees?

> I was really under pressure to determine which principles we should use to make the decisions as to who to lay off. I took the decision, which no one understood, that we would not fire anyone over 50. Neither would we fire people who were so essential that we didn't think we could survive without them. But other than that, we would let those people go who we thought would have the best chance of getting another job quickly – even though these were obviously the ones, I would have preferred retaining. I just couldn't look into the eyes of all of the people that we would kick into prolonged unemployment in order for the rest of us to make money and prosper. I just couldn't do that. I must admit that I simply made these decisions and I didn't really think about where they came from, which was from my conscience.

Lars Kolind's sense of responsibility extended to each and every person who was laid off:

> I talked to every single person that was to be laid off and told each of them that they were going to be fired and that we would work with

them to get a new job the best we could. I was experiencing all their bad feelings as I was confronting myself with the doubts and fears of all of these people. To me it would have been an act of cowardice to let others do this for me.

As a result of the spirited culture he created and his inspiring vision for the company, Oticon rose from the ashes to become one of the leading designers and manufactures of hearing aids in the world – with an amazing growth in market capitalization. In 1990 the value of the company was 150 million Danish Crowns (approximately US$19 million); by 2002, when we interviewed Lars Kolind, it had grown to 20 billion Danish Crowns (approximately US$2.5 billion), an annual growth rate of more than 25 per cent.

External pressures

Increasingly, there are demands on companies from external stakeholder groups to live up to certain responsibilities. For example, these include the quality and safety of products; human rights and working conditions of employees within the company and in its supply-chains; environmental sustainability and animal rights; support and respect for the local communities in which the company is located; employment policies that promote opportunities for minorities and the handicapped.

So we meet a question very similar to that raised as to responsibilities to living up to internal pressures: To what extent are leaders and organizations responsible to society and those who make demands on behalf of society's interests? Those making these demands have no problem at all when they speak of *corporate responsibility*. They do not reflect on whether responsibility is an individual matter or whether it is an organizational matter. They make sweeping demands on the leadership, and the more vigilant of such observers, particularly the NGOs, keep a wary eye on the activities of the company – calling for the instant guillotine on the television news if they observe behaviour they consider to be irresponsible or unethical.

Reacting to these pressures from external sources, leaders may be tempted to focus on convincing such external stakeholder groups that the company is responsible, rather than on actually being responsible. For example, Dena Merriam, Vice-Chairman of Rudder-Finn, a global public relations firm, told us in an interview:

> To me spirituality is being so in tune with a universal spirit that you are not acting from a place of ego or desire or greed, but you are acting from a place that is on behalf of the welfare of the totality. We are a communications company, and organizations come to us when they are in trouble. In our work, we play a double role: we counsel our clients

and we help them communicate to the public. Often, they don't come to ask how to be a good corporate citizen; they just want to tell the public something so that they can get out of the trouble. We show them how this would do them more harm. Then we show them what they need to do.

This obstacle presents a major challenge to corporate leadership – to balance the pressure for maintaining an image of responsibility with a heart-felt need to develop an identity founded in a culture of responsibility (Pruzan 2001c). Emphasizing an external image of responsibility, at the expense of actually being responsible, ultimately undermines trust in the company as well as the broader trust between society and the business community that is so vital for the future of our societies.

A leader who has met such challenges from his spiritual basis is Dr A.K. Chattopadhyay, former Senior Vice-President of ACC Limited Refractories Division in India. In our interview with him, he told us:

> Spirituality is the manifestation of the perfection that is already there within us. I also believe there is a superpower who creates things in a systematic and organized manner, and I can align my thoughts with this.

Extreme external pressures were put on him when one of his factory employees lost his hand in a conveyer belt accident:

> I stayed in the operation theatre the whole night that he was being operated on, in order to give moral courage to his family members. The newspaper came to write stories against me since I was head of the plant, saying that not enough safety measures were being applied. There were some local union leaders who wanted to influence the head of the local police to arrest me. All of these things happened while I was sitting inside the hospital.
>
> Personally, I felt a strength inside of me because I knew what I was doing was good for this man and for his family.

It turned out that proper safety measures had been in place but, unfortunately, the employee had not followed them. Dr Chattopadhyay did not spend his energy defending the company with this fact. Instead, he focused on being responsible for the future of this employee:

> I called his family together and explained that I would take full responsibility to take care of this man and them. I explained that, 'No, we cannot get back his hand, this is most unfortunate. However, we can give the monetary compensation that needs to be given and we can give him a job where he can still work peacefully without his hand.'

I called groups in our company together and explained what had happened and how we handled it. Later, after all of this was over, I reflected back on this strength that I felt and realized it came from my connection with what I call a *superpower*.

Ego

Ego is the Latin word for *I*. Our sense of *I* shapes and informs our focus and attention on *my* physical and psychological well-being, material success and wealth, reputation, power and so on. It is a phenomenon of human consciousness that we can expand or limit our sense of *I*-dentity. The narrowest sense is that we identify ourselves with our bodies and personal psyche: 'I am this individual body and personality'. But we often, and easily, expand that identity to include others, so that the *I* becomes a *we* that we treat more-or-less as ourselves. Thus identified with our family or favourite sports team, we might exclaim, 'We won the lottery!' or 'We won the championship!' We often identify ourselves with the company we work in: 'We achieved 20 per cent growth this year'. Our sense of identity can expand more to include our nation: 'I am a Greek. We hosted the last Olympics'. It can expand even further to include all humanity, or even all of creation: 'We are at a crossroad of human history'.

To what extent are leaders and corporations responsible to others, beyond the self-interest of themselves as individuals or of themselves as members of a *special interest group*? When dramatic change takes place, our egos get most threatened and we tend to move towards self-centred behaviour. How does a leader deal with this from a spiritual basis? A good example is that of Ashoke Maitra when he was head of Human Resources for NOCIL, an Indian petrochemical company. When NOCIL acquired and merged with a competitor, Ashoke was put in charge of integrating two large firms that were quite diverse organizationally and culturally. To manage the merger from his spiritual point of view, he exercised a sense of responsibility to the people in both organizations while addressing the ego clashes inherent in a merger between two fierce competitors. In our interview he told us:

> There was a lot of hatred between them because for years they had fought each other to prove who was better. Now one of the companies was merging into the other and would be losing its identity.
>
> My definition of spirituality is that each soul is potentially Divine. The goal is to manifest this Divinity, by any means that suits you. I thought the best way to merge would be to integrate people at the spiritual level; therefore, I experimented.

Whether he was working with the top management group or other employees, Ashoke Maitra focused on fostering introspection and a personal sense of purpose:

Spirituality is all about introspection. When you put people in an introspective mode in an exercise, then they start to question their own life and their own reason for existence, such as what they are here to do and how they will achieve it. I think the reason they accepted what I said is because they saw I was not concerned about the company; I was concerned about them and their grief.

With the top management, he expanded this into a sense of group purpose grounded in a spiritual connection among all of them.

At first there were a lot of grievances that surfaced. By the afternoon we said okay, it is the worst thing to happen in life, but it has happened. Now what do we do? We started examining the question of purpose and in three days time we came to a top management integration of the purpose of the combined companies. Ultimately, we had one of the smoothest mergers in the history of India of two competitive petrochemical companies.

Maximizing personal wealth

Taken together, the obstacles of time, distance, internal and external pressures, and ego culminate in an obstacle that we call the *desire to maximize personal wealth*. That raises the question, 'To what extent are leaders and organizations responsible for creating wealth for the largest possible group/community/society rather than for their own personal benefit?'

In her provocative book *The Divine Right of Capital*, Marjorie Kelly compares the primacy of shareholder rights to that of the landed gentry in pre-industrial times; she refers to it as 'a form of entitlement out of place in a market economy' (2001: 4). From the viewpoint of this new aristocracy, shareholders have a claim to wealth they do little to create, in the same way that nobles claimed privileges they did not earn. Just as a feudal estate was considered to be a piece of property, so too the modern corporation is considered to be property (not a human community) that can be bought and sold by the propertied class for one major purpose: to return to shareholders as much as possible, even if this means as little as possible to employees.

Many readers may take exception to this last statement. But this *new aristocracy* viewpoint follows logically from the rationalist perspective that the primary goal of companies is to maximize shareholder wealth – which can lead to insensitivity to the values and aspirations of all other stakeholders, including the employees.

When the corporation is implicitly reduced to a profit-generating machine, employees and other stakeholders are reduced in the managerial mindset to be merely instruments to achieve financial goals. This leads to a concomitant radical reduction in the scope and meaning of *responsible leaders and responsible companies*, whereby wealth maximization becomes a major obstacle to realizing a more inclusive individual and corporate responsibility. This position is strongly reinforced by remuneration systems relying heavily on stock options, so that leaders become leader-owners with short-term financial interests and a corresponding narrow concept of *success* and *responsibility*.

How might the issue of wealth maximization be dealt with from a spiritual basis? Consider Anita Roddick (2001), founder and former co-chairperson of the major retailer of natural skin and hair-care products, The Body Shop International. She started The Body Shop as a one-woman show in the late 1970s; it has now more than 2,000 shops in 54 countries throughout the world. In 2003, the Queen of England honoured her with the title Dame Commander of the British Empire for services to retailing, the environment and charity.

When we interviewed Dame Anita Roddick for our research project on spiritual-based leadership, she described her spiritual basis this way:

> My definition of spirituality is no more complicated than Gandhi's definition: *To be in service to the weak and the frail.* That is absolutely my path. My spiritual theme is kindness. Tenacious and fierce kindness! Kindness, which makes you re-think many actions. Kindness is my religion.

She shared with us her views about the purpose of business and gave us an example of how she views corporate wealth:

> Everything changed when we went on the stock market; we were then expected to be measured by financials, but that was not what we were interested in. Our success was not only how many people we were employing, but also what we could do with the money we were making. With profits, the purpose of business is to do something remarkable within the community, because it is the community of your customers that gives you your wealth.
>
> We opened up a soap-factory, *Soapworks*, in the Easterhouse district of Glasgow, Scotland, an area that had the worst examples of unemployment in Western Europe. We set up the best model of a soap-factory. 127 people worked there making nearly 12 million bars of soap a year. We wanted to pay the best wages, give them the best day-care facilities, the best food and put 25 per cent of the profit back into the community. Even before we opened up the Soapworks, we built an adventure playground for kids. In the next stage we built a drop-in centre for the elderly. You think you are doing the right things and will get the right reactions, but the financial journalists said that we were taking money from our shareholders' pocket.
>
> I remember one year at a meeting where I had to talk about profits, I was challenged by these guys, and I just said, 'That's the way I want

to run this place. I want to make this workplace breathless, I want to make it believable, I want to make it human.' And they couldn't answer to that.

What about her personal wealth as the founder and major stockholder of, as she says, 'one of the top 27 brands in the world and number seven in terms of trust'?

To be wealthy is indeed to be glamorous, according to the financial analysts. My husband and I publicly say that for us to die rich is to be obscene. There is no value in accumulating wealth; accumulated wealth is like water in a vase that has gone rancid. I think that my responsibility for the last 20 years of my life is to get my hands really dirty giving it away on a proactive basis, and seeing the fruits of that. We have to find leaders who can use these funds well.

Conclusion

Based on our observations, experience and research, we have addressed four fundamental questions: What is responsibility? Can organizations be responsible? Why be responsible? What obstacles are there to being responsible? Along the way, we have explored four different perspectives on responsible leadership and corporate responsibility – rational, humanist, holistic and spiritual-based. In addition, we discussed six obstacles: time, distance, internal pressures, external pressures, ego and the desire to maximize personal wealth.

As we have reflected on the four perspectives, the rational perspective seems to have the least capability to surmount these obstacles to being responsible. It embraces the shortest time frame and distance, is most reactive, has the narrowest I-dentity, and is most concerned with maximizing personal wealth. By contrast, the spiritual-based perspective seems to offer the greatest capability for overcoming the obstacles to individual and collective responsibility. This perspective embraces the longest time frame and broadest distance, is the most proactive, has the most expanded and inclusive I-dentity, and is the least concerned with maximizing personal wealth as a top priority.

Certainly there are many business leaders today who are eager to try to project an image of social responsibility – for example, by developing *triple-bottom-line* reports. This is most often simply a rational, economically instrumental way of reacting to pressures from an increasing number of challenges from internal and external stakeholders to demonstrate an image of responsibility. We might say that this is a pattern of adopting the ethic of *responsibility from the outside in*.

But rather than writing off this pattern as a cynical representation of responsible corporate behaviour, we suggest that we can instead be optimistic. The very fact that the leaders of mega-corporations are introducing the word *responsibility* into their business vocabulary, and are attempting to operationalize this concept, is highly encouraging. If a company maintains this effort for an extended period of time, even as a reaction to pressures, it is likely to lead to a greater awareness of and sensitivity to the need for responsible behaviour (Zadek 2004).

Beyond this, we are optimistic that there is a new wave and new generation of leaders who sincerely ascribe to responsibility in themselves and their companies from an ever-broadening sense of I-dentity. As they identify with not just themselves and their companies, but with their communities and society at large, with the environment and with future generations, they have begun to naturally embody responsibility from *the inside out*.

While the impact of any one leader's, or any one company's actions, can seem limited, nevertheless the cumulative effect of such an expansive sense of responsibility can have a significant impact on the well-being of societies, nations and the world as a whole. As the late Willis Harman, Emeritus Professor at Stanford University and former president of the Institute of Noetic Sciences, once explained:

> Leaders in world business are the first true planetary citizens. They have worldwide capability and responsibility ... their decisions affect not just economies, but societies; not just the direct concerns of business, but world problems of poverty, environment and security ... world business will be a key actor in the ultimate resolution of the macro-problem.
>
> (Harman 1998: 147)

In the evolution from the rational perspective on responsibility to the spiritual-based perspective, we find an increasingly inclusive sense of responsibility – a spiritual openness that ultimately embraces humanity and the planet. Stephen Rockefeller, Chairman of the Rockefeller Brothers Fund stated that this responsibility requires an evolution of our spiritual consciousness:

> Some would argue that it is humanity's spiritual destiny to build a just, sustainable and peaceful world community. I believe that. However, to achieve this ideal a further development in the evolution of our ethical and spiritual consciousness must occur. ... It is doubtful whether humanity can find any lasting solution to the big problems it faces without taking this spiritual challenge to heart.
>
> (Rockefeller 2004)

Ultimately, when leaders and organizations are operating from the spiritual-based perspective – from a deep awareness of their spiritual nature – they naturally behave responsibly beyond their own self-interest. That is, they naturally serve themselves, their employees, customers, owners, competitors, suppliers, society, the environment and all of creation.

The strongest future for responsible leadership and responsible corporations will result when the spiritual roots of this and of future generations of business leaders are nourished. This will occur when *all* of us nourish our *own* spiritual roots by living in accord with our spiritual nature in thought, word and deed. The result will be business leadership that is spiritually uplifting to all, tangible in its results for all, humanly respectful to all, and socially responsible to all.

Questions

1 What is your spiritual view of life and how is that expressed in your leadership?
2 From your spiritual perspective, what is the meaning and scope of responsibility to you as a leader?
3 From your spiritual perspective, why is it important to you to be responsible and to have your organization be responsible?
4 From your spiritual perspective, how could your organization foster a culture of collective responsibility?
5 What do you feel are the major obstacles to exercising responsibility – for yourself as a leader and for your organization – and how could you transcend them from a spiritual-based perspective?

Bibliography

Amplified Bible (1987) Grand Rapids, MI: Zondervan.
Anderson, S. and Cavanagh, J. (2000) 'Corporate Watch 2000'. Online. Available HTTP: http://www.globalpolicy.org/socecon/tncs/top200.htm (accessed 11 April 2005).
Brundtland, G.H. (ed.) (1987) *Our Common Future: the world commission on environment and development*, Oxford: Oxford University Press.
Chakraborty, S.K. (1991) *Management By Values: towards cultural congruence*, New Delhi: Oxford University Press.
De Pree, M. (1987/2004) *Leadership as an Art*, revised edn, New York: Currency Doubleday.
Freeman, E. (1984) *Strategic Management: a stakeholder approach*, Boston, MA: Pitman.
Friedman, M. (1962) *Capitalism and Freedom*, Chicago, IL: University of Chicago Press.
Global Reporting Initiative (2002) 'Global reporting initiative guidelines'. Online. Available HTTP: www.globalreporting.org/guidelines/2002.asp (accessed 11 April 2005).
Greenleaf, R.K. (1998) *The Power of Servant Leadership: Essays*, ed. L. Spears, San Francisco, CA: Berrett-Koehler.
Harman, W. (1998) *Global Mind Change: the promise of the 21st century*, 2nd edn, San Francisco, CA: Berrett-Koehler.

Harman, W. and Porter, M. (1997) *The New Business of Business: sharing responsibility for a positive global future*, San Francisco, CA: Berrett-Koehler.

Hendricks, G. and Ludeman, K. (1997) *The Corporate Mystic*, New York: Bantam.

Hewlett, W.R. and Packard, D. (1980) *The HP Way*, Palo Alto, CA: Hewlett-Packard Corporation.

Huxley, A. (1946/1990) *The Perennial Philosophy*, reissued edn, New York: Perennial.

Kelly, M. (2001) *The Divine Right of Capital*, San Francisco, CA: Berrett-Koehler.

MacGregor, D. (1960) *The Human Side of Enterprise*, New York: McGraw-Hill.

Miller, W. and Miller, D. (2002) 'Spirituality: the emerging context for business leadership'. Online. Available HTTP: www.globaldharma.org/sbl-publications.htm (accessed 11 April 2005).

Pruzan, P. (1998) 'From control to values-based management and accountability', *Journal of Business Ethics*, 17: 1379–94.

Pruzan, P (2001a) 'The question of organizational consciousness: can organizations have values, virtues and visions?', *Journal of Business Ethics*, 29: 271–84.

Pruzan, P. (2001b) 'The trajectory of power: from control to self-control' in S.K. Chakraborty and P. Bhattacharya (eds), *Leadership and Power – Ethical Explorations*, New Delhi: Oxford University Press, 166–81.

Pruzan, P. (2001c) 'Corporate reputation: image and identity', *Corporate Reputation Review*, 4(1): 47–60.

Rockefeller, S.C. (2004) 'Interdependence and global ethics', lecture given at the University of the Philippines, Diliman, Quezon City, 31 August 2004. Online. Available HTTP: www.rmaf.org.ph/Foundation/Press-Releases/Lecture Rocke feller.htm> (accessed 19 April 2005).

Roddick, A. (2001) *Business as Unusual*, London: Thorsons.

Taylor, F.W. (1911/ 1998) *The Principles of Scientific Management*, New York, London: Harper & Brothers; reprinted 1998, New York: Dover.

United Nations (1948) *Universal Declaration of Human Rights*. Online. Available HTTP: http://www.un.org/Overview/rights.html (accessed 11 April 2005).

Varughese, S. (2004) 'New Age Trailblazers', *Life Positive*, 8(11): 32–6.

Wheeler, D. and Sillanpää, M. (1997) *The Stakeholder Corporation: a blueprint for maximizing stakeholder value*, London: Pitman.

Zadek, S. (2004) 'The path to corporate responsibility', *Harvard Business Review*, 82(12): 125–32.

Part II

What makes a responsible leader?

6 Integrity, responsible leaders and accountability

George G. Brenkert

Introduction

A great deal has been written recently about integrity, responsible leadership and accountability. There are widespread calls for integrity on the part of business and its leaders, as well as for other professionals and private individuals. Bill George says that 'we need authentic leaders, people of the highest integrity, committed to building enduring organizations' (2003: 5). Joseph Badaracco and Richard Ellsworth say that 'the concept of integrity is a nexus of ideas and guidelines that is central to business leadership' (1989: 96) and that 'integrity lies at the very heart of understanding what leadership is' (ibid.: 98). The web pages of dozens of businesses both present and past, including Enron, trumpet the importance of integrity. Suresh Srivastva notes that 'stakeholders of all kinds ... are crying out for integrity' (1988: 5). The non-governmental organization Transparency International has developed national integrity pacts to fight corruption, other groups speak of the importance of developing cultures of integrity.

The reasons for this focus on integrity are fairly obvious and, though important, are only worth briefly repeating here. They are focused on two distinct but related problem areas in business. First, in any number of very significant cases involving major businesses' failures, the lack of personal and organizational integrity has been said to be a primary contributing factor that has led to fraud, deception and the loss of billions of dollars. Second, the role of large organizations in our lives, and the social and political processes we take part in, all seem to pose challenges to our integrity. Both leaders and employees must face the challenge of maintaining their integrity while meeting the demands of their jobs.

In response to these two problem areas, we are told that integrity and the guidance it provides are at least part of the solution. Badaracco and Ellsworth stress the importance of integrity as a form of guidance for leaders (1989: 98). Lynn Sharp Paine suggests that 'integrity strategies ... can help prevent damaging ethical lapses while tapping into powerful human impulses for moral thought and action' (1994: 107). And Srivastva contends that 'integrity is the pivotal force behind organizational existence itself ... [The] executive mind is impotent without power, power is danger-ous without vision, and neither is lasting or significant in any broad human sense without the force of integrity' (1988: 2). In short, talk about integrity touches a nerve for many people and there are good reasons why this is the case. Most importantly, having integrity seems to be part of the solution.

In this chapter I will elaborate on the following: first, I want to explore the notion of integrity and what special contribution, if any, it can make to the discussion of the above kinds of problems. Many claims are made for and on behalf of integrity. I think that much of this is over-blown and confused; second, I will elaborate on the relationship between integrity and responsible leadership, and why the two exist in tension rather than in a harmonious relation that some seem to postulate. I do not discuss corporate or organizational integrity directly here, although I believe that much of what will be said here can be applied to that issue; finally, I will draw out a number of implications from the preceding discussion, including the role of accountability as one of the important measures whereby a responsible leader may seek to ensure his or her integrity.

Contrasting views

Although there are many calls for integrity, what they amount to and how their answers may help to address the problems noted above is much less clear. Badaracco and Ellsworth comment that 'everyone thinks they know what integrity is, and in a broad sense they are probably right. But the familiarity of the notion can mislead' (1989: 96). In fact, the uses of the term *integrity* are so wide and seemingly so various, we must ask whether anything meaningful can be said about integrity. In short, is there anything substantive about such talk that might play an important role in business ethics? Accordingly, one criterion of a successful account of integrity is that it offers something specific and unique that cannot be said better with other terms. We might begin by noting the contrasting views that some promi-nent thinkers have held on integrity. Doing so will reinforce the question as to what contribution talk of integrity may play in our discussions of business ethics and responsible leadership.

John Rawls identifies integrity in terms of such virtues as 'truthfulness and sincerity, lucidity and commitment, or, as some say, authenticity' (1971: 519). These virtues are insufficient for dealing with morality and justice, since even though they 'are virtues and among the excellences of free persons', 'their definition allows for most any content: a tyrant might display these attributes to a high degree, and by doing so exhibit a certain charm, not deceiving himself by political pretences and excuses of fortune' (ibid.: 519). Hence integrity is hardly linked uniquely with responsible leadership. These virtues and, hence, integrity only come into their own when 'joined to the appropriate conception of justice, one that allows for autonomy and objectivity correctly understood' (ibid.: 520). It is for these reasons that Rawls views integrity as a secondary virtue. People turn to these virtues, he claims, 'in times of social doubt and loss of faith in long established values' (ibid.: 519). At those times when people cannot agree on what values should replace the traditional ones, 'we can in any event decide with a clear head how we mean to act and stop pretending that somehow or other it is already decided for us and we must accept this or that authority' (ibid.: 519).

Richard DeGeorge's view of integrity is quite different from that of Rawls. For DeGeorge, 'acting with integrity is the same as acting ethically or morally' (1993: 5). Quite explicitly, he contends that 'acting with integrity means both acting in accordance with one's highest self-accepted norms of behaviour and imposing on oneself the norms demanded by ethics and morality' (ibid.: 6). He argues that integrity requires individuals and businesses to rise above any moral minimum and engage in, 'at least to some extent', actions that are not merely morally required, but also 'morally praiseworthy' that is, actions that fall within an ideal sphere (ibid.: 7). Finally, DeGeorge maintains that integrity requires 'acting in accordance with moral norms willingly, knowingly, purposefully, and because one is in command of one's action' (ibid.: 7). Accordingly, DeGeorge rejects Rawls's view about the tyrant who has integrity. 'It is a misuse of the term to talk about the integrity of a Hitler who acted on his beliefs in order to achieve racial purity through genocide, or of a Mafia hit man who lives up to the code of his profession' (ibid.: 6).

It might be tempting to argue that either Rawls or DeGeorge is mistaken in the view each holds of integrity. However, since *integrity* is a systematically ambiguous term I think another course of action is more productive. Instead, I suggest that there are three primary ways in which people talk about integrity. Firstly, there is a systemic sense of the wholeness or unity of some set of separate parts. This may be related to material systems, e.g. the integrity of a pipeline, a phone system or even the software of a communications system. It is also relevant to psychological systems where we may speak of the wholeness or extent to which a person's feelings, thoughts and actions are integrated. Secondly, there is a functional sense of integrity as seen when we speak of an individual who focuses on and adheres strictly to some non-moral value, e.g. aesthetics, religion, and does not allow anything else to deter him from pursuing that value. Thirdly, there is the moral sense of one who is conscientious and acts according to certain moral beliefs. This moral sense is sometimes linked with the whole of morality, as DeGeorge does. On other occasions, it is linked with only a part of morality. When this occurs, integrity is linked in particular with values or virtues such as fairness and honesty. In both these moral cases, what is crucial is not wholeness or unity so much as commitment to some particular moral standard or standards, or perhaps even the whole of morality.

Each of these senses of integrity is distinct, though we can imagine various ways in which they might be related. Still, distinguishing these

views can help sort through the previous disagreement as well as other contemporary discussions regarding integrity and responsible leadership.
Furthermore, each of these senses is important in their own ways in business as well as everyday life. As such, integrity is a systematically ambiguous concept. In short, I do not think that any of these senses is privileged
such that we could reject the other, nor could we claim that a particular
understanding of integrity is of primary value or significance.

However, inasmuch as our talk about integrity has to do with recent
scandals in business or scandals involving the behaviour of business leaders,
it is appropriate for us to concentrate on the moral sense of integrity. While
we do not expect business leaders to be saints, we certainly expect them to
adhere to certain moral standards and to transmit these into acts of responsible leadership. It is in this sense that Badaracco and Ellsworth claim that
'integrity lies at the very heart of understanding what leadership is'
(1989: 98).

Having noted various ways in which people understand integrity, I want
to contend now that it is mistaken to equate integrity simply with morality
and hence, DeGeorge's views of integrity should not be accepted. The basis
for my argument would be to draw on a principle I suggested at the outset to
the effect that if we invoke a concept such as integrity, it should be so that we
can refer to various situations or conditions that cannot be captured better
by other concepts. In short, we should ask what can be said specially or
uniquely using the term *integrity*. Invoking a phrase of the pragmatists,
'What is its "cash value"?' It has been said that integrity is a modern virtue;
that the Greeks did not talk about it, even though they talked about morality
and ethics. Hence, what special contribution does integrity bring to the table
and what is its special link with responsible leadership?

One answer to this question, the one that DeGeorge gives, is that *ethics*
has negative connotations and *morality* may suggest to some people moral-
izing (1993: 6). Even though integrity is 'an ethically charged term', acting
with integrity 'does not carry with it the overtones of naiveté that acting
ethically sometimes does' (ibid.: 6–7) Accordingly, DeGeorge speaks of
integrity because of the positive associations with this word, as opposed to
the negative associations with the words *ethics* and *morality*. He then pro-
ceeds to link integrity with 'living up to one's highest standards, and since
these standards are self-imposed, acting with integrity emphasizes the
autonomy of the firm and of the top managers' (ibid.: 6).

The arguments raised by DeGeorge are tactical or practical reasons if we
want to talk about morality in certain business contexts. But they are not
substantial or theoretical reasons. I think that if we want to invoke
integrity, it must be for other and better reasons than this. DeGeorge's view
of integrity covers up and makes more palatable what we really are talking
about, that is, ethics, morality and autonomy. It is a camouflage concept
for the superlatively moral or, at the least, the morally upright.
Accordingly, though DeGeorge is right that integrity does have moral

associations, the reasons he gives for focusing on integrity do not relate to any special substantive contribution that integrity itself offers. In this sense, Rawls' view that we do not equate integrity and morality seems preferable, since we already have a long-established and rich discourse on morality.

Paine (1994) gives a different answer to the question, why speak about integrity? She invokes integrity in her paper on 'Managing for organizational integrity' as a contrast term with compliance. In compliance, you are doing something that someone else tells you to do. On the contrary, Paine links integrity with self-governance and hence speaks of integrity strategies in contrast to compliance strategies. Paine notes different organizational integrity strategies but does not present a theory of self-governance for organizations that is clearly moral. Indeed, portions of her integrity strategies have close similarities to compliance strategies. Even if we allow that integrity, in her view, is a way of referring to moral uses or forms of self-governance, what is special in her talk about integrity is its reference to self-governance. Again, integrity proves to be a term of convenience; it is not clear what its own contribution is since we have already established significant ways of speaking about self-governance.

A new view of integrity

I have suggested that we need to identify what is important about integrity in its own right and that it is best not simply to equate it with morality, though it does have a moral dimension to it. There are, of course, many aspects of integrity such as cohesiveness (as opposed to simple unity or wholeness) that I am unable to address here. I thus propose we take special note of four prominent features of integrity.

An axiological dimension

Integrity involves a value structure by which the individual's identity is framed. There is, in short, *an axiological dimension* to integrity. There are three aspects to this dimension. First, although integrity does not equate simply with a full or maximal view of morality, it does presuppose some minimal view of morality that involves values or principles such as honesty and fairness. It should be noted that this allows a person to have a wide variety of other values with regard to which this person acts and lives. In this manner, integrity fits the pluralism of our times. The upshot is that a person of integrity takes seriously (at least within the minimal moral aspects of this dimension) the impact of his/her judgements on others. A person of integrity who was wholly indifferent to the impacts of his or her decisions on other people would be a strange individual.

Secondly, the values and principles one identifies with embody a distinction between core values and non-core values. The rationale for this is that if each and everything a person valued were a matter of that person's integrity, then that person would face the problem of successfully living with others. Both core and non-core values must meet the moral minima just suggested. Still, to have integrity is to recognize that some values or norms are more important than others.

Finally, since the principles or values part of this axiological dimension are bound up with who we are, they are not distant, impersonal abstract principles or rules. A person of integrity is one who acts honestly and meets certain other minimal moral standards, such as treats others fairly or does not impose unnecessary harm on others. This person acts in these ways because that is who they are, not because they are merely responding to some external obligations or commands. Nevertheless, integrity remains largely under-specified when it comes to its axiological and/or moral content. It can be given different contents within this minimal moral framework. Integrity itself does not fully specify that content.

A temporal dimension

Integrity is not a momentary thing, but rather an ongoing cohesiveness regarding one's values and actions over time. Like other virtues, it can be damaged by actions contrary to one's core values. Though, theoretically, it can be lost in a moment if the ruptures are serious enough, most commonly loss of one's integrity requires various actions over time. Those people of high integrity are able to maintain the cohesiveness of their core values and actions over time to a greater degree than others. Accordingly, one cannot tell, upon meeting a person at some moment, whether he or she is a person of integrity or not. One needs to hear from other people what their experience with this person has been over time. Over time it becomes clear whether this person is a person of integrity. In short there is also *a temporal dimension* to integrity.

A motivational dimension

Integrity is realized in the face of special challenges, threats and opportunities that it faces. In this way, it makes sense to see courage as linked to integrity. People of integrity are prepared to speak truth to power. They do not readily compromise in the face of threats, opportunities or counter-incentives. There is, then, also *a motivational dimension* to integrity. There is a sort of *toughness* to it. This motivational attribute of integrity need not be continually tested; but until a person has confronted conflicts, temptations, threats, etc. that person, and others around him, may not know the extent to which that person has integrity.

A social dimension

Finally, one's integrity is bound up, paradoxically perhaps, with others. It is only in our relations with others that our integrity is not only known or tested, but also manifested. In short, integrity has *a social dimension.* Consider, for example, Robinson Crusoe on an abandoned island – Crusoe would be hard-pressed to speak of his integrity without referring to how he was esteemed by others, even though those people were absent. It is therefore in social situations with others that one's integrity comes into play and by which it is maintained.

It is not surprising, then, that one's integrity is not something that one can determine simply by introspection. If a person says she has a pain, she has a pain. If she claims to be a person of integrity, she may or may not be so. One may be blind in various ways regarding whether one is behaving in a manner that demonstrates integrity. Thus, part of one's integrity is the reason-giving and dialogue with others concerning what one is doing, or proposing to do. Of course, some may refuse to do so. They may even claim that to give such reasons is, implicitly if not explicitly, to question their integrity. Such individuals confuse challenges to one's integrity with the challenge of being a person of integrity, a condition that requires of people that they give, or are able to give, accounts of their behaviour to others. And the rationale for this is, as noted above, that one's integrity is not something one can determine simply alone since it is realized in relations with others and not simply by oneself.

Implications of this view

What does such an account of integrity then tell us regarding the special uses or contribution of integrity and its importance for leadership? First, integrity does not itself provide moral directions in the manner that various moral principles and values do. Instead, integrity is a meta-virtue or condition. In this sense Rawls was right: a person of integrity is one who acts in accord with certain core values, does so candidly, while meeting certain other minimal moral standards. But what it is to be a person of integrity is not simply specified by core and minimal moral standards. Instead, having integrity is a way of acting on one's own basic principles. Responsible leaders cannot turn to integrity as they might turn to a principle of utility or a principle of distributive justice to tell them what to do.

Second, integrity can serve as a guide in the same manner that repeated experience makes it easier, more natural and more obvious what to do in familiar and unfamiliar situations. Through the adherence to certain central values or principles that one maintains in those experiences, as well as in the face of conflict and challenge, one's integrity may cut off certain distractions and temptations. Integrity helps one to focus; it maintains one on course. It is for this reason that people sometimes refer to integrity, metaphorically, as a kind of gyroscope. The gyroscope, however, is the wrong metaphor since gyroscopes are mechanical devices, and there is nothing mechanical about integrity and the guidance it provides.

Accordingly, rather than identifying integrity with this or that principle and their directions, it is better to link integrity with a person's ability to make good judgements based upon one's lived commitments, subject to core and minimal moral requirements.

Third, the preceding discussion focuses our attention on two different challenges that are particularly linked with talk about integrity. The first challenge arises when one's basic values or principles seem to require that one does something different from what the situation one faces demands. In short, some sort of compromise of the ways in which those values and principles are enacted is called for. The second challenge occurs when the values and characteristics of people successful in certain positions are at odds with their integrity. The characteristics attributed to some leaders may make having integrity difficult or impossible for such persons. In both cases, though in different ways, one's integrity is at stake. It is in addressing these kinds of challenges that integrity provides its special contribution. In the following I will treat each of these challenges briefly.

Challenges to our values and integrity

A frequent challenge to a person's integrity occurs when the characteristics of a person that make him or her successful are ones that may undermine his or her integrity. Alice Rivlin, for example, has expressed concern that of the characteristics she has identified as common among leaders, some are at odds with integrity. For example, the leaders she examines believe they must do certain things in order to lead the organization: they tend to be optimistic about results; they will shade the truth, minimize downside risks while taking risks and resist admitting mistakes; they are very competitive and rely on their power of over-simplified rhetoric to persuade others (Rivlin 2003). These personal characteristics may lead them to do things that others see as incompatible with integrity as well as that of their organization. Furthermore, many times these leaders do not see this. Hence they do not see their behaviour as compromising their integrity. They fail to see the conflicts of interest they are involved in raise questions of fairness, or that their shading of the truth undercuts their honesty. But such behaviour undermines claims that they fulfil the above conditions of having integrity.

It is plausible to believe, then, that at least part of the story behind the problems that Skilling, Lay, Fastow, Koslowski, Ebbers and others had was due, not simply to greed or a desire for boundless power, but to various positive features they possessed such as optimism and willingness to take risks. By this, I mean to suggest that the positive *and* negative features of these individuals might have played a role in their failure. The moral irony of our times is thus that some of the very features that lead a person to be successful as a leader may be the very features that cause them problems when it comes to questions of integrity.

Rivlin argues that the answer to this problem 'lies in requiring more information and asking more probing and sceptical questions' (2003: 353). She notes that in the United States in the public sphere, 'the separation of powers provides some protection against misleading forecasts put out by presidents' (ibid.: 352). And in the private sector, she maintains that 'that job falls on corporate boards, regulators, and, above all, investors' (ibid.: 353).

I suggest that the answer also lies with our views on integrity and leadership. First, it simply is not the case that great leaders must possess the grand-ego dimensions of many of those who have brought themselves and their companies into trouble by shading the truth, exaggerated optimism, etc. Jim Collins (2001) argues that the characteristics of the leaders of the most successful corporations he identifies do not have the larger-than-life egos Rivlin portrays, but much greater humility and willingness to accept responsibility.

Second, the characteristics Rivlin attributes to these individuals may also be seen to stem from, or be fostered by, the offices or positions one holds and the perceived expectations of those offices. In these offices or positions, one is challenged to engage in certain actions which undermine, if not undercut, one's integrity.

There are two extreme situations here. At one extreme is a person who is willing to do anything regardless of his/her principles or values to be successful or make his/her organization successful. This person is the arch-hypocrite. At this same end of the spectrum is the person who possesses or adopts values that lead to success but does so without regard for moral minima or the impact of his or her decisions on others. Rivlin's examples tend to be of this kind of person.

At the other extreme would be a person who seeks to protect his or her values by being simply unyielding. If a leader believes that compromise is wholly out of the question, then such a person will be rather rigid or intransigent. Of course, if everyone in an organization were equally rigid about what is compatible with their integrity, then the organization would be disrupted and become dysfunctional.

Hence the challenge is to come up with some middle ground where compromise is not integrity destroying, and integrity is not destructive of others, organizations, and society. That middle ground cannot be defined by seeking out additional moral principles or algorithms. How, then, can we know whether some action which we might otherwise have judged incompatible with our values or principles is not actually incompatible with them, or that in performing these actions we won't give up our integrity at the same time?

First, the person must draw appropriate distinctions between what is basic and what more marginal to his/her set of values. Is the person aware of the implications and consequences of these distinctions? A person who insists that everything that is different or opposed to each of one's values threatens his or her integrity is a person that has transformed integrity into an end in itself, rather than a manifestation of the values and principles to which that person is committed. Such a person is either so brittle that he fears any accommodation, or so rigid that he cannot allow it.

Second, compromise is possible regarding certain actions and/or policies if they can be seen as part of an overall structure that maps those measures or actions onto one's other important values and what is essential to the value being challenged. Integrity is a global or general condition, even if it need not be linked with the whole of one's life (Benjamin 1990). Accordingly, we must ask whether particular actions fit within an ongoing interpretation of the patterns that one's core values have hitherto constituted. If one stopped a movie as it neared its end, one could imagine a variety of different endings. Some of those would fit or be in harmony with the previous actions and patterns of behaviour, others would not; with other endings there would be question and dispute. A person of integrity must make this judgement of coherence, consistency and continuity regarding the basic values he or she has. Of course there may be disputes regarding this; and what the person says may not be final. We do not always know what our own values or principles require, and hence the necessity of engaging others. Still, whether a person could publicly affirm the proposed action without a sense of shame or embarrassment is also an indicator of the integrity-affirming or destroying nature of a particular action.

Third, we recognize that there are differences over the implications of moral principles and values. I have argued that there is a minimalist moral ground that involves honesty and perhaps other values such as fairness and not harming others unnecessarily. A person of integrity must fulfil those minimal standards. This determination involves others' perceptions and external evaluation. Hence we must ask whether one's values and principles require patterns of actions that are inconsistent with the minimalist external nature of integrity. The social side of integrity is relevant here since it is at this point that accountability enters into both integrity and responsible leadership. A leader who is not willing to be subject to conditions involving giving an account of his or her behaviour to others is a person whose integrity lacks necessary anchoring in one's social context since one's proposed compromises must be tested against others. They may perceive personal biases, self-deception, and so on, that one cannot oneself see. Integrity and accountability share this inner connection.

Finally, a responsible leader of integrity will have to balance all of the preceding considerations. In doing so, it is important to note that the challenge to our integrity is frequently portrayed as involving significant threats and portentous occasions. The truth may be far less exciting; it may instead occur in our daily humdrum activities and everyday choices that seem ordinary. It is through the small actions and compromises we make that we are prepared for larger ones. The power, praise and congratulation that leaders receive can foster as well as corrupt them. This means they must be on guard against if they are to secure their integrity.

Business and leadership implications

What are the implications for business and educational institutions of such an understanding of integrity? In the remainder of this chapter I shall point out a few of these implications.

First, can integrity be taught? It certainly is not taught by informing a person about various moral principles or important values in an organization or society. Preparation for integrity ought to begin early in life. On the other hand, this does not mean that one cannot later be forewarned through teaching about various situations in which one's integrity might be tested. Hence learning about conflicts of interest, which are uniquely part of this or that position, might play an instructional role in how a person responds with integrity in those situations. Similarly, learning about various subtle influences that may compromise a person can prepare a person to respond appropriately. A salutary learning experience also occurs when potential leaders are made aware of various self-deceptive biases that all people have that may obscure to them their own compromises of their integrity.

It is clear that various organizational and social conditions might foster individual integrity more so than others. In this sense as well, integrity can be taught or inculcated. Not all teaching is classroom teaching: this is not how one learns to swim or to have integrity. Paine (1994) and others have forcefully made the point that the organizational structures and cultures within which people live and work play a direct role in fostering integrity. Consider merely that aspect of integrity having to do with courage. A person of integrity must have trust and confidence in his or her values, judgement, etc. These are matters of self-trust, self-confidence and, indeed, courage. But people have different levels of each. Bad structures can reduce the number of people who have sufficient courage to act on their values; good structures may encourage and enhance those who will. Good role models, effective mentors and instructors may lead them to take their fate and that of others in their own hands.

Second, given the social dimension of integrity, the accountability structures in an organization will also provide feedback for maintaining individual integrity. Sometimes it takes a person willing to say, 'no, that's what you think, but that's not what you are really doing', to make people aware of their lack of awareness about themselves and how their integrity is at stake. Having to provide an account of their behaviour, either informally or formally, may make a person understand that his or her integrity is at stake. Accordingly, measures such as Sarbanes-Oxley and the US Federal Sentencing Guidelines need not be seen simply as ways in which the integrity of business leaders and organizations is questioned, but as ways in which that integrity may be supported.

Thirdly, the view of integrity advanced in this chapter has direct implications for the theories, images and metaphors through which we understand ourselves and business relations. For example, those who paint business as a form of warfare in which the object is to win, paint a picture in which deceit, subterfuge and dishonesty against one's competitors may have an important place. If this is the view that is inculcated into students as well as new employees, then one may well imagine that integrity will occupy a low priority in such a business organization. This is not to say that people in the military have low levels of integrity. Rather, the stakeholders in business are quite different from the stakeholders in the military: military people have enemies in ways that business people do (or should) not, and may be called upon to act in ways that people in business do (or should) not. Integrity demands different courses of action in different areas of life. We should be wary that the metaphors we use confuse the two.

Conclusion

The scandals and corruption society faces in business and other major institutions of society today have led to calls for integrity on the part of businesses and their leaders. However, what these calls amount to is much less clear. I have urged that we must sort out what special contribution integrity can play, as opposed to other familiar features of morality or responsibility.

I have proposed four major dimensions – axiological, temporal, motivational and social – that define integrity. In this account, integrity is a secondary virtue or condition regarding the way in which people and organizations work out other basic values and principles with which they identify. However, this view has several implications with regard to the guidance that integrity can offer as well as the ways in which integrity can be fostered in individuals and in organizations, be they educational or commercial.

The integrity of leaders of organizations may be challenged by positive characteristics of those leaders as well as the pressures stemming from their offices and positions. When evaluating the characteristics of leaders, we should not be misled by popular images of what leaders ought to do in order to be successful. And when weighing up the pressures they face, we should consider the moral minima we are all subject to, the larger schemes that our proposed actions fit into, and the organizational structures within which those actions take place. It will take some moral imagination to accomplish this, but such is what we expect from people of integrity.

Questions

1   How does the present account of integrity relate to how you viewed integrity prior to reading this chapter?
2   Do the positions that leaders occupy make it more difficult for them to maintain their own integrity?

3   In what ways can integrity be taught?
4   Some have suggested that integrity is particularly a Western concept. If not, do other cultures have very different understandings of integrity? What are the implications for business and business leaders?
5   What is the relation of the personal integrity of a business leader and the integrity of the organization he or she leads?

Bibliography

Badaracco, J.L. and Ellsworth, R.R (1989) *Leadership and the Quest for Integrity*, Boston, MA: Harvard Business School Press.

Benjamin, M. (1990) *Splitting the Difference*, Lawrence, KS: University of Kansas Press.

Collins, J. (2001) 'Level 5 leadership', *Harvard Business Review*, 79(1): 66–77.

DeGeorge, R. (1993) *Competing with Integrity*, New York: Oxford University Press.

George, B. (2003) *Authentic Leadership*, San Francisco, CA: Jossey-Bass.

Paine, L.S. (1994) 'Managing for organizational integrity', *Harvard Business Review*, 72(2): 106–17.

Rawls, J. (1971) *A Theory of Justice*, Cambridge, MA: Harvard University Press.

Rivlin, A. (2003) 'Greed, ethics and public policy', *Public Integrity*, 5: 347–54.

Srivastva, S. (1988) *Executive Integrity*, San Francisco, MA: Jossey-Bass.

7 Leadership, character and virtues from an Aristotelian viewpoint

Alejo José G. Sison

Introduction

The author proposes Aristotelian rhetoric as the model for the art of leadership. True leadership requires professional competence and moral integrity. It is a relationship that results not only in the achievement of noble goals but also in the moral growth of both leaders and followers. For this reason, authentic leadership cannot be based on charisma alone; above all, it calls for a trustworthy character. In essence, trustworthiness is a virtue or a combination of virtues.

We learn from Aristotle that virtue is that specific human excellence found in a person's actions, habits and character. Each of these levels of functioning has its own criteria of moral goodness. Furthermore, a feedback loop or reinforcement mechanism, usually called *learning* or *habituation*, exists among them.

Leadership is fundamentally the art of persuasion. Aristotle teaches that basically the means available to the speaker or potential leader are three: his speech or arguments (*logos*), the emotional disposition of his listeners (*pathos*) and the character (*ethos*) that he projects. The speaker's character, as in the case of the leader, is the controlling factor; and he would be convincing only to the extent that he displays practical wisdom (*phronesis*), good will (*eunoia*) and virtue (*arete*). Aristotle thus demands that technical competence in crafting speeches and capturing an audience's benevolence be inseparable from moral excellence in the ideal rhetorician. So, too, with the ideal leader.

Leadership: character or charisma?

As we go about our work, in the exercise of our profession, there comes a time in which, either individually or as an organization, we enter into uncharted territory with no apparent rules, or where the rules we knew no longer apply. Before we could just have gone with the flow, driven by routine, but suddenly, these guides seem to have vanished. We find ourselves at a crossroads and without a clue ... We're lost!

This is the time for leadership: when someone has to make a crucial decision, with hardly any guide, and summon strength to carry it out. It would indeed be wonderful if things just went ahead as planned and the call for leadership never arose, given the fearful chance for abuse. Yet this is mere wishful thinking. Leadership necessarily involves discretionary acts or prerogatives; notwithstanding the care to avoid arbitrariness and behaving in a self-serving fashion. A leader fills some very real needs: a need for vision, clear objectives and effective strategies, and a need for drive and energy to put such strategies into practice. The alternative to not having a leader is chaos and paralysis.

Leadership is one of the most observed yet least understood human phenomena (Bennis and Nanus 1978: 4). Practically each generation has come up with its own definition of leadership, with varying points of emphasis. In the 1990s, perhaps the most widely accepted definition was that of Joseph Rost, for whom 'Leadership is an influence relationship among leaders and followers who intend real changes that reflect their mutual purposes' (Rost 1993: 102). Rost's definition hits the mark on two main aspects of leadership. Firstly, in recognizing that leadership is a reciprocal relationship or a partnership between leader and followers. Not only do followers depend on their leader, but so does the leader on his followers, for he cannot accomplish anything without them. Secondly, Rost is also right in that leadership goals have to be agreed upon by leader and followers. Only a voluntary followership is acceptable to true leadership.

Rost's merits aside, the real issue is not how well leadership is defined, but how well it is practised, as Joanne Ciulla remarked (Ciulla 1998: 13). We should then inquire on how good leadership, in its double sense of morally good and technically effective, is achieved. In the measure that we figure out what sort of person should lead, to that extent we advance in our understanding of leadership. This conjunction between technical competence and moral excellence is what Ciulla refers to when she affirms that 'ethics lies at the very heart of leadership' (Ciulla 1998: xv, 18).

Former US President Harry Truman once gave the following litmus test of leadership: 'the ability to get other people to do what they don't want to do, and like it' (Solomon 1998: 91). Earlier we said that the need for leadership is most keenly felt when an organization has to move on, yet finds no rules for proceeding. Because of this puzzlement and inaction, an organization's members may feel depressed and discouraged. A leader is then needed to provide vision and energy. This task is easy when group members agree with the leader or when they pose little resistance to his initiatives. But this is hardly ever the case. Often, special leadership skills are needed to get other people to do what they initially disliked, while respecting their freedom. Moreover, leadership lies in getting people to actually like and even enjoy what at first they had not even imagined doing. How can one do this?

History has bequeathed us with a variety of pathways to leadership. Machiavelli posed the well-known alternative of leading through love or fear. Fear, like love, is indeed a very strong motivator; but unlike love, fear prevents people from feeling good about their work. Under the influence of fear, they focus more on avoiding punishment than on getting work done and doing it well. Besides love and fear, other routes to leadership are wealth, status, intelligence and skill. These are different forms that power, the capacity to effect change, adopts. At this juncture, the question of whether these qualities are innate or something that the leader has acquired often arises. The best response, perhaps, is that everyone has the potential to become a leader at least in some special circumstance. Very few, unfortunately, ever take the trouble of developing this capacity.

Leadership cannot develop merely as the result of external pressure, coercion or intimidation; it cannot be decreed. Its converse, followership, has to spring naturally from the minds and hearts of people, in response to their having felt recognized, respected and valued. Leadership is 'a complex moral relationship between people based on trust, obligation, commitment, emotion, and a shared vision of the good' (Ciulla 1998: xv); it is never a simple mechanical reaction to a superior force.

Above all, leadership consists in exerting moral influence over one's followers. Others express this influence in terms of moral authority (Casson 2000: 6). That the leader's moral influence benefits followers is the source of his authority; it legitimizes his power. Moral influence, in turn, could be understood in a double direction. First, from followers to leaders. Moral attributes such as honesty, integrity, credibility and trustworthiness are the qualities most desired by people in their leaders (Kouzes and Posner 1993: 255). Followers therefore can encourage and demand moral behaviour from their leaders. Second, from leaders to followers. Since all human decisions have a moral dimension, leaders shape the ethical choices of their followers, enhancing or inhibiting their personal growth. James MacGregor Burns saw this point lucidly: leadership is a two-way transformative and intrinsically moral relationship between leader and followers (Burns 1978). The two parties involved – leaders and followers – morally transform and elevate each other through their interaction. Hence, leadership becomes a major driving force for people and organizations to become ethical. Leadership nurtures personal ethics, allowing it to grow and shape a supportive organizational culture.

Stewardship and servant-leadership stem from the assumption that leadership is a reciprocal, morally uplifting relationship between leaders and followers. Stewardship represents a pivotal shift in leadership thinking, for it acknowledges a leader's deep moral accountability to the organization and its workers (Block 1993). In accordance with stewardship, no leader should behave despotically, going about his tasks as if he were the organization's sole proprietor. A steward-leader recognizes the power of workers to make decisions regarding their own jobs, as well as their capacity to influence the organization's goals, systems and structures. A steward-leader empowers workers instead of controlling them, so that they could become in turn leaders themselves.

Servant-leadership is even more revolutionary than stewardship, for it turns traditional leadership thinking, with its emphasis on high-profile figures, on its head. A servant-leader should not only acknowledge the interests of others in the organization; he is also duty-bound to serve them, transcending his self-interest (Greenleaf 1977). His obligation is to provide those under his care with a chance to grow and develop as persons, furnishing them with opportunities to enrich themselves, both materially and morally, through their work in the organization. The integral fulfilment of everyone in the organization is the servant-leader's aim and the standard according to which his very self-fulfilment is to be judged.

Many construe ethical leadership as an emotional relationship based on charisma – etymologically, the quality of being *touched by grace*. Charisma is that mysterious and extraordinary power possessed by people who are successful in influencing others. Being a non-rational characteristic, charisma is extremely difficult to define, lending itself at most to vague descriptions. In general, charisma has to do with a leader's message, how he says it, and the whole gamut of emotions (e.g., hopes, fears, enthusiasm) he evokes. Charm, intelligence and sincerity also contribute to the overall perception of charisma. Nonetheless, in the words of Robert Solomon,

> charisma doesn't refer to any character trait or 'quality' in particular, but is rather a general way of referring to a person who seems to be a dynamic and effective leader. And as a term of analysis in leadership studies, I think that it is more of a distraction than a point of understanding.
>
> (Solomon 1998: 98)

In place of charisma, Solomon proposes trust as the basis of ethical leadership (ibid. 8: 101, 105). An ethical leader is one who establishes and sustains a framework of reciprocal trust between himself and his followers and among his followers themselves. Without trust, no dialogue, understanding, cooperation, commerce or community would be possible. That's why despite the cynicism and suspicion accumulated through negative experiences, human beings still tend to have an open and trusting attitude towards others. Open-mindedness is absolutely necessary for future dealings. The more successful subsequent transactions are, the better the parties involved get to know each other, and the deeper their trust. Trust lowers transaction costs, facilitates entrepreneurial initiatives and boosts economic competitiveness (Casson 2000: 17–18). But what is the source of trust on which ethical leadership is founded? It is none other than virtue.

Virtue as excellence of character

Virtue is excellence of character, the possession and practise of habits appropriate for a human being within a particular sociocultural context. Nowadays, its meaning could be expressed by the word *integrity*, suggesting wholeness and stability in a person on whom others can rely. Virtue is a form of capital, moral capital (Sison 2003), because it is a productive capacity that accumulates and develops through investments of time and effort. Virtue however is unique in that it perfects the human being as a whole and not just in a limited aspect. It is not what makes a person strong, smart or successful, but what makes him good as a human being.

Excellence of character depends on cultivating the right habits. As Aristotle explains in the etymology of the word *ethics*, 'Virtue of character results from habit; hence its name "ethical", slightly varied from "ethos"' (*Nicomachean Ethics*, henceforth, NE, 1103a). Virtuous habits result from the repetition of virtuous actions, and virtuous actions spring from a person's having nurtured suitable inclinations in accordance with his nature.

There is a feedback mechanism among these different levels of functioning: character, habits and actions. We normally say that actions arise from a person's inclinations, yet actions themselves also weaken or reinforce inclinations. Similarly, habits do not only constitute character, but character likewise predisposes or disengages a person from certain habits. This circularity is as essential to Aristotelian teaching. Let us now consider the three main analogues of virtue: actions, habits and character.

Actions

Actions, which arise from a person's inclinations, are the building blocks of moral life. Not all actions, however, are morally significant, nor do they all have the same ethical value.

First, we must distinguish between involuntary and voluntary actions. Involuntary actions do not have moral significance, that is, they are exempt from praise or blame. Aristotle explains that 'what comes about by force or because of ignorance seems to be involuntary. What is forced has an external origin, the sort of origin in which the agent or victim contributes nothing' (NE 1110a). Only voluntary acts are morally significant, admitting praise or blame. They proceed from an internal principle (appetite, feeling, desire or will) and are accompanied by the agent's knowledge and consent: 'what is voluntary seems to be what has its origin in the agent himself when he knows the particulars that the action consists in' (NE 1111a). These actions are performed intentionally and deliberately, thus fully committing their agents.

Virtue lies in good voluntary actions and its goodness springs from three sources: the object or the action itself, the agent's end or intention, and the circumstances in which the act is carried out. These criteria should be considered in succession when judging a voluntary act.

The first criterion refers to the object or the action itself. It is what the agent does as a humanly meaningful whole and not the mere series of movements he goes through: for example, it's killing a man, and not simply aiming a gun and pulling the trigger. The object principally determines whether an action is good or evil. Certain actions are evil by their very object and are prohibited without exception: lying, theft, murder and so forth. As Aristotle observed, 'there are some things we cannot be compelled to do, and rather than do them we should suffer the most terrible consequences and accept death' (NE 1110a).

The second criterion examines the agent's intention, whether it is oriented towards his final end. At times, an action choice-worthy in its object becomes ethically flawed due to the agent's intention. To be virtuous an action has to be performed with a noble end. For instance, it is not enough to give alms; one should also wish to help the poor rather than do it merely for show.

Finally we have the circumstances surrounding actions. Seemingly *favourable* circumstances cannot change the moral quality of an action from evil to good. For example, no act of torture could be justified even if the fate of a hundred people depended on it. Circumstances affect the degree to which actions are good or evil, making them better or worse.

The moral excellence or virtue of actions requires the integral goodness of object, intention, and circumstances. Any defect would render a voluntary human act evil, debasing its agent.

Habits

Every voluntary act leaves a trace or mark that remains in the agent. This by-product is called *habit*: a stable disposition or manner of being and doing acquired by a subject. Habits vest human nature with a new, improved and reinforced tendency, a *second nature*. After good actions, good habits are the next analogue of virtue.

How do habits arise and take root? Following Aristotle, we start with a contrast between habits and nature:

> if something arises in us by nature, we first have the capacity for it, and later display the activity. ... Virtues, by contrast, we acquire, just as we acquire crafts, by having previously activated them. For we learn a craft by producing the same product that we must produce when we have learned it, become builders, e.g., by building and harpists by playing the harp; so also, then, we become just by doing just actions, temperate by doing temperate actions, brave by doing brave actions.
> (NE 1103a–b)

A purely sequential mode of thinking is inappropriate for understanding how habits develop. Unlike in nature, where the capacity precedes the activity, in habits, the activity itself creates the capacity. The creation of the capacity and the exercise of the activity occur simultaneously and are mutually reinforcing. Habits comprise an integrated feedback loop in human beings.

An analogy with crafts is useful in explaining the acquisition and growth of habits. To play the guitar one needs, aside from the instrument, certain faculties like arms, hands, fingers, an ear for music, a capacity to read a musical score, and so forth. Yet all these would be useless if one did not want to learn; the decision to learn is indispensable. The first time one picks up the guitar and strums a few chords, foreseeably, he would produce horrific noise. The tips of his fingers, his whole hand would get sore, pressing on the strings, reaching for the chords and strumming. The experience would not be enjoyable.

However, with perseverance and practice, the notes come out each time with less pain and effort. That's when the music begins. Later he could try more complicated scores and even improvise, leaving a personal mark. He would really be enjoying himself for the pleasant sounds now come out naturally. A little while longer and he could turn into a virtuoso. Not only would he have acquired the craft of guitar playing but he would have also perfected it. The dynamics of guitar playing is similar to the development of any other moral virtue or good habit. These enable us to do more things with greater perfection.

As habits, craft expertise, virtues and vices arise from the repetition of actions. This is what the phrase 'just as in the case of a craft, the sources and means that develop each virtue also ruin it' (NE 1103b) means. For crafts and virtues not any sort of action will do, 'for building well makes good builders, building badly, bad ones' (NE 1103b). Only the right sort of actions produces craft expertise; good actions alone produce virtues. For example, when faced with the same terrifying situation, those who have the habit of courage react bravely and confidently, those who have the habit of cowardice, fearfully. 'The same is true of situations involving appetites and anger; for one or another sort of conduct in these situations makes some people temperate and gentle, others intemperate and irascible' (NE 1103b). The right sort of habituation produces virtues, the wrong sort, vices. How do we distinguish virtues from vices?

First, to acquire proper habits, 'actions should express correct reason' (NE 1103b). Not in theory or in the abstract, but in each particular case, as expert doctors or navigators know in practice. Second, right habituation equally shuns excess and defect:

> Too much or too little eating or drinking ruins health, while the proportionate amount produces, increases and preserves it. The same is true, then, of temperance, bravery and the other virtues. For if, e.g.,

someone avoids and is afraid of everything, standing firm against nothing, he becomes cowardly, but if he is afraid of nothing at all and goes to face everything, he becomes rash. Similarly, if he gratifies himself with every pleasure and refrains from none, he becomes intemperate, but if he avoids them all, as boors do, he becomes some sort of insensible person. Temperance and bravery, then, are ruined by excess and deficiency but preserved by the mean.

(NE 1104a)

Third, proper habits come from experiencing appropriate pleasure or pain. 'For if someone who abstains from bodily pleasures enjoys the abstinence itself, then he is temperate, but if he is grieved by it, he is intemperate. Again, if he stands firm against terrifying situations and enjoys it, or at least does not find it painful, then he is brave, and if he finds it painful, he is cowardly' (NE 1104b).

An apparent contradiction now surfaces. Perhaps virtue is a natural state impossible to acquire, for in order to become just, one must first do just actions. Yet just actions could only be done by one who is already just! Either one is already just, and thus performs just actions, or one is not, and being incapable of just actions, no amount of habituation would do.

Aristotle offers clarifications which, apart from undoing this paradox, serve to establish the limits of the craft analogy. In the crafts, one may produce an object that conforms to expertise only in appearance. It could have been produced 'by chance or by following someone else's instructions' (NE 1105a); that is, without accompanying knowledge. Furthermore, 'the products of a craft determine by their own character whether they have been produced well' (NE 1105b). In craft products there is an objective goodness without reference to the craftsman.

This is not the case with virtues: 'for actions expressing virtue to be done temperately or justly [and hence well] it does not suffice that they are themselves in the right state. Rather, the agent must also be in the right state when he does them. First he must know [that he is doing virtuous actions]; second, he must decide on them, and decide on them for themselves; and third, he must also do them from a firm and unchanging state' (NE 1105a). There is no objectively virtuous action independent of the person. A virtuous act could not be separated from the virtuous habit that it emerges, nor from the virtuous person who possesses the habit. For an action to be virtuous it has to be performed as a virtuous person would (see Figure 7.1).

Character

Character describes an individual's personality or moral type. It results from the combination of different habits that a person develops. Initially, there may be some confusion whether virtue of character is a feeling, a capacity or a state of the soul. Indeed virtue of character allows us to

Actions   Habits   Character

Figure 7.1 The dynamics of virtue

experience certain feelings, positive or negative, regarding particular objects or actions. Yet we don't know if virtue of character lies in the feeling itself, in the capacity for such feeling, or in the acquired state from which that capacity derives.

By feelings Aristotle understands 'appetite, anger, fear, confidence, envy, joy, love, hate, longing, jealousy, pity, in general, whatever implies pleasure or pain' (NE 1105a). He quickly disqualifies feelings, though, because they arise without our consent and we are neither praised nor blamed for merely experiencing them. With feelings we play a passive role, while virtues require that we be active. Aristotle's reasons for precluding capacities as virtues of character are similar: 'the virtues are not capacities either; for we are neither called good nor bad in so far as we are simply capable of feelings. Further, while we have capacities by nature, we do not become good or bad by nature' (NE 1106a). Virtue of character is acquired, not innate; it cannot be a natural capacity for feelings or actions. Character states emerge, then, as the proper condition for virtue by elimination (NE 1106a).

An individual's character is like a fabric composed of several strands. First we have the physiological elements, referring to bodily traits that influence one's manner of being and acting. Next come a person's feelings, affections and emotions, representing the psychological component. These elements are unstable and do not strictly follow reason. Lastly, sociocultural factors such as a person's family, work, economic and political backgrounds also contribute to character. Aside from nature nurture too plays an important role in moulding personality. A person's character could then be described as a unique mix of physiological, psychological and sociocultural elements.

We may also differentiate a person's natural temperament or pathos from his acquired character or ethos. Pathos refers to an innate, spontaneous and pre-moral personality. Ethos results from deliberate and intentional acts, and is the object of moral responsibility. The transformation from pathos to ethos occurs through a lifelong process of learning. A person could deliberately change his character through the cultivation of appropriate habits.

Aristotle enumerates five main groups in classifying virtues of character. The first concerns virtues related with feelings: bravery governs fear and confidence, temperance, pleasures and pains (NE 1107b). The second group refers to virtues describing our relationship with external goods. Generosity or magnificence is the desirable character trait in the giving and taking of money, magnanimity, in honour and dishonour (NE 1107b). The social life requires its own set of virtues of character: mildness, between an excess and a deficiency of anger; truthfulness, between boastfulness and self-deprecation; wit, between buffoonery and boorishness; and friendliness, between being ingratiating and quarrelsome (NE 1108a). Next comes a group of desirable intermediate states which are not exactly virtues: having the right dose of shame, without being ashamed about everything or having no sense of disgrace; or proper indignation, between envy and spite (NE 1108a–b). Lastly comes justice, which is highly complex and demands a fuller explanation in its dimensions of lawfulness (general or universal justice) and fairness (particular justice) (NE 1129b).

How are we to acquire virtue of character? Since it lies in the mean, Aristotle admonishes us to avoid the more opposed extreme: 'For since one extreme is more in error, the other less, and since it is hard to hit the intermediate extremely accurately, the second-best tack, as they say, is to take the lesser of the evils' (NE 1109a). Regarding courage, for example, it would be better to err on the side of rashness than on cowardice, the more contrary extreme. Secondly, one should avoid the easier extreme depending on his natural drift. 'For different people have different natural tendencies towards different goals, and we shall come to know our own tendencies from the pleasure or pain that arises in us. We must drag ourselves off in the contrary direction' (NE 1109b). Aristotle also warns that we be careful with pleasures, 'for we are already biased in its favour when we come to judge it' (NE 1109b). Finally, Aristotle tells us that the rules do not, however, give exact and detailed guidance for action. Virtues of character deal with concrete, contingent actions and feelings beyond the scope of general, theoretical accounts: 'for nothing perceptible is easily defined, and [since] these [circumstances of virtuous and vicious action] are particulars, the judgment about them depends on perception' (NE 1109b). We are remitted, in the end, to the perception of an already virtuous person who alone is the competent judge in concrete situations.

Rhetoric as the art of leadership

All along, as we examined the art of leadership, we have been looking at what was known in the classical world as rhetoric. In the words of Aristotle, 'Let rhetoric be an ability, in each case, to see the available means of persuasion' (*Rhetoric*, henceforth, Rh, 1355b). Having excluded force as a legitimate means of influence, the only instrument available to the potential leader is reason. Words are nothing more than vehicles for reason. A leader has to persuade his audience to act through words. Yet words only move listeners once they have been understood; they are effective tools of persuasion exclusively among free and rational agents. However, words alone do not move; they require the complicity of feelings and emotions. That is why Aristotle directed his treatise on rhetoric or civic discourse to the citizens of the fledgling Athenian democracy who discuss the public good. It would not have made sense to teach rhetoric to slaves or irrational animals. Unlike citizens, they do not participate in deliberations about the public good or in government.

Today, as in Aristotle's time, there are people with a gift for communication and persuasion. Others, however, seem bereft of it. Nevertheless, both types of people stand to gain by studying the principles of speech and composition, observing and imitating successful speakers and writers, and constant practice. Aristotle was well aware of the controversy surrounding rhetoric and its teaching. Socrates, first, and Plato, like him, both thought that rhetoric as practised by the Sophists amounted to mere flattery, the use of empty words and misleading arguments to one's advantage, a brazen appeal to emotions without regard for truth. By contrast, Plato described his ideal rhetorician in the Phaedrus as a virtuous person with firm knowledge of the subject matter; one who has mastered the logical techniques of exposition and understands his audience well, leading them to the truth. For Plato, the only valid form of rhetoric was one that wedded persuasive skills with personal virtue and love of truth.

Aristotle, for his part, held that rhetoric as a communication art was morally neutral. It could be used for good or for evil; it was independent of both truth and virtue. With this spirit he wrote his treatise. He was careful, however, not to separate rhetoric from ethics; rather, he insisted on its subordination to the architectonic discipline of politics (NE 1094b). Aristotle argues that the study of rhetoric is useful for three main reasons (Rh 1355a–b). Firstly, because without rhetoric, the truth can be easily defeated in debate, for true knowledge alone may not be enough to persuade certain audiences who rely on uncontrasted feelings and opinions. Secondly, rhetoric helps the speaker understand the real state of an issue by giving him a chance to consider both sides, enabling him to refute an opponent with more ease. And thirdly, rhetoric permits one to defend oneself without recourse to violence, as in cases of false accusation.

According to Aristotle, three instruments are available to the speaker or potential leader to persuade his public (see Table 7.1): the speech or

Table 7.1 The means available to the Aristotelian rhetorician-leader

1   The speech or argument itself (*logos*)
2   The emotional disposition of listeners (*pathos*)
3   The character of the speaker (*ethos*)
   a   practical wisdom (*phronesis*)
   b   virtue (arete)
   c   good will (*eunoia*)

argument itself (*logos*), the character (*ethos*) of the speaker and the emotional disposition (*pathos*) of the listeners (Rh 1356a).

Speech or argument plainly persuades in the measure that it shows the truth in a particular case. The truth however may prove insufficient in convincing others who are unable to follow complicated reasoning and are dependent on hearsay. This does not mean that true reasoning has to be abandoned; one should simply realize its limitations.

Persuasion also occurs when the public is led by speech to experience appropriate emotions. These emotions, in turn, become the triggers of action. Those who hold a purely technical view of rhetoric focus exclusively on listeners' emotions. Yet it is also relevant to consider to whom a particular emotion is directed and for what purpose. Aristotle strikes a balance recognizing, on one hand, the role of emotions in human judgement and making it clear, on the other, that emotions are not the deciding factor in persuasion. Insofar as human judgement is affected by emotions, it is not an entirely rational act, but neither should the influence of emotions be exaggerated.

The character of the speaker is what Aristotle considers the controlling factor in persuasion: 'we believe fair-minded people to a greater extent and more quickly on all subjects in general and completely so in cases where there is not exact knowledge but room for doubt' (Rh 1356a). Listeners are convinced mainly by the image of trustworthiness that a speaker or potential leader projects. And what better way to assure an image of trustworthiness than by being trustworthy in fact?

Aristotle lists three personal qualities that an aspiring leader should possess to be credible before an audience: practical wisdom *(phronesis)*, virtue (*arete*) and good will (*eunoia*) (Rh 1378a). A leader's trustworthiness results from the confluence of these traits. Practical wisdom permits one to form correct opinions over concrete, contingent issues; virtue prods him to express his views justly and fairly; and goodwill ensures that he give the best advice to his listeners. A person who displays these characteristics necessarily becomes persuasive. Most likely, he'll be a successful and effective leader as well.

These qualities of a persuasive speaker – identical to those of a good leader – could then be employed for any of the following purposes (Rh 1358b). First, in a deliberative mode, to exhort or to dissuade from future action, by showing its potential advantage or harm. Second, in a judicial mode, to approve what is just or to condemn what is unjust in past actions. And thirdly, in a demonstrative mode, simply to indicate what is honourable or shameful in a thing or a person, without calling for any action.

Whatever be a leader's purpose, it would indeed be helpful that he learn to present his arguments well and that he elicit sympathetic feelings from the audience. For this he must turn to rhetoric. But by themselves, these techniques would not work if he lacked virtue, and in this regard there is no substitute for ethics.

Concluding remarks

Aristotle provides a basis for understanding leadership or the task of government through the distinction between production (*poieisis*) and action (*praxis*) (*Metaphysics* 1254a). Action and production refer to changes wrought by human intervention on individual, concrete and contingent realities; they are not the result of mere reflection on universal and abstract ideas. Action and production are activities carried out under the guidance of reason in its practical use.

Leadership is akin to action or praxis, and is thus superior to production or poieisis. In action, the emphasis lies on the qualitative change in the subject – for example, the cultivation of a virtuous character – while in production, the external object of the subject's activity is given more importance. In action – unlike in production – it is not possible to perfectly codify a set of objective rules and separate them from the personal dispositions of the agent, in a manner that guarantees the quality of the activity's performance. There are no valid recipe books or instructions manuals for good action or virtue, unlike for good production. To perform a good action, aside from the rules, an agent also has to ensure the right intention and moral dispositions. The excellence of action is called prudence: the excellence of production, technique or art. Prudence in leadership not only requires knowledge of the proper end, but also the right choice of means to that particular end. As a form of action, leadership comes close to the metaphysical model for a perfect, immanent act, where the end is internal to the activity itself (*Metaphysics* 1048b).

The error of most approaches to leadership consists in understanding this task as one of production, subject to technique, rather than action. The end then becomes the formulation of codes, the setting up of structures and the design of processes instead of governing the firm well. Together with this overdependence on codes comes the neglect for the virtues of mind and character in the education of the ruler or executive. Not that Aristotle holds written laws in disdain; they are a safeguard against arbitrariness and exert a powerful influence in moulding habit and custom. But he nevertheless upholds the superiority of habit and custom over the law, for absent coercion, it is from habit and custom that the law draws strength.

The contents of codes – rules, structures and procedures – represent at most only a third of the solution to the challenge of good leadership or governance. The rest would have to come from the other elements of corporate culture, the virtues of character or the good habits that leaders cultivate, and the ends or goods they pursue. As we have seen, good habits arise from the repetition of good actions, facilitating and improving their performance, as well as perfecting the agent, that is, bringing him closer to his final end in accordance with reason. The good that business leaders pursue can not be profit alone; otherwise, they would all be dealing drugs, where profits are astronomical and tax free. Rather, the true purpose of a firm, the primary good that corporate leaders have to look after, is to earn profits chiefly as a reward for offering quality goods and services that society demands. Virtues, precisely, are what integrate the rules with the goods of praxis or action.

Questions

1   Why is charisma insufficient for true leadership? Why wouldn't coercion or manipulation qualify as means for authentic leadership?
2   Explain the reinforcement mechanism among actions, habits and character with regard to virtue.
3   What are the criteria for goodness or virtue in actions? In habits? In character?
4   In what way is craft expertise similar to moral virtue? How do they differ?
5   How are technical competence and moral integrity related in the Aristotelian leadership model?

Bibliography

Aristotle (1971) *Aristotle's Metaphysics*, trans. C. Kirwan, Oxford: Clarendon Press.

Aristotle (1985) *Nicomachean Ethics*, trans. T. Irwin, Indianapolis, IN: Hackett.

Aristotle (1991) *Aristotle on Rhetoric: a theory of civic discourse*, trans. G.A. Kennedy, Oxford: Oxford University Press.

Bennis, W. and Nanus, B. (1978) *Leaders: the strategies for taking charge*, New York: Harper & Row.

Block, P. (1993) *Stewardship: choosing service over self-interest*, San Francisco, CA: Berrett-Koehler.

Burns, J. M. (1978) *Leadership*, New York: Harper & Row.

Casson, M. (2000) *Enterprise and Leadership: studies on firms, markets and networks*, Cheltenham, UK and Northampton, MA, USA: Edward Elgar.

Ciulla, J.B. (1998) 'Leadership ethics: mapping the territory', in J.B. Ciulla (ed.) *Ethics: the heart of leadership*, Westport, CN: Praeger.

Greenleaf, R.K. (1977) *Servant Leadership: a journey into the nature of legitimate power and greatness,* Mahwah, NJ: Paulist Press.

Kouzes, J.M. and Posner, B.Z. (1993) *Credibility: how leaders gain and lose it, why people demand it*, San Francisco: Jossey-Bass.

Plato (1953) *The Dialogues of Plato*, trans. B. Jowett, Oxford: Clarendon Press.

Rost J. (1993) *Leadership for the Twenty-First Century*, Westport, CN: Praeger.

Sison, A.J.G. (2003) *The Moral Capital of Leaders: why virtue matters,* Cheltenham, UK and Northampton, MA, USA: Edward Elgar.

Solomon, R.C. (1998) 'Ethical leadership, emotions, and trust: beyond "charisma"', in J.B. Ciulla (ed.) *Ethics: the heart of leadership*, Westport, CN: Praeger.

8 Leading responsibly across cultures

Sonja A. Sackmann

Introduction

The issue of leading and leadership has been of particular interest to practitioners and scientists since the end of the nineteenth century. Many models and theories of leadership have been developed since then (e.g. Bass 1990) and applied in practice with more or less satisfaction. In recent years, however, the focus on leading and leadership has received new impetus due to increasing rates of internationalization and globalization on the one hand and issues of fraudulent business conduct on the other.

Several indicators show that the world has become more international and multinational if not global. Modern means of transportation allow travel in all regions of the world on a daily basis. Since the early 1990s, the internet or world wide web connects people all over the world with 934,480,000 users in 2004 and expected users of about 1 billion in 2005 (Computer Industry Almanac 2004, Juliussen 2004). Nations have formed political and business regions such as the European Union, EFTA, NAFTA, Mercosur, ASEAN, CARICOM, Central American Common Market or the Andean Group. Multinational organizations such as the UNO, associated NGOs and Bretton Woods Institutions, the World Bank, WTO, IMF and ILO have been formed to address issues on a global level. Furthermore, business has also moved globally, as figures of foreign direct investments (FDI) indicate. During the 1990s, international investments increased by more than tree times and China replaced the United States in 2001 as the leading recipient of FDI. In 2001, worldwide exports of merchandise were almost US$6 trillion. To stay competitive in such a business context, firms have chosen different kinds of strategies to internationalize or *go global*. They have developed locations in other parts of the world, acquired firms, merged with firms or developed networks, and new organizational arrangements have emerged as a consequence.

The resulting work context can be characterized by an increasingly inter- or rather multi-national and multi-cultural workforce with employees holding various cultural backgrounds. They may work in different locations within the boundaries of such inter-, multinational or global firms or even side by side within one location of such firms. This multicultural work context poses challenges and new requirements on leaders and their leading skills as we will explore in this chapter.

In the past few years, business scandals like Enron, Tyco, WorldCom, Barings Bank, Ahold, Parmalat or Adelphia have shaken the world, resulting in an outcry for more responsibility in business conduct. Consequently, corporate governance structures have been scrutinized; the Sarbanes Oxley Act and other institutional frameworks and guidelines in regard to corporate governance have been installed. In addition, topics like corporate citizenship, corporate social responsibility, corporate ethics and responsible leadership have been addressed by practitioners as well as management scholars and organization researchers alike. The issue of responsible leader-ship is being explored in the various chapters of this book and is also explored from different perspectives in a recent publication edited by Doh and Stumpf (2005). While responsibility in leadership embraces institutional, structural, cultural and behavioural aspects that are located at different levels of analysis (Sackmann 2005), we will focus here predominantly on issues of responsibility at the individual and cultural level.

The chapter addresses several concepts that need some explication and positioning since their specific use has implications for practice and research. If we take a cognitive, social constructionist perspective (e.g. Sackmann 2004a), we can assume that our models of the world on topics such as leadership and culture influence our behaviour. Such a stance requires us to first explore the concepts of responsibility in leadership and leading as well as the concept of culture. Based on a multiple cultures perspective we will then propose a dynamic model of leadership. This model is further investigated in terms of leading responsibly across cultures with implications for practice.

Conceptions of leadership – leading responsibly

The topic of leadership is as old as mankind. Scientists have started to address it systematically since the end of the nineteenth century. Since that time, numerous models and theories have been developed, researched and applied in practice (e.g. Bass 1990). While the first wave of research assumed that leaders are born, that is, leaders bring with them a specific genetic set-up that enables them to lead as compared to others, the next wave of research was influenced by the behavioural paradigm that dominated most social sciences from the 1920s to about the 1970s. According to the behavioural paradigm, it was assumed that leaders are made and that every person can learn appropriate leadership skills regardless of their genetic make-up.

In the late 1970s, the human mind was rediscovered and *mind was brought back* into the social sciences (Pondy and Boje 1980). The cognitive approach to organizational analysis had gained grounds (e.g. Sackmann

2004a) and cognitive theories such as social cognition and attribution theory were applied to the topic of leadership (e.g. Sims and Lorenzi 1992). In addition, some authors started to stress the close connection and interaction between action and thinking (e.g. Weick 1979, 1983, 1995). Another stream in the wave of new leadership theories reintroduced a focus on the personality of the leader – be it from a psychoanalytical perspective (e.g. Kets de Vries 2003, Kets de Vries and Engellau 2004), a humanist perspective (e.g. Bennis 1998, Bennis *et al.* 2001, Bennis and Nanus 2003), with a focus on charisma (Conger and Kanungo 1998) or a focus on charisma and vision in terms of transformational leadership (e.g. Bass 1997, Avolio and Yammarino 2002, House and Shamir 1993). A different group of researchers focused on the exchange between leaders and subordinates (Graen and Cashman 1975, Vecchio and Gobdel 1984) and others construed leadership as a relational enterprise on the basis of a social constructionist perspective (e.g. Biedermann 1995, Dachler and Hosking 1995, Shotter 1995).

Despite this wide variety in available leadership theories, only few have been directly associated with responsibility. One may assume that the role of leadership automatically entails responsibility. Those who become leaders or assume leadership roles are implicitly expected to act in responsible ways. As recent business cases have shown, this implicit assumption can no longer be taken for granted. Research on ethical leadership, the field of business and moral philosophy has indirectly addressed issues of responsibility in leadership. While moral philosophy provides a basis for ethical decisions (for example, Ferrell *et al.* 2000, Robertson and Crittenden 2003), three different perspectives have been identified. Two of them locate responsibility in the person of the leader with a normative appeal, for example, the focus on virtues or morals and the focus on ethical conduct in terms of the Golden Rule. The third perspective focuses on legitimate actions based on dialogue (see Kuhn and Weibler 2003), with responsibility being considered the outcome of a communication process that occurs between leader and followers.

In the first two perspectives, responsibility is seen as a personal virtue in reference to traditional ethics. A responsible leader has the right morals based on his or her virtues that guide his or her behaviour. The great man theory as well as charismatic and transformational leadership theories can be related to this moral philosophy, since responsibility is seen as a property of the leader. Integrity, honesty, trustworthiness and being just are responsibility-related traits that can be found in both streams of leadership theories. In addition, in the recent GLOBE Leadership Studies (House *et al.* 2004), these traits have been found to be associated with desirable leadership behaviour in many countries of the world (e.g. Den Hartog *et al.* 1999).

Ethical leadership, on the other hand, draws on Kant's philosophy and considers responsibility first and foremost as an obligation of the leader who acts on the basis of a certain set of acquired values and who can be held accountable for his or her action (for a more detailed discussion see Sackmann 2005). The importance of values in leadership and value-based leadership has also received recent attention both in the managerial and academic communities (e.g. Sackmann forthcoming, Vogelsang and Burger 2004). Leaders are expected to adhere to certain values that prevent them from acting solely in their own self-interest. Value based leadership is based on shared and strongly internalized ideological values espoused by the leader while employees strongly identify with these values (House *et al.* 1999: 2). It is assumed that these ideological values such as responsibility and personal morality allow their carriers a moral or ethical assessment of right and wrong.

The third perspective places Kant's intrapersonal dialogue in the context of interpersonal interaction. Resulting actions are considered responsible if underlying reasons have been discussed, if these reasons are understood and if the resulting choice is seen as the most responsible one under given circumstances (for a more detailed discussion see Kuhn and Weibler 2003). This perspective can account for the fact that the work context in which leadership occurs may be characterized by different and partially conflicting interests, contradictions and even paradoxes. Hence, responsible choices are made with the awareness of these differing and partially contradicting streams of interest.

These three perspectives can be combined in a dynamic model of leading responsibly as shown in Figure 8.1. In this model, the person of the leader is considered to have and adhere to a set of acquired values associated with a sense of responsibility and responsible behaviour that is perceived at various degrees by the interaction partner who may be a subordinate, a colleague, a superior or a person outside the organization such as a customer, supplier or investor. In addition, the leader is seen to have a perceived range of responsibility that he or she enacts on the basis of an intrapersonal as well as interpersonal dialogue. This may also imply that choices and resulting actions are negotiated with the respective interaction partners. The visible behaviour is compared by the interaction partner with that of other leaders and also evaluated against other potential courses of action. The resulting consequences of actions taken are evaluated against the potential consequences of alternative courses of actions by the leader with feedback loops to his or her sense and range of perceived responsibility and its enactment. Simultaneously, the interaction partner evaluates perceived consequences to alternatives and considers the entire context of perceived consequences. The resulting judgement feeds back into his or her evaluation of the leader's perceived integrity and range of responsibility and may reinforce prior perceptions of the leader, his or her integrity, trustworthiness and honesty and his or her perceived sense of responsibility.

This dynamic model combines both personal and situational aspects as well as the perspectives of the actor and the perceiver(s) and related

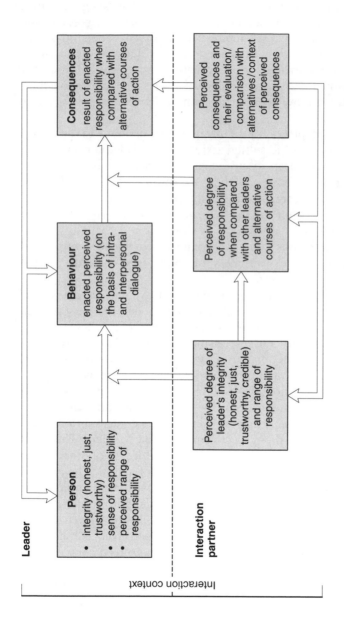

Figure 8.1 A dynamic model of leading responsibly

attributions as well as potential attribution errors. The model implies, for example, that the same leader may be perceived differently by different interaction partners – as a *person* in terms of integrity (e.g. being honest, just and trustworthy) and on the basis of his or her *behaviour* and the resulting *consequences*. It also implies that the leader and relevant interaction partner(s) may evaluate the same consequences differently in terms of responsibility since they may use different personal and contextual frames of references.

In the following section we want to explore some of the implications of this model for a leader who works in different cultural settings and who leads people with different cultural backgrounds.

Leading across cultures: the concept of multiple cultures

As we have pointed out in the introduction, the everyday work setting of a leader is becoming increasingly inter- and multinational due to companies' more international and global presence and due to technological, political, economic and societal changes that enable people to be mobile and move around. Resulting workforces are diverse in background. To give an example, at BrainLAB, a company that develops and globally distributes software and integrated medical solutions for minimally invasive therapies, the 270 employees at their Munich headquarters come from 26 different nations. The new organizational arrangements that are formed by companies in order to stay competitive in this globalizing world will require leaders increasingly to cross cultures in their daily work activities.

Culture in this context has been most frequently equated with national culture (e.g. Boyacigiller *et al.* 2004) and the sensitivity and attention to cultural differences at the national level has dramatically increased both in the business and in the academic world over the past years. The ground breaking work of Hofstede (1980a, 1980b, 1997, 2003) has sensitized researchers and practitioners alike to the fact that culture has an impact on interactions between people who come from different nations. In addition, his work and the work of Trompenaars (1993) and Trompenaars and Hampden-Turner (1998) have provided practitioners and researchers with dimensions that can be used to analyze, investigate and understand potential differences between people of different nations or cultures and deal with them more effectively.

Only recently, however, several researchers and practitioners have indicated that the new workplace realities of firms that act in the context of a globalizing economy go beyond cultural differences at the national level. Today's organizations and organizational arrangements may be composed of multiple cultures that co-exist simultaneously within organizational boundaries (e.g. Sackmann and Phillips 2002, 2004). The resulting cultural context of an organization may be rather complex and organizational members may be at the same time members of several cultural subgroups.

That is, national culture may only be one of several other cultural influences as June Delano, an executive from Eastman Kodak Company, described:

> people of many nationalities ... lead multi-cultural teams, work on multicountry projects, and travel monthly outside their home countries. In any year, they may work in Paris, Shanghai, Istanbul, Moscow, or Buenos Aires with colleagues from a different set of countries.
>
> (Delano 2000: 77)

If we define culture as 'basic assumptions or understandings commonly-held by a group of people that influences their thinking, feeling and acting' (e.g. Sackmann and Phillips 2004: 379) culture may emerge whenever a group of people works together over an extended period of time. As a consequence, work organizations may consist of several co-existing subcultures. These subcultures may emerge at the sub-organizational level and form according to functional domain (e.g. Sackmann 1991), work group or ethnicity (de Vries 1997). They may exist at the organizational level such as a single business culture (Ybema 1997). Subcultures may transcend the organization's boundary such as professions (e.g. Kwantes and Boglarsky 2004), networks (Lawless 1980) or race (Jones 2002), or they may exist at the supra-organizational level such as nation, industry (Phillips 1994), geographic region (Jang and Chung 1997), or ideology/religion (Aktouf, 1989). For a more detailed discussion of this multiple cultures perspective see Sackmann and Phillips (2002, 2004).

The challenges that result from this multiple cultures perspective for leaders who work and manage across cultures are manifold, as we discuss in the following section.

Leading responsibly across cultures: a dynamic model

We have pointed out in the previous section that leading responsibly across cultures requires not only sensitivity towards national differences and respective skills. It also requires sensitivity to the entire cultural context that is relevant for a given interaction and the appropriate skills in dealing with them responsibly. Figure 8.2 shows the dynamic model of leading responsibly (Figure 8.1) from a multiple cultures perspective. According to this model, both leaders and interaction partners bring with them a set of cultural identities that are influenced by socialization processes at the national/societal and regional level. If a leader has lived an extended period of time in another or several other countries, the result may be a hybrid cultural identity at this level. In addition, socialization into a certain profession may have a strong impact on the way they think, the way they approach problems and the way they structure interactions with

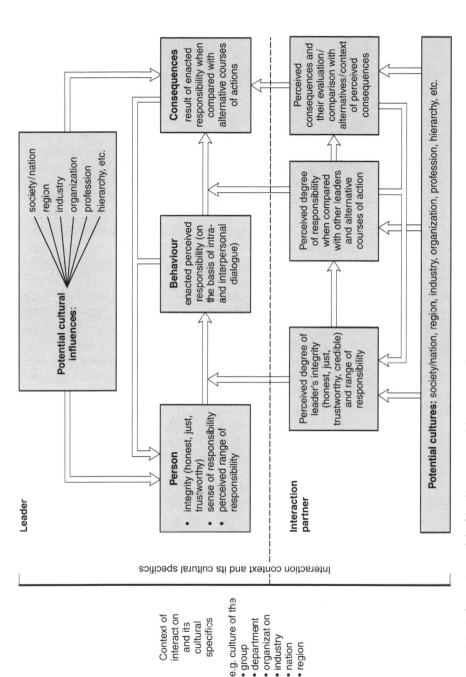

Figure 8.2 A dynamic model of leading responsibly across cultures

subordinates, superiors, colleagues, customers and other people outside the organization (e.g. Kwantes and Boglarsky 2004). These culture frames also influence the perceptions of what is considered responsible leadership behaviour and what is expected from a responsibly acting leader – at an institutional, organizational and individual level.

Culture at the industry level (e.g. Brodbeck *et al.* 2004, Phillips 1994), the organizational level, the hierarchical level as well as gender may provide additional cultural identities that may become salient depending on the issue at hand and hence influence their interaction with others. Recent research indicates, for example, that managers' moral reasoning may be less influenced by personality traits than previously assumed, while gender showed a difference in the study by Forte (2004) and age and management levels were found to influence perceptions of organizational climate in this study.

While both parties involved – leader and interaction partner(s) – bring with them their specific multiple cultural identities that influence their perceptions, their expectations and enactments of responsibility, their mutual interaction takes place in a certain context that has its own cultural specifics. Prior research has already suggested that individuals' behaviour is largely contextually determined and that values may be situationally suspended (Zimbardo 1972/2001). A more recent study on value congruency between personal and business values supports this notion that context matters and that business values are less stable across situations than previously assumed. In the laboratory study by Watson *et al.* (2004), for example, layoff decisions were justified and legitimized to maintain self-concepts in situations where personal values contradicted business related decisions.

When leading in a multiple cultures setting, the specific interaction context may be influenced by the group's culture, the department/division culture, the organization's culture, by culture at the industry, regional and national level. With only two people involved, three different kinds of cultural set-ups may come into play and influence the interaction process that may become rather complex from a cultural perspective. It goes far beyond the traditional perspective of bi-cultural (or rather bi-national) interaction. Instead, interacting and leading across cultures may turn into a challenge in dealing with a potential multitude of differing culture perspectives without knowing exactly when which kind of culture perspective becomes salient.

Some implications of the dynamic model for leading responsibly across cultures

Leading responsibly across cultures thus requires from the leaders' perspective knowledge of their cultural identities, of their interpretations of responsibility in leadership and the respective biases involved. It requires knowledge of the interaction partners' cultural identities and their expectations about responsibility, and it requires knowledge of the cultural specifics of the interaction context. What are, for example, some of the institutional requirements in regard to responsible leadership? What kind of behaviour is legally required from a responsible leader and also sanctioned and where is room for interpretation in regard to responsible behaviour? What is expected from a responsible leader by the organization with its specific culture? What expectations are held of leadership at different levels and functions? At Hilti AG, a Liechtenstein based company that develops, produces and supplies products for construction professionals worldwide, members of the board of directors are for instance expected to engage actively in the company. That means that they are expected to spend between 20 and 40 days per year working in and for the company to gain profound knowledge of the company's business and of the customers' needs so that they can ask critical questions and make informed decisions.

Available models and concepts that address the content of culture at different levels may serve as guides for a first orientation in regard to potentially existing cultural differences. Several models are available for understanding culture and cultural differences at the national and organizational level. For a first orientation at the national level, Hofstede's (2003) five bi-polar dimensions can be used, which were derived empirically (e.g. individuals–collectivism, femininity vs. masculinity, power distance, uncertainty avoidance and Confucian dynamism). Or Trompenaars' six theoretically based dimensions can help in reading some of the cultural differences at the national level (e.g. universalism vs. particularism, affective vs. neutral, specific vs. diffuse, individualism vs. collectivism, ascription vs. achievement, and time orientation). In regard to leadership, the dimensions included in the GLOBE Leadership Studies (e.g. House *et al.* 2004) may be of particular interest. These are performance, future, and humane orientations, gender egalitarianism, assertiveness, individualism and collectivism, power distance and uncertainty avoidance. Recent publications (House *et al.* 2004) discuss data from 62 nations in regard to these dimensions.

For culture at the organizational level, other sets of dimensions have been developed that may help in a first orientation of culture specific content at this level. The empirically developed dimensions by Sackmann (1991) or Schein's (1995) model of culture and five culturally relevant assumptions can be used for orientation (e.g. humanity's relationship to nature, the nature of reality and truth, the nature of human nature, the nature of human activity and the nature of human relationships). The issue of responsibility may run, however, across all five dimensions and the collective expectations in regard to responsible leadership behaviour are organization specific and need to be empirically determined. In addition, the standards for responsibility may change over time, as the cases of Bearings Bank or Enron have shown. Normative models of culture exist (e.g. Kobi and Würhrich 1986, Sackmann 2004b) and at the industry level, the framework developed by Phillips (1994) may be of help for a first orientation of cultural specifics in a particular setting.

Leaders should, however, be aware that information about perceived cultural differences gained with the help of these dimensions bears the danger of being reduced to stereotypical information – even if employed dimensions become finer grained and help further differentiation, such as the integrated cultural frameworks approach suggested by Boyacigiller and Phillips (2003) for analyzing culture at the national level. These models and dimensions may help and serve as a first orientation but they cannot replace open perception, open interaction and *customized treatment* of each individual interaction partner with his or her specific cultural socialization and related expectations. Hence, what is considered responsible leadership behaviour may vary depending on the interaction partner, the issue(s) at hand and the context in which the interaction occurs. What is considered responsible behaviour in a given context needs therefore to be explained, negotiated and re-negotiated over time between parties involved in that particular context.

The above discussion shows that knowledge about potential cultural differences in regards to these possibly existing multiple cultures is not sufficient. A leader who intends to act responsibly needs also sensitivity and awareness to be able to detect these potentially existing differences, changes over time and situations as issues may shift. In addition, a leader who wants to be perceived as responsible also needs to reflect and assess his or her own actions and outcomes with their potential impact on interaction partners.

Conclusion

In today's increasingly multicultural work settings, leading responsibly across cultures is an endeavour that requires several skills from leaders. They include knowledge of cultural specifics and differences at the national level but go far beyond this knowledge (e.g. Phillips and Sackmann 2002). First of all, leaders need to be aware of their own cultural identity and related cultural biases in regard to the issue of responsibility. They need to be sensitive to the cultural identities of their interaction partners and their expectations in regard to responsible leadership. They also need to be aware that people most likely hold multiple cultural identities and that their priorities may shift depending on the salience of issues at stake. Dahler-Larsen (1997) has shown this, for example, in a strike at SAS. Depending on the issues at stake, flight attendants identified with their work organization, their profession/function, or their nation. Responsible leaders are also sensitive to the cultural specifics of the context in which they interact and the potentially existing expectations in regard to responsible leadership behaviour. In addition, they have acquired diagnostic skills that help them identify these potentially important cultures at different levels. They have also sufficient social skills that help them navigate their behaviour in such a multiple cultures context in responsible ways – from their perspective, from the perspective of their interaction partner(s) and from the expectations of the context in which they interact. Potentially existing dilemmas are openly addressed, discussed and explained.

Questions

1   What are important components of your cultural identity (gender, nationality, profession, organization, industry etc.?) Think of a situation when different components of your cultural identity were challenged. What did you do?
2   If people have multiple cultural identities what are the challenges of leading people with different cultural backgrounds?
3   What is your understanding of a *responsibly acting* leader?
4   What are the implications of the dynamic model of leading responsibly for a leader who works in different cultural settings?
5   Think of a situation when your understanding of leadership responsibility was challenged or differed from that of another person. What did you do?

Bibliography

Aktouf, O. (1989) 'Corporate culture, the catholic ethic, and the spirit of capitalism: a Quebec Experience', in B.A. Turner (ed.) *Organizational Symbolism*, Berlin: de Gruyter.

Avolio, B.J. and Yammarino, F.J. (2002) *Transformational and Charismatic Leadership: the road ahead*, Amsterdam: Jai Press.

Bass, B.M. (1990) *Bass & Stogdill's Handbook of Leadership*, 3rd edn, New York, London: Free Press.

Bass, B.M. (1997) *Transformational Leadership*, Mahwah, NJ: Lawrence Earlbaum.

Bennis, W.G. (1998) *On Becoming a Leader*, London: Arrow.

Bennis, W.G. and Nanus, B. (2003) *Leaders: strategies for taking charge*, New York: Harper Business.

Bennis, W.G., Spreitzer, G. and Cummings, T. (2001) *The Future of Leadership*, Newbury Park, CA: Sage.

Biedermann, C. (1995) *Subjektive Führungstheorien (Subjective Leadership Theories)*, Bern: Haupt.

Boyacigiller, N. and Phillips, M.E. (2003) 'Cultural scanning: an integrated cultural frameworks approach', in N.A. Boyacigiller, R.A. Goodman and M.E. Phillips (eds) *Crossing Cultures: insights from master teachers*, New York, London: Routledge.

Boyacigiller, N., Phillips, M.E., Kleinberg, J. and Sackmann, S.A. (2004) 'Conceptualizing culture', in B.J. Punnett and O. Shenkar (eds) *Handbook for International Management Research*, 2nd revised edn, Oxford, Cambridge: Blackwell.

Brodbeck, F.C., Hanges, P.J., Dickson, M.W., Gupta, W. and Dorfman, P.W. (2004) 'Societal culture and industrial sector influences on organizational culture', in R.J. House, P.J. Hanges, M. Javidan, P.W. Dorfman and V. Gupta (eds) *Culture, Leadership, and Organizations: the globe study of 62 societies*, London, Thousand Oaks, CA: Sage.

Computer Industry Almanac Inc. (2004) 'Worldwide internet users will top 1 billion in 2005', available HTTP: www.c-i-a.com/pr0904.htm (accessed 5 May 2005).

Conger, J.A. and Kanungo, R.N. (1998) *Charismatic Leadership in Organizations*, Newbury Park, CA: Sage.

Dachler, H.P. and Hosking, D.-M. (1995) 'The primacy of relations in socially constructing organizational realities', in D.-M. Hosking, H.P. Dachler and K.J. Gergen (eds) *Management and Organization: relational alternatives to individualism*, Aldershot: Avebury.

Dahler-Larsen, P. (1997) 'Organizational identity as a "Crowded Category": a case of multiple and quickly shifting "we" typifications', in S.A. Sackmann (ed.) *Cultural Complexity in Organizations*, Newbury Park, CA: Sage.

de Vries, S. (1997),'Ethnic diversity in organizations: a Dutch experience', in S.A. Sackmann (ed.) *Cultural Complexity in Organizations*, Newbury Park, CA: Sage.

Delano, J. (2000) 'Executive commentary to J.S. Osland and A. Bird, "Beyond Sophisticated stereotyping: cultural sensemaking in context"', *Academy of Management Executive*, 14(1): 77–8.

Den Hartog, D.N., House, R.J., Hanges, P.J., Ruiz-Quintalnilla, S.A., Dorfman, P.W. and 170 co-authors (1999) 'Culture specific and cross-culturally generalizable implicit leadership theories: are attributes of charismatic/ transformational leadership universally endorsed?', *Leadership Quarterly*, 10(2): 219–56.

Doh, P. and Stumpf, S. (eds) (2005) *Handbook of Responsible Leadership and Governance in Global Business*, London: Edward Elgar.

Ferrell, O.C., Fraedrich, J.P. and Ferrell, L. (2000) *Business Ethics: ethical decision making and cases*, 4th edn, Boston, MA: Houghton Mifflin.

Forte, A. (2004) 'Antecedents of managers' moral reasoning', *Journal of Business Ethics*, 51(4): 313–47.

Graen, G.B. and Cashman, J.F. (1975) 'A role-making model of leadership in formal organization: a developmental approach', in G. Hunt and L. Larson (eds) *Leadership Frontiers*, Kent, OH: Kent State University Press.

Hofstede, G.H. (1980a) *Culture's Consequences: international differences in work-related values*, 1st edn, London, Newbury Park, CA: Sage.

Hofstede, G.H. (1980b) 'Motivation, leadership, and organization: do American theories apply abroad?', *Organizational Dynamics*, 9(1): 42–63.

Hofstede, G.H. (1997) *Cultures and Organizations: software of the mind: intercultural cooperation and its importance for survival*, revised edn, London, New York: McGraw-Hill.

Hofstede, G.H. (2003) *Culture's Consequences, Comparing Values, Behaviors, Institutions, and Organizations Across Nations*, 2nd edn, London, Newbury Park, CA: Sage.

House, R.J. and Shamir, B. (1993) 'Toward the integration of transformational, charismatic, and visionary theories', in M.M. Chemers and R. Ayman (eds)

Leadership Theory and Research: perspectives and directions, New York: Academic Press.

House, R.J., Delbecy, A. and Taris, T.W. (1999) *Value Based Leadership: an integrated theory and an empirical test*, Sidney: University of New South Wales Press.

House, R.J., Hanges, P.J., Javidan, M., Dorfman, P.W. and Gupta, V. (eds) (2004) *Culture, Leadership, and Organizations: the globe study of 62 societies*, London, Thousand Oaks, CA: Sage.

Jang, S. and Chung, M.-H. (1997) 'Discursive contradiction of tradition and modernity in Korean management practices: a case study of Samsung's new management', in Sackmann, S.A. (ed.) *Cultural Complexity in Organizations: inherent contrasts and contradictions*, Thousand Oaks, CA: Sage.

Jones, V. (2002) 'Beyond black and white: race and social identity in Brazil', paper presented at the IIB Conference 'Identifying Culture', Institute of International Business, Stockholm School of Economics, Sweden, June 2002.

Juliussen, E. (2004) *Worldwide Internet Users will Top 1 Billion in 2005: USA remains #1 with 185M internet users*, a market research report by eTForecasts. Online. Available HTTP: www. etforecasts.com/pr/pr904.htm (accessed 5 May 2005).

Kets de Vries, M.F.R. (2003) *Leaders, Fools and Impostors: essays on the psychology of leadership*, New York, Lincoln, NB, Shanghai: iUniverse.

Kets de Vries, M.F.R. and Engellau, E. (2004) *Are Leaders Born or Are They Made: the case of Alexander the Great*, London, New York: Karnac Books.

Kobi, J.M. and Wüthrich, H.A. (1986) *Unternehmenskultur verstehen, erfassen und gestalten* (Understanding, assessing and managing corporate culture), Landsberg/Lech: Verlag Moderne Industrie.

Kuhn, T. and Weibler, J. (2003) 'Führungsethik: Notwendigkeit, Ansätze und Vorbedingungen ethikbewusster Mitarbeiterführung', *Die Unternehmung*, 57(5): 375–92.

Kwantes, C.T. and Boglarsky, C.A. (2004) 'Do occupational groups vary in expressed organizational culture preferences? A study of six occuptions in the United States', *International Journal of Cross Cultural Management*, 4(3): 335–54.

Lawless, M.W. (1980) 'Toward a theory of policy making for directed interorganizational systems', doctoral dissertation, Graduate School of Management, University of California, Los Angeles, in *Dissertation Abstracts International* (University Microfilms No. 8111245).

Phillips, M.E. (1994) 'Industry mindsets: exploring the cultures of two macro-organizational settings', *Organization Science*, 5(3): 384–402.

Phillips, M.E. and Sackmann, S.A. (2002) 'Managing in an era of multiple cultures', The Graziadio Business Report, November 2002. Online. Available http://gbr. pepperdine.edu (accessed 5 May 2005).

Pondy, L.R. and Boje, D.M. (1980) 'Bringing mind back in', in W.M. Evan (ed.) *Frontiers in Organization and Management*, New York: Wiley.

Robertson, C.J. and Crittenden, W.F. (2003) 'Mapping moral philosophies: strategic implications for multinational firms', *Strategic Management Journal*, 24(4): 385–92.

Sackmann, S.A. (1991) *Cultural Knowledge in Organizations: exploring the collective mind*, Newbury Park, CA: Sage.

Sackmann, S.A. (2004a) 'Der kognitive Ansatz' (Cognitions in Management), in G. Schreyögg and A.V. Werder (eds) *Handwörterbuch Unternehmensführung und Organisation* (Handbook of Corporate Leadership and Organization), 4th revised edn, Stuttgart: Schäffer Poeschel.

Sackmann, S.A. (2004b) *Erfolgsfaktor Unternehmenskultur* (Success Factor Corporate Culture), Wiesbaden: Gabler.

Sackmann, S.A. (2005) 'Responsible leadership: a cross-cultural perspective', in J.P. Doh and S. Stumpf (eds), *Handbook of Responsible Leadership and Governance in Global Business*, London: Edward Elgar.

Sackmann, S.A. (forthcoming) 'Die Rolle und Bedeutung von Werten im Führungsprozess' (The role and implications of values in leadership processes), in U. Meier (ed.) *Mit Werten in Führung gehen*, Regensburg: Pustet Verlag.

Sackmann, S.A. and Phillips, M.E. (2002) 'Multiple cultures perspective: an alternative paradigm for international cross-cultural management research', *Proceedings of the International Western Academy of Management*.

Sackmann, S.A. and Phillips, M.E. (2004) 'Contextual influences on culture research: shifting assumptions for new workplace realities', *International Journal for Cross-Cultural Research*, 4 (3): 371–92.

Schein, E. (1995) *Organizational Culture and Leadership*, San Francisco, CA: Jossey-Bass.

Shotter, J. (1995) 'The manager as a practical author: a rhetorical-responsive, social constructionist approach to social-organizational problems', in D.-M. Hosking, H.P. Dachler and K.J. Gergen (eds) *Management and Organization: relational alternatives to individualism*, Aldershot: Avebury.

Sims Jr, H.P. and Lorenzi, P. (1992) *The New Leadership Paradigm*, Newbury Park, CA: Sage.

Trompenaars, F. (1993) *Riding the Waves of Culture: understanding cultural diversity in business*, 1st edn, London: Nicholas Brealey.

Trompenaars, F. and Hampden-Turner, C. (1998) *Riding the Waves of Culture: understanding diversity in global business*, 2nd revised edn, New York: McGraw-Hill.

Vecchio, R.P. and Gobdel, B.C. (1984) 'The vertical dyad linkage model of leadership: problems and prospects', *Organizational Behavior and Human Performance*, 34: 5–20.

Vogelsang, G. and Burger, C. (2004) *Werte schaffen Wert: Warum wir glaubwürdige Manager brauchen* (Values Create Value: why we need credible managers), Munich: Ullstein.

Watson, G.W., Papamarcos, S.D., Teague, B.T. and Bean, C. (2004) 'Exploring the dynamics of business values: a self-affirmation perspective', paper presented at International Association for Business and Society, Jackson Hole, WY, March 2004.

Weick, K. (1979) *The Social Psychology of Organizing*, 2nd edn, New York: McGraw-Hill.

Weick, K. (1983) 'Managerial thought in the context of action', in S. Srivastva and Associates (eds), *The Executive Mind*, San Francisco, CA: Jossey-Bass.

Weick, K. (1995) *Sense Making in Organizations*, Newbury Park, CA: Sage.

Ybema, S.B. (1997) 'Telling tales: contrasts and commonalities within the organization of an amusement park – confronting and combining different perspectives', in S.A. Sackmann (ed.) *Cultural Complexity in Organizations*, Newbury Park, CA: Sage.

Zimbardo, P.G. (1972) 'The pathology of imprisonment', *Society,* 9(6): 4–8; reprinted in J.M. Henslin (ed.) (2001) *Down to Earth Sociology*, 11th edn, New York: Free Press.

9 Towards responsible leadership through reconciling dilemmas

Tong Schraa-Liu and Fons Trompenaars

Introduction

Today, in an age of economic globalization, leaders in the corporate world find themselves in a dynamic and complex multicultural business environment in which there is an increasing interconnection between technology, people, organizations and society at large. Established models of leadership, conceived for more traditional and stable eras, have broken down. We must consider what new facets of leadership are required to serve today's executives.

From a holistic perspective, the competing and often conflicting demands of clients, suppliers, customers, shareholders, communities, NGOs and the environment for resources give rise to a whole series of tensions that need to be reconciled. In addition, the internal challenge is to lead an increasingly diverse workforce across distance, businesses, countries and cultures; to select, develop and retain people from different backgrounds; and to leverage their potential in order to create an inclusive environment.

In this global multi-stakeholder society, a purely financial view of bottom-line performance is too limited to capture the quality of leadership and success of organizations in the long run. There is no line in the regular profit and loss statements that represents *responsibility* as either an income or expense. The challenge for today's leaders is to perform effectively in an environment of uncertainty and ambiguity while reconciling the diversity of interests, needs and demands of multiple stakeholders.

To rise to a position of responsible leadership in today's business world is to experience numerous and various claims upon your allegiance: organizational goals versus the long-term needs of society, globalism versus localism, employee orientation versus accountability to shareholders, self- versus company-interest, and service to customers and community. As a leader you are no longer only in your own business, but in interaction with external stakeholders. You must, of course, satisfy shareholders, but how can you do this without first enthusing your own people, who then delight customers, who then provide the revenues you all seek?

In this chapter, we present and justify our definition of responsible leadership in the above context. We explain the key dilemmas responsible leaders face in a global multi-stakeholder society and why it is appropriate to present cross-cultural competence as the fundamental construct for responsible leadership. Analyzing the data and cases we have collected over the years in our consulting practice as well as our research demonstrates that competence in reconciling dilemmas is the most discriminating feature that differentiates successful from less successful leaders, and responsible from non-responsible leaders. Having explored this key competence of responsible leadership, we discuss how to develop responsible leadership characteristics and how to develop the propensity to reconcile with external stakeholders. Finally, we explore what is the *inner* path to responsible leadership.[1]

How can responsible leadership be defined?

An enormous amount has been written and researched in leadership. Frameworks to capture the essence of leadership have been developed on the basis of personality traits, cognitive and behavioural competencies, situational and context models, models of transformation, as well as military and head versus heart ideologies. Almost as much confusion exists about the concept of *followership*.

At this point we neither want to discuss the different leadership approaches nor conduct an in-depth analysis of their strength and weaknesses (see Rost 1991). However, we need to share an observation from a cross-cultural point of view: many approaches that claim universal applicability for their findings and ideas ignore cultural differences and are as such ethnocentric; they often only apply to the culture of the country or organization in which they were studied.

Kouzes and Posner (2002), for example, have tried to identify finite characteristics of good leadership. From their American perspective, they listed five universal keys to effective leadership: pave the way, inspire a shared vision, challenge the process, enable others to act, encourage the heart. In their book *Les Grand Patrons* (1998), French authors Christine Ockrent and Jean Pierre Séréni shed a completely different light on what makes leaders effective. Here attention is given to the personal background of the leader, her education and her family background. If we turned to the Asian literature on leadership, we would find different competences again. (see e.g. Mannari 1986).

If the French manage in France, the Japanese in Japan, and the Americans in the United States there might be less of a problem of using the single national frame of reference. However, such models cause a great deal of confusion for the trans cultural leader who manages a multi cultural business. How does one deal with multicultural groups and stakeholders with multiple frames of reference and mental models? Which principles should they follow if they need to act in a multicultural setting? Which framework should they follow? Which meaning should they create?

Based on our extensive research and consulting where we have examined the professional practice of leaders across the globe, we have derived the following core proposition that evolves from the analysis of our evidence: namely, that *successful leaders in the twenty-first century apply their propensity to reconcile dilemmas to a higher level.*

Our research studies reveal clearly that competence in reconciling dilemmas is the most discriminating feature that differentiates successful and less successful leaders. Leaders increasingly need to *manage culture* by continuously fine-tuning dilemmas. Thus, our definition of responsible leadership is that leaders are those who take responsibility towards the bottom-line and shareholders of the organization, while at the same time – through reconciliation – take responsibility towards integrating a diverse workforce, multicultural customers and suppliers, local and global communities, NGOs, environmental concerns and society at large. These leaders recognize and respect multiple demands, interests, needs and conflicts stemming from diverse responsibilities and reconcile them by mobilizing and successfully engaging the organization and varying stakeholders.

What is dilemma reconciliation?

The word *dilemma* originates from Greek, meaning *two propositions in apparent conflict*. Take the example of gift-giving. Suppose my American or West European Headquarter has a Code of Conduct banning gifts, which are considered forms of bribery. Suppose an important supplier gives me a piece of jade as a gift, not because he seeks to corrupt us but because we mentioned over lunch that my young daughter collects jade figurines. The gift is small in value, a token of friendship and respect. It is even inscribed with birthday greetings. Should I *Follow the Code of Conduct* prescribed from 8,000 miles away? Or *Be Flexible* and follow the norms of East Asian friendship networks? At the moment we lack the logic to decide such issues. Philosophers of science tell us that values are mere 'exclamations of preference', akin to liking or disliking strawberry ice-cream. Economists tell us that all values are subjective and relative, until an objective price is fixed by markets, at which point their value becomes verifiable.

In contrast, the logic of dilemma resolution is circular or cybernetic. *Follow the Code*, forbidding all reception of gifts, needs to learn from East Asian flexibility, that some gifts are not bribes but tokens of friendship. In short, that there are reasonable exceptions to this rule. So the rule is modified – now the prohibition is against accepting bribes, defined as gifts exceeding $75 in value. This modified rule allows executives abroad both to *Follow the Code* and *Be Flexible* about friendship tokens. No longer do we have to insult gift givers by returning their presents.

Another variation of the modified rule is to accept gifts *equal in value to an evening meal for two at a good restaurant* but no more. This makes sense because Westerners tend to treat entertainment expense as a non-bribe, while others who do not make this distinction are puzzled by our acceptance of meals and refusal of gifts.

The ideal of reconciliation upholds the important free-market principle that the best product should win the business and bribes distort this outcome. Yet, since service is important, small gifts may also be used to show friendship, consideration and good relations. Now, clearly some gifts are bribes but many are not. By thinking carefully about these exceptions, you learn to develop rules that will work in foreign countries, by moving along the continuum of *New Rules–New Exceptions*. This is the way to make your rules better while appreciating the truly exceptional.

Consider two international businesses and how these confront two very common dilemmas of overseas operations.

Competing strongly   vs.   Making friends
Following rules   vs.   Finding exceptions

Let us suppose that one of our businesses is extremely successful and the other is teetering on the edge of bankruptcy. Can we explain their good and ill fortunes by the relative fervour with which they compete or follow rules? Not really – a failing company may be competing with desperate intensity and clinging to the rules as it would to a life-raft. Feeling very strongly about any of these values cannot distinguish triumph from disaster.

So where does the difference lie? Not in each value itself, nor in the strength of one or both. The answer lies between them, in the patterns of competing strongly and making friends, in the patterns of following rules and finding exceptions. In successful wealth creation, these two pairs of values are integrated and synergistic; hence the judgement that such leaders have 'integrity'. In wealth or value destruction, the two pairs of values frustrate, impede and ultimately confound each other. We call the first a virtuous circle and the second a vicious circle.

In the example above, the dilemma of making friends and competing fiercely on the merits of our product and service has been synergized. The exception of gift-giving is permitted under the revised rules, which allow genuine expressions of respect but no bribes. All four values work together. In the vicious circle, however, one value is deemed *right* – sticking to the rules – while the opposite – making an exception for small gifts – is deemed 'wrong'. As a result, competitiveness falls, business is in jeopardy, friendship has failed, and out of desperation, someone will probably be willing to pay a bribe. The result is a downward spiral – rules exclude more and more of what is necessary to survive, driving competitiveness ever lower, and making friendship more costly and unwise. While in virtuous circles the values are mutually reinforcing, they are in vicious circles estranged and they exacerbate each other.

Value cannot be added because it does not accumulate transitively. Values are differences: they need to be reconciled and connected in a virtuous manner. Outstanding leaders take apparent opposites – dilemmas like rules and exceptions, globalism and localism, mass markets and customized markets, self- or company-interest and service to customers, individual creativity and group dynamics – and integrate these so that they benefit each other (Trompenaars and Hampden-Turner 2001).

What, then, are the implications for the leadership of an organization? Too often, a company overplays its strong card and finds out that it is undermined by its weak suit. The leader ought to act instead as a critic and diagnostician of the status quo, one who restores balance, say, between dream vacations and paying propositions, between the dreary task of insurance and the caring task of health provision. The best leaders are fiercely inner-directed yet lightning fast at reacting to and pre-empting changes in the business environment. To act responsibly and be successful at the same time, leaders need to alter their mindsets towards viewing challenges as open problems and expressing them as dilemmas. Only then can they begin to seek a reconciliation of the dilemmas leading to integration of two seemingly opposing values into integrity. In the following, we look at some examples of key dilemmas that leaders are likely to encounter in a global stakeholder society and describe a method of framing these dilemmas to reconcile them over time.

Stakeholder perspectives: the outer path to responsible leadership

Leaders of corporations are beset by a series of dilemmas, each being a pair of (apparently) conflicting propositions, demands, objectives and interests, and (cultural) value differences. Based on our research data we propose that responsible leadership depends on the capacity to integrate these demands in a multi-cultural setting and create powerful strategies that unite them.

We have found with our clients in the last five years of research and consulting that leaders are facing multiple stakeholder dilemmas. Figure 9.1 shows the major stakeholders of the organization, with the leader at the centre. From this, we can distinguish four organizational perspectives facing responsible leaders, as represented by each of the stakeholders (see Figure 9.1).

The human asset component includes employee and corporate cultural attitudes related to both individual and corporate self-improvement. In any organization, *people* – the foremost repository of knowledge – are its main asset. In a climate where competition is fierce and rapid changes demand constant innovation, it is commonly agreed that any failure to make the best use of its people will have serious consequences for the organization. Organizations know that a business that fails to ensure that all employees

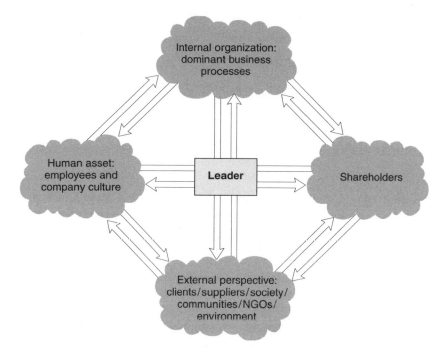

Figure 9.1 Four basic organizational perspectives

play a full and active part cannot hope to optimize productivity, competitiveness and sustainability.

The internal business and organization component refers to internal business processes. Standards of measurement for internal business processes allow managers to know how well their business is doing, and whether their products and services conform to customer requirements. These metrics have to be carefully designed by those who know these processes best – that is, by people within the organization. Ultimately, these metrics define the efficiency of the organization.

The external stakeholders include clients, suppliers, communities, NGOs, the environment and society at large. In a (global) stakeholder society, commercial viability and long-term business success depend on responsible leadership with respect to commerce, multiple stakeholders, society and the environment. The challenge for leadership is to transform their business into a responsible corporate citizen, create a high-performing organization from an ethical, social, environmental and business perspective, and ultimately develop an appropriate mindset within themselves as well as in their employees and future leaders (Maak and Pless 2006).

The shareholder component recognizes that we cannot discount the need for financial information; leadership has to focus on other stakeholder needs too. Nonetheless, we would add that there is currently an over-emphasis on financial data with regard to other components in measuring the success of an organization.

Each component is connected to at least three others, illustrating the conflicts in values between them and hence the dilemmas which have to be reconciled over time. Let's have a look at three dilemmas and what leaders can do to reconcile them.

Dilemmas responsible leaders face

Dilemma 1: internal organization versus external stakeholders

This first major dilemma concerns the coordination between external larger societal demands/needs and internal organizational goals. Is the internal allocation of resources in line with the long-term demands of society? Are business processes in line with the actual needs of clients? Obviously the sustainable and responsible organization needs to reconcile this potential dilemma, which is expressed in the following dilemma grid (see Figure 9.2).

Take for example the British United Provident Association (BUPA), a private health insurer and provider. Its approach to training its call-centre staff is by mining the experience of its own people in helping their family members confront illness. When customers call, they expect prompt attention to a medical emergency. The person they speak to on the other end of the telephone could be someone whose father also has Alzheimer's disease, or whose mother has had a mastectomy or heart bypass operation, or who has nursed a child through leukaemia. The understanding will be deep and

Figure 9.2 Society versus internal goals dilemma

poignant, the advice personal, the attachment real. Moreover, the call-taker is more likely to be motivated to speed medical assistance on its way and take personal charge of the case. In this instance, taking an inventory of your cultural resources and matching these to customers' needs is the best strategy. Development consists of sharing with fellow workers your ordeals as a carer so as to discover the ordeals that others have survived. The leadership of the company has thus reconciled an internal company process with its customers' needs and perspectives.

Dilemma 2: internal organization versus shareholders

This dilemma is perhaps one of the most underestimated. Resulting from the separation of powers between owners and managers, many dilemmas are created between a fair return in the short term and an even better return in the long term. In the analysis of the dilemmas with our clients, we found that the quality of internal organization is too often sacrificed for the sake of short-term returns for shareholders (see Figure 9.3).

Trying to steer a company by the profitability of successive quarters is like trying to steer a ship by the shape of its wake left several miles astern. It fails to alert the company to recent errors, whose consequences may only be realized months or years later. Indeed, the cumulative profitability of seven fat years may blind managers to the onset of seven lean years; managers may well be into this latter trend before it shows up on their bottom line.

The health-care products firm, Johnson & Johnson has made abnormally high returns for their shareholders for most of the twentieth century.

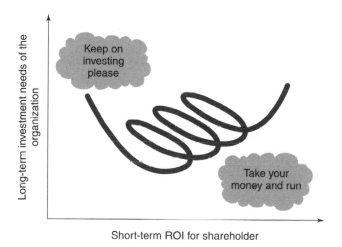

Figure 9.3   The long-term (LT) organizational and short-term (ST) shareholder dilemma

How strange is it that a major principle of their *Credo*, written back in 1943, is 'Shareholders come last'? This cannot mean that shareholders are least important to the company, otherwise the high returns paid to them would be inexplicable.

Rather, this is a reference to the *sequence in which wealth is created*: leaders and employees first motivate each other and innovate, then the company, guided by standards and benchmarks and employing machinery of some kind, acts strategically on behalf of its customers. Through its goods and services, customers become satisfied or dissatisfied with the company and signal their response, most immediately through changes in their consumption patterns and hence the revenue flow. Only then are monies available to pay out to shareholders. We can picture this sequence as a cycle (see Figure 9.4). It might be objected that a circle does not begin from any one segment and that shareholders finance the rotation. This is quite true. But if we are concerned with leadership and how companies might be better steered, then you have to look for *leverage points in the learning loop*.

There are many ways of altering human resource interaction in the first segment. There are many ways of raising the measurable quality of work in the second segment. Recipes for better relationships and closeness to customers abound in the third segment. Yet shareholders buy, sell or hold, and their conduct is usually a result rather than a trigger, although they many intervene in times of crisis or restructuring. For all such reasons, the view of shareholder reward as a *consequence of earlier activities* is a sound one

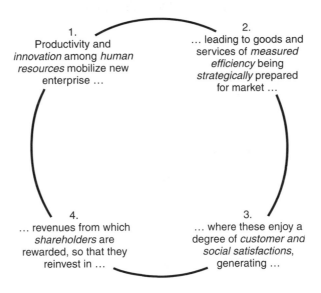

1.
Productivity and *innovation* among *human resources* mobilize new enterprise ...

2.
... leading to goods and services of *measured efficiency* being *strategically* prepared for market ...

4.
... revenues from which *shareholders* are rewarded, so that they reinvest in ...

3.
... where these enjoy a degree of *customer and social satisfactions*, generating ...

Figure 9.4 Sequential wealth creation

and ways of judging companies by how well they are being led and how well they are functioning may be more profound than looking at the totals of past successes.

Dilemma 3: shareholders versus external stakeholders

There are differing views on what the primary role of a corporation should be in society, let alone the views among different cultures. One view is that it serves the enrichment of its shareholders and the remuneration of its employees. The corporation is instrumental to these ends. At the other extreme, there is the view that the role of the corporation should be its own development, its learning and growth as a community, and its service to other communities, public and private. The corporation is not an instrument but an expression of these ends (see Figure 9.5).

Can we not reconcile these different human passions to undo the knots and solve the puzzles of our world and business? In this perspective, we need to use learning loops to connect what many people see as different or as even opposed viewpoints. It is the creative connection between these seeming oppositions, recognition of, respect for, reconciliation of and finally, realization of such differences that provides new, exciting meanings. For example, if a new form of safety harness for young children in automobiles means that annually roughly 2,000 will not be flung through windshields in a collision, then technical prowess plus social value would have created new meanings, with the capacity to give precious lives new direction and purpose.

Many activities that appear at first glance humble and prosaic may turn out to be neither when we trace their full ramifications. Let's take the Belgian-French company Suez Lyonnaise des Eaux, which enjoys more than

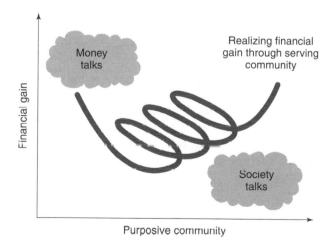

Figure 9.5 The shareholder versus society dilemma

50 per cent share of the world market in foreign operated water utilities. How did it achieve this? First, it prioritized the seemingly utilitarian task of building sewage systems. The dramatic rise in life expectancy around the world has been due less to advances in medicine than to the simple provision of clean drinking water. This company has not only transformed public health in impoverished communities around the world, it also embarked on a 'post-colonial' strategy, using French embassies to sell their vision. Suez Lyonnaise des Eaux believes that every country should own its own infra-structure. It therefore secures 20-year concessions to rebuild water and sanitation systems in countries or cities. Furthermore, it trains an indigenous workforce to operate and maintain these newly installed systems, after which the system is handed back to national or municipal ownership. So, even low technology solutions can have wide social ramifications and broad meanings for the challenge of human development and public health, while at the same time growing the market share and business of the company.

Whereas managers have to cope with problems they need to solve; responsible leaders operating in a global multi-stakeholder environment deal with dilemmas that they need to reconcile on a higher level. This section has provided examples of dilemmas that executives face in leading an organization and its people.

Dilemma reconciliation reduced to a multi-step procedure

Thinking about dilemmas and resolving them is in practice a complex task. We suggest in this section how this process can be reduced to six simple steps (Hampden-Turner and Trompenaars 2000):

1   Elicit the dilemma. Find issues and check for dilemmas.
2   (a) Chart the dilemma in a dual axis system as shown above and (b) label the axes according to the most relevant dimensions according to the 7-dimension model of Culture. In addition, add labels that reflect the (seemingly) opposing values of the dilemma.
3   Stretch the dilemma and list positives and negatives of both of the axis.
4   Define possible (including non-desirable) solutions.
5   Reconcile the dilemma. There are five aspects to the dilemma resolving process. Each aspect builds upon the previous one.
    (a) *Processing*. Treat one axis of the dilemma as if it were a process of organizing the other axis, e.g. turn universal changes into universalizing.
    (b) *Contextualizing*. Treat one side of the dilemma as context surrounding a text.
    (c) *Sequencing*. The dilemma will seem insolvable if we assume that both values must be managed simultaneously. Realize one value first and then realize the other after that.
    (d) *Waving or circling*. Realize one value through the other. By joining the ends of the sequence we can create a circle.

(e) *Synergizing.* To represent synergy, from the Greek syn-ergo 'to work with', we improve the circle and develop values so that it becomes a helix.

6 Define an action plan to realize the 'reconciled value'.

While the multi-stakeholder approach focuses on the dilemmas that the leader needs to reconcile in the *outside* world, we will now focus on reconciling dilemmas that exist *inside* the world of the leader – the starting point to developing responsible leaders. The inner state and world of the leader, which Kets de Vries (2001) called 'the inner theatre', defines a leader's effectiveness in dealing with various external relationships and challenges. From there, the responsible leader is capable of connecting the outcomes of internal reconciliation processes with external events. He or she transcends work–life and material–spiritual balances, enriches work through private activities and assigns meaning to material things. It is the inner and outer process of enrichment that makes the leader a person of ultimate responsibility and integrity, as we will show in the following section.

The inner path to responsible leadership

Where does the path to responsible leadership start? We argue that responsible leadership to stakeholders starts from the very core of the leader herself. Responsible leadership is built on the foundation of a leader's inner urge to serve and enable others, accompanied by human empathy and compassion (see e.g. Ciulla, Maak and Pless, Pruzan and Miller in this book). The urge to serve goes beyond serving one's own interests, purpose and position. As Robert Greenleaf said, love of oneself in the context of pervasive love for one's fellow man is a healthy attribute and necessary for the fulfilment of a life; the crucial point is humanness, the leader as a thoroughly humane person (Greenleaf 1977/2002). We would add that it is necessary for the fulfilment of responsible leadership. The sense of responsible leadership originates from a deep sense and recognition of unity with all living beings and the external environment. It is the belief that, behind our apparent differences, we are all alike in human heart, soul and feeling, and from the same source and origin. Given this unity, the responsible leader views people as beings to be trusted, believed in, loved and served, rather than as objects to be used, judged or against whom we compete.

In order to be able to serve others, employees, clients and the community, one needs to have an understanding of the value of other people, to respect them, as well as to value oneself. Thus, we postulate firstly that leaders need to understand and know themselves. Self-knowledge and awareness includes understanding one's impulses, drives and motives, and being conscious of how the self is steering one's actions and choices. It is also the awareness and conscious development of one's ideal – a goal with a higher purpose, a set of value systems and a clarity regarding life's purpose. Manfred Kets de Vries (2001), psychoanalyst and leadership expert, explores in his studies the 'inner theatre' of leaders – personality styles, dysfunctional patterns in leadership, the impact of narcissism etc. – themes that are key to understanding their behaviour. This approach helps explain unusual and even inappropriate responses to associates, excessive compulsions and self-defeating behaviours that are obstacles to acting responsibly towards one-self and the stakeholders one is responsible to.

Leading other people in a mature way requires leaders to reconcile their inner dilemmas. How well has one mastered reconciling the inner being with the outer self? How diligently is one working on cultivating one's personality by being conscious of one's character flaws? How well is one actualizing the firm's ideal and values while meeting the demands of everyday life? How effective is one reconciling the instant impulse with deeper motives, one's mind with one's heart, feeling with reason, body with soul, internal journey with external action? How conscious is a leader of reconciling his or her personal developmental goals while pursuing other goals? Given the complexity of human nature and life, has the leader reconciled in a humane manner the multiple stakeholders and perspectives within him- or herself?

Only if leaders know themselves and are able to reconcile their *inner* dilemmas can they maturely fulfil their *external* responsibilities, such as creating sustainable and trustful relationships with different stakeholders (clients, employees, shareholders, community), acting as a corporate citizen and creating an inclusive culture of diversity where people from different backgrounds feel recognized and respected and empowered to contribute to their full potential (see Pless and Maak 2004, 2005).

We also postulate that people are not born as responsible leaders, but can develop qualities over time based on thorough self-understanding: understanding one's innate nature and temperament, one's outer self and inner being, one's various layers of self and ego (the mind, heart and soul), one's limitations and aspects that need to be transformed, one's various mental models and lenses on life and the world established over the years of life experiences. Of course, a lot is already developed during the early stages of socialization as child and young adult. However, even managers and leaders can still develop themselves on a lifelong basis. To cope with the increasingly demanding challenges of the business environment, corporate leaders need to manage their work-life balance, schedule time for self-reflection and contemplation, and discover their intuition.

The art of personality is much neglected in today's world; people, intoxicated with cupidity and competitiveness, are bound to commercialism and kept busy in the acquisition of their everyday needs. Beauty, the need of the soul, is lost from view. The Indian musician and mystic Hazrat Inayat Khan, who lived in the 1920s, once said, 'The human heart must first be melted, like metal before it can be molded into a desirable personality' (Khan 1993).

The art of personality is like the art of music, wherein ear and voice training are indispensable in discerning the pitch of a tone and its interval from another for the purpose of establishing harmony. When relating this same ideal of harmony to our fellow humans, it is obvious that the beauty of the personality shines out in such tendencies as a friendly attitude in word and action, spontaneity in the art of offering one's help without any expectations of return, and in the awakening of the true sense of justice. The art of personality is a precious secret in life – and in responsible leadership.

Examples of remarkable and responsible leadership include Nelson Mandela and Mahatma Ghandi, who as responsible leaders fulfilled their ideal of humane personality development and the cultivated compassion and love. Although we do not (and cannot) expect all business leaders to act like these great people, we think that such qualities are nevertheless crucial in business life before people can internalize the meaning of true responsibility. In the present corporate world, it is difficult to explore this inner aspect of responsible leadership and give space and attention to develop the heart quality and personality of leaders. The reason for this tendency has to do with the notion that leading and managing a business relies on logic, reason and analytical skills; heart quality is interpreted as too emotional, soft and not quantifiable, and therefore it should be eliminated from the managing of business. On the contrary, heart quality refers to a level of maturity that results from the reconciliation of reason and feeling, mind and heart, inner being and the outer self.

Many of the above arguments have been confirmed by various scientific disciplines. The cognitive scientist Francisco J. Varela in his study of consciousness investigated conscious experience at the personal level (see e.g. Varela and Shear 1999, Depraz *et al.* 2003). He advances such an investigation along several fronts of introspection, phenomenology and meditative psychology, and builds bridges to cognitive science, psychiatry and the scientific study of meditation techniques. He argues that the objective scientific paradigm is insufficient to serve the study of human consciousness and inner state; the methodology of first-person accounts is needed in studying and making sense of internal consciousness experiences. In order to make sense of the internal consciousness experiences, whether for cognitive science researchers or ordinary people who seek greater self-mastery, it requires the cultivation of a sustained discipline of observation and introspection.

In the field of psychology, drawing on brain and behavioural research, Daniel Goleman (1995) shows the factors at work when people of exceptionally high IQ flounder while those with normal intelligence do surprisingly well. He termed these factors *emotional intelligence*, which includes self-awareness, self-discipline and human empathy. These aspects of personality can be nurtured and strengthened throughout adulthood – with the immediate benefit to a person's inner peace, health, relationship with others and work performance. In the corporate world, IQ, which refers to cognitive intelligence, logical reasoning and mathematical skills, is traditionally over-valued and over-emphasized. Studies on emotional intelligence, referring to the healthy state of one's inner life and emotional maturity, give extra evidence to our argument on the responsible leader's tasks in addressing the challenges *within* himself and leading from the very core of himself before exercising the responsible leadership externally.

Maak and Pless (2006) propose that responsible leaders not only need emotional intelligence in order to interact successfully with a diversity of people, but *ethical intelligence*, which they understand as 'recognizing and reflecting on one's own and others' values, norms, interests, situations, behaviour etc. from an ethical point of view, distinguishing between right and wrong, being able to cope with *grey areas* and using this information to derive ethically appropriate behaviour'. According to them, a responsible leader uses both emotional and ethical abilities in his or her interaction with various stakeholders in and across different cultures to make decisions, to find solutions for conflicts of interest cope and reconcile dilemmas in the face of today's and tomorrow's leadership challenges. They call this approach *relational intelligence* (Pless and Maak 2005):

> Relational intelligence is the ability to relate to and interact with people based on a combination of emotional and ethical abilities that involves being aware of and understanding one's own and others' emotions, values, interests and demands, discriminating among them, critically reflecting on them, and using this information to guide one's actions and behaviour with respect to people.

We therefore believe that responsible leadership towards multiple stakeholders starts from the leader: leading from within based on regular introspection, leading one's own life consciously, truthfully as a result of cultivating one's heart and personality with self-discipline; walking the talk and embodying the truth responsibly in one's own life. This *inner expertise* (Varela, in Goleman 2003) of reconciliation needs to and can be nurtured and developed in leaders so that they may fulfil with compassion their responsibility to the external stakeholders and society at large.

Conclusion

Responsible leaders recognize, respect and reconcile the multiple demands, interests, needs and opposites stemming from their intrinsic responsibility towards employees, customers, suppliers, communities, shareholders, the society at large, NGOs and the environment. As we have demonstrated, the propensity to reconcile these dilemmas is the most discriminating competence that differentiates successful from less successful leaders today. Leaders, their organizations and the society at large improve and prosper not by choosing one end over the other, but by reconciling both ends. Dilemma reconciliation serves to connect the opposites into a virtuous circle where they sustain and enrich each other at a higher level.

Reconciling outer dilemmas starts with the inner world of leaders, embodying the true responsibility in one's own life before one is able to fulfil the responsibility with compassion towards the external stakeholders and the society at large. All the above requires self-understanding, self-discipline and self-mastery as well as emotional and ethical abilities that inform *relationally intelligent* behaviour displayed by leaders in interaction and their capacity to responsibly reconcile dilemmas (Pless and Maak 2005).

All in all, responsible leadership does not only have to restrict itself to corporate leaders, but it can be applied to every responsible human soul. Everybody can act as a responsible leader in his and her own way to bridge existing and new gaps, starting by leading from within based on regular introspection, leading one's life consciously, truthfully, as a result of cultivating one's heart and personality.

Questions

1   What are the main challenges and major dilemmas that leaders encounter in a global stakeholder society?
2   Which cross-cultural and/or moral dilemmas did you encounter in your own (professional) life? How did you solve them?
3   Pick a dilemma you experienced and follow the six-step procedure laid out in this chapter to reconcile it.
4   Think about other challenging dilemmas and try to reconcile them on a higher level.
5   In your view, how are the inner and outer path to responsible leadership connected?

Note

1   We would like to offer our words of thanks for the excellent contribution and support from Jo Spyckerelle and other colleagues at THT-consulting and in particular the great minds of Charles Hampden-Turner and Peter Woolliams to whom we owe so much.

Bibliography

Ciulla, J.B. (2006) 'Ethics: the heart of leadership', in T. Maak and N.M. Pless (eds) *Responsible Leadership*, London, New York: Routledge.
Depraz, N., Varela, F.J. and Vermersch, P. (eds) (2003) *On becoming Aware: a pragmatics of experiencing*, Amsterdam: John Benjamins.
Golcman, D. (1995) *Emotional Intelligence*, New York: Bantam.

Goleman, D. (2003) *Destructive Emotions: a scientific dialogue with the Dalai Lama*, New York: Bantam.

Greenleaf, R.K. (1977/2002) *Servant Leadership: a journey into the nature of legitimate power and greatness*, 25th anniversary edn, New York, Mahwah, NJ: Paulist Press.

Hampden-Turner, C. (1990) *Charting the Corporate Mind: from dilemma to strategy*, Oxford, Cambridge, MA: Blackwell.

Hampden-Turner, C. and Trompenaars, F. (2000) *Building Cross-Cultural Competence: how to create wealth from conflicting values*, New Haven, CT, London: Yale University Press.

Kets de Vries, M.F.R. (1989) *Prisoners of Leadership*, New York: Wiley.

Kets de Vries, M.F.R. (2001) *Struggling with the Demon: perspectives on individual and organizational irrationality*, Guilford, CT: International Universities Press.

Khan , H.I. (1993) *The Dance of the Soul*, Delhi: Motilal Banarsidass.

Kouzes, J.M. and Posner, B.Z. (2002) *The Leadership Challenge*, 2nd ed, San Francisco, CA: Jossey-Bass.

Maak, T. and Pless, N.M. (2006) 'Responsible leadership: a relational approach', in T. Maak and N.M. Pless (eds) *Responsible Leadership*, London, New York: Routledge.

Mannari, Hiroshi (1986) *The Japanese Business Leaders*, Tokyo: University of Tokyo Press.

Ockrent, C. and Séréni, J.P. (1998) *Les Grands Patrons. Comment ils voient notre Avenir*, Paris: Plon.

Pless, N.M. and Maak, T. (2004) 'Building an inclusive diversity culture: principles, processes and practice', *Journal of Business Ethics*, 54: 129–47.

Pless, N.M. and Maak, T. (2005) 'Relational intelligence for leading responsibly in a connected world', in K.M. Weaver (ed.) *Proceedings of the Sixty-fifth Annual Meeting of the Academy of Management*.

Pruzan, P. and Miller, W.C. (2006) 'Spirituality as the basis of responsible leaders and responsible companies', in T. Maak and N.M. Pless (eds) *Responsible Leadership*, London, New York: Routledge.

Rost, J.C. (1991) *Leadership for the 21st Century*,Westport, CT, London: Quorum.

Trompenaars, F. and Hampden-Turner, C. (2001) *21 Leaders for the 21st Century*, London: Capstone.

Trompenaars, F. and Woolliams, P. (2002) 'Just typical: avoiding stereotyping in personality testing', People Management, Chartered Institute of Personal Development, London, December: 2–15.

Varela, F.J. and Shear, J. (eds) (1999) *The View from Within: first-person approaches to the study of consciousness*, Thorverton: Imprint Academic.

10 Leading in a world of competing values: a strategic perspective on corporate social responsibility

Daniel Diermeier

Introduction

For over three decades the debate over the moral responsibility of firms has been dominated by Milton Friedman's (1970) article 'The social responsibility of business is to increase its profits'. Recent critiques of the Corporate Social Responsibility movement, for example in *The Economist* (Crook 2005), are not much else than a rehash of Friedman's main argument. Even scholars who vehemently disagree with Friedman still frame the debate in terms of what the role and responsibilities of the firm should be (see Margolis and Walsh 2003). The debate is essentially normative: it is about what firms ought to do.

Recently, we have witnessed the emergence of a separate line of research, the *doing well by doing good* literature (such as Porter and van der Linde 1995). This literature is empirically motivated. It tries to establish whether it pays to adopt socially responsible business practices, e.g. those that are environmentally sustainable. According to this approach, responsible business practices are simply a form of sound management, especially in the long-run and especially for large corporations. The evidence for the latter claim is mildly positive (see e.g. Dowell *et al.* 2000). However, there are both conceptual and methodological problems with this approach, which I will address below. At least this line of research has started to focus the debate on the managerial problems of corporate social responsibility.

In this essay I will argue for a different perspective that focuses on the leadership problem of what to do in an environment where companies are increasingly held accountable to standards other than shareholder value maximization. The underlying premise is that the latter claim is indeed a fact. Whether managers like it or not, and whether such demands are beneficial for society or not, is largely besides the point. Firms and industry need to learn how to compete in an environment of moral values. Yet, existing scholarship has little to offer in this regard. I also will argue that both existing approaches – the normative and the empirical – are missing in the key problems that need to be addressed. That does not mean that the approaches are not important in their own right, but in terms of their relevance for providing guidance to management they are limited.

Values everywhere

My first task is to demonstrate the reality of a value-based environment. First, there has been an explosive increase in CSR activities. From survey response, to the money invested in socially responsible investment funds, to the growth in shareholder resolutions that focus on social and environmental issues, CSR is gaining in popularity. Even Walmart has recently started to be concerned about its reputation as a corporate citizen. The following figure provides one such measure: the publication of corporate social responsibility reports (see Figure 10.1). Of course, these activities may be just another fad, or, as many NGOs would argue, a corporate *fig leaf* that is nothing more than an exercise in public relations. Yet, these criticisms beg the question why we see this trend now and why firms feel the urgent need to at least appear socially responsible.

My claim is that there is something deeper at play. And its evidence comes from an area of research largely ignored by both researchers and practitioners of CSR: the empirical literature on value change. Since the 1970s a group of researchers, largely political scientists and sociologists has used large cross-national surveys such as the World Value Surveys to

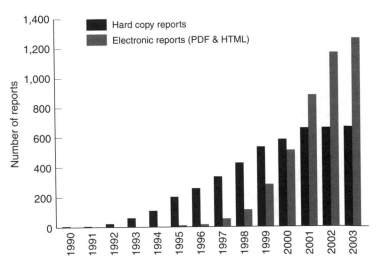

Number of hard copy and electronic reports produced 1990–2003

Source: CorporateRegister.com June 2004 (based on a sample of 4,528 hard copy and 4,295 PDF reports)

Figure 10.1 Growth of corporate citizenship reports

demonstrate a significant, broad-based value shift in advanced industrial societies. These researchers have found younger respondents are more likely to report an emphasis on *post-materialist values* (Inglehart 1990) or *emancipative values* (Inglehart 1997, Welzel *et al.* 2003) such as self-expression, concern for the environment, tolerance and so on, while their parents care more about *materialist* and *conformative* values, such as material success, security, individual accomplishments. Moreover, these value orientations stay constant over a life-span for a given cohort; they are not merely an expression of youthful idealism that fades over time. The findings suggest that such value orientations are formed early in life and then do not change much. Inglehart and others suggest that this phenomenon can be explained by reference to theories of human development such as Maslow's hierarchy of needs (Maslow 1943). The argument is that people aspire to satisfy the most pressing needs first. Therefore, children growing up in more resource constrained environments will have a more *materialist* value orientation, while those growing up in more affluent environments will tend to put a stronger emphasis on *post-materialist* values. This would explain the value shift in Europe where a generation that, shaped by the Second World War years and post-war reconstruction, exhibited a materialist orientation has been followed by a generation driven by post-materialist and emancipative values. Recent cross-national research has confirmed this thesis by showing that countries where people in their childhood suffered from severely constrained resources tend to be dominated by values that emphasize material well-being, security and conformity, but these countries slowly change in their value orientation as resource scarcity is alleviated (Inglehart 1997).

This has three important consequences for our understanding of CSR. First, the CSR movement is for real. In fact, it is an epi-phenomenon of more fundamental value shifts that have expressed themselves in various forms such as social movements (women's, civil rights, environmental, etc.), the growth of NGOs and social activists and so forth. Just as other institutions such as party systems, legal rules and regulations, even political constitutions have adapted to those changes, so will firms.

Second, companies will have to respond to an environment of contested values. One of the implications of the value shift hypothesis is that we should expect value conflict between an older segment of the populations that values goals such as economic growth, stability, efficiency and conformity, and a younger generation with a more post-materialistic orientation that values social justice, tolerance and concern for the environment. Companies will have to learn how to manoeuvre in this space of contested values. It will create new challenges and new opportunities.

Third, there will be cross-national variation in the importance of CSR. The value shift research suggests that while environmental issues will be of importance to the populace in Europe, they will be of much less importance in emerging economies such as Eastern Europe, India and China. It also implies that, assuming sustained economic growth, environmental issues will be important to the next generation of Eastern Europeans, Indians and Chinese who would have been born in an era of rapid economic progress. This pattern has been documented, for example in Japan (Inglehart 1997).

For companies operating in a global environment, this presents serious challenges. For example, the pressure to seek low-cost suppliers or to outsource various business functions is leading to a whole range of concerns in OECD countries ranging from social justice to global workers' rights and environmental concerns. Some of these challenges are already apparent in the debates over child and slave labour as well as in the anti-globalization movement.

Taking values seriously

Competitive positioning

If values matter, corporate leadership needs to take them into account. Specifically, this means that firms need to adopt appropriate strategies in all markets where they compete, whether over customers, capital or talent.

Consider first the competition over consumers. This case is often considered in the context of *socially responsible brands*. Examples include The Body Shop, Patagonia, Ben & Jerry's, etc. Let us assume for a moment that the owners/shareholders of the business unit in question are only interested in maximizing long-term profits. (We will consider the case of ethically motivated owners and managers below.) From a strategic management perspective these are examples of product differentiation on non-price attributes. Similar to differentiation on quality or location, the business unit tries to attain a competitive advantage over other firms in the industry that cannot be easily imitated.

A business unit has a competitive advantage in a market when it has a higher rate of profitability than the *typical* business unit in that market. This can be achieved through a *benefit position*, i.e. creating higher value for customers, or through a *cost position*, i.e. producing at lower cost than competitors (Porter 1985). Socially responsible brands thus fall in the benefit position category. They are intended to create and capture value of customers concerned about the social and environmental aspects of producing, marketing and consuming goods and services.

To attain a competitive advantage through a product differentiation strategy, at least three conditions need to hold. First, there must be a segment of customers willing to sufficiently pay more for the socially responsible product to cover the additional costs of providing it. The following figure illustrates this point. If the variable cost of providing a socially responsible brand is higher than for a customary brand, the additional willingness of consumers must be sufficiently high and the segment must be sufficiently large to cover the fixed costs (see Figure 10.2).

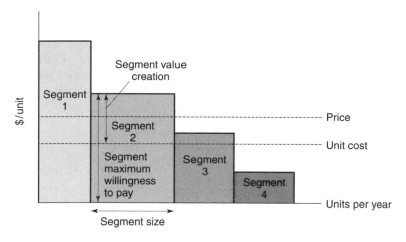

Figure 10.2 Market segmentation and competitive advantage

Second, to qualify as a competitive advantage, socially responsible brands cannot be easily imitated. This suggests that in markets where there is room for socially responsible brands we will find product differentiation. This is indeed the case in all the examples listed above. For example, US ice-cream brand Ben & Jerry's is differentiated from Haagen-Daaz on the socially responsibility dimension, while both are differentiated from e.g. Dreyer's on the quality dimension. Modern competitive strategy (e.g. Tirole 2002) suggests that such differentiated outcomes may constitute equilibria in markets with various customer segments.[1] That is, no competitor has an incentive to imitate the other and both can be profitable.

Note that this last insight points out the methodological flaws in the *doing well by doing good* literature, i.e. the line of empirical research that tries to demonstrate that in the long run socially responsible businesses out-perform their competitors. Recall that this literature tries to show that *on average*, socially responsible brands do better. But in a differentiated market both the socially responsible *and regular* firms can be profitable, just as both Tiffany and Walmart may be highly profitable in retailing, one adopting a high-quality/high-cost strategy, the other a low-quality/low-cost strategy. If empirical studies in the *doing well by doing good* literature have not managed to prove their hypothesis, this may be because they fail to take into account the existence of differentiated markets. By pooling all firms in an industry together, the measured marginal effect of socially responsible brands will be close to zero, giving the misleading answer that adopting a strategy based on socially responsible brands does not pay.[2]

In contrast to other non-price attributes such as quality, convenience or location, consumers cannot directly verify whether a company or product makes good on its promise of social responsibility. In the language of strategic management, they constitute *credence goods* – they possess consumer relevant attributes that cannot directly be experienced in the act of consumption (Feddersen and Gilligan 2001).[3] Rather, the credence good quality must be *believed*. This suggests that companies that try to differentiate themselves along a social responsibility dimension need to invest in building a reputation. This in turn makes it difficult for other firms to quickly imitate such a positioning strategy.

Reputation management

An important shortcoming of the current debate on social responsibility and competitive advantage is that it focuses exclusively on benefit-driven strategies. The discussion is centred on the ways in which socially responsible brands offer socially conscious customers a higher *consumption value* because they are better aligned with their ethical principles. However, this leaves out the other dimension on which companies compete: cost. This issue has received some attention in the context of environmentally sustainable business practices (e.g. Porter and van der Linde 1995). The basic idea is that a judicious use of natural resources not only is good for the environment, but also saves costs. This argument is completely independent of any value-orientation (by customers or others); it is simply an application of cost-efficient production techniques.

But consider another example: BP. Since 1997, BP, under the leadership of Lord Brown, has engaged in an aggressive repositioning strategy that combined advertising with an emphasis on sustainability, policy decisions (e.g. the withdrawal from the oil industry's anti-Kyoto coalition), changes in business practices (e.g. committing to unilateral cuts in emissions) to portfolio choices (e.g. the investment in solar technology). But BP is not a *boutique business* trying to identify a specific consumer segment with strong environmental values; it is one of the world's largest corporations. So, what is driving its strategy?

The answer is reputation. Companies such as BP believe that CSR can be an important means to manage reputational risks. For example, while the segment of the population that is willing to pay more for gasoline because of a company's reputation for environmentally friendly business practices may be quite small, a much larger segment will be willing to stop purchasing from an oil company that has a tainted reputation.[4] One of the most famous cases is the confrontation between Royal Dutch Shell and the environmental activist group Greenpeace over the issue of deep-water disposal of the Brent Spar oil platform. After an acrimonious battle between activists and the company, where sales in Germany and other European countries dropped by as much as 50 per cent, Shell UK who had operating responsibility for the Brent Spar decided to abandon the deep-water disposal plan and seek a license for on-shore disposal (see Diermeier 1996 for more details).

Only one year later Royal Dutch Shell was targeted again, this time over human rights issues related to Shell Nigeria. Royal Dutch Shell subsequently engaged in an extensive reorganization and value-based change process to avoid similar issues in the future. This is in effect a cost-based strategy. To lower the long-term expected costs from reputational damage, the company *invests* in socially responsible business practices. This will improve its competitive position if the costs of complying with such practices are on expectation smaller than the expected savings from the avoidance of reputational damage.[5] Moreover, since reputations cannot be built over night, the ability to imitate such a strategy in the short-term is rather limited.

While clearly an important driver of managerial decision making, our understanding of how to effectively manage reputational risk is still quite limited, even if we focus just on consumers. (We will discuss industry and non-market issues below.) One problem is that a company's reputation on social issues is to a large extent mediated by third-party actors such as the media, activists and public institutions. In contrast to other kinds on corporate communications (such as many forms product advertising), companies have much less control over the messages that their current and potential customers will receive.

Using Baron's theory of the media (Baron 2006), we can identify some of these difficulties. News coverage is largely driven by two forces: audience interest and societal significance. Audience interest drives the amount and likelihood of coverage, while the societal significance dimension determines how an issue is covered, e.g. whether an issue is merely reported or whether its wider significance is explored (see Figure 10.3).

In Figure 10.4 we combine these two dimensions into a rough typology of media coverage. Depending on an issue's location in the interest-significance space, news coverage will change significantly. The most dangerous location for management is the high-audience-demand/high-societal-significance quadrant (*north-east*). This is the area where in the United States, *60 Minutes* or *48 Hours* are located – hard-hitting television news

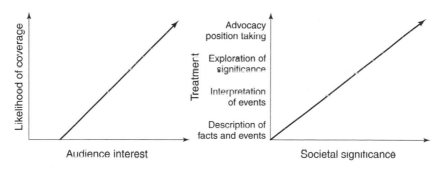

Figure 10.3 Perception drivers

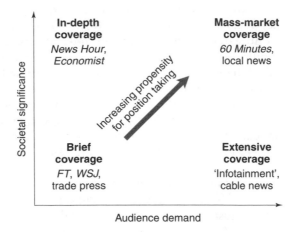

Figure 10.4 Reputation and the media

programmes that address controversial social issues but need to present them in a format that is attractive to a mass audience. This format focuses on drama, individual cases (*victims*), easy to understand moral conflicts (*good* versus *evil*) and testimony instead of data. In this media environment complicated arguments (e.g. the scientific rationales for choosing deep-sea dumping over on-shore disposal) are very difficult if not impossible to communicate. An approach that focuses solely on technical or legal aspects will almost always fail. Rather, the company must tell a compelling, credible story that can stand up to images with direct emotional impact.

These tactical considerations have important strategic consequences. Consider the Brent Spar controversy as an example. To generate sufficient attention to their issue, activists need to obtain media coverage in the north-eastern corner. This is difficult. Competition for air and print space is fierce and many environmental issues, such as the Brent Spar disposal, involve complicated, technical issues. *Before* Greenpeace took action, the Brent Spar issue was located in the south-western corner with little to no coverage in the media. Thus Greenpeace needed to stage its protests in a way that increased *both* audience interest and social significance. The Brent Spar occupation was an ideal means to increase audience interest. It provided drama, high stakes and great visuals. Moreover, by taking a confrontational approach, e.g. turning on the water canons, Shell directly played into the hands of the activists by providing dramatic images of a high-stakes confrontation.

But increasing audience interest was not enough for Greenpeace. The activists also needed to provide the German public with a simple, straightforward reason to act. Ingeniously, Greenpeace framed the whole issue as a recycling issue, something German citizens care passionately about. The activists' message, 'Here I am dutifully recycling my garbage, and there comes big business and simply dumps its trash in the ocean', made the choice for German citizens an easy one. Since every upstanding German citizen recycles, Shell, by dumping the Brent Spar into the deep ocean, cannot be a good *corporate* citizen. It is important to recognize that by framing the issue as one concerning the moral duties of corporate citizens, the scientific and technical arguments that Shell brought to the discussion were made powerless. They looked like feeble attempts by the company to avoid its onerous duty as a good corporate citizen.

This example illustrates some of the strategic role of corporate social responsibility in managing reputational risks. First, we need to distinguish between industries where the product itself is highly controversial (e.g. tobacco, weapons) from industries where the product is not controversial, but the way it is produced or marketed may give rise to concerns. Examples are labour practices in the apparel industry, such as the Nike boycott, or the issue of dolphin-safe tuna. It follows that, for example, tobacco companies have less incentive to adopt responsible business practices to protect their reputation than, for example, Nike.[6]

Second, industries where consumers are more likely to switch products (e.g. gasoline) are more at risk than industries with high switching costs (e.g. entertainment industry). Activists have a notoriously difficult time in targeting firms in the entertainment industry, for instance. An example is the attempt by the conservative Christian group, the Southern Baptist Convention, to target Disney over the violent films distributed through Miramax.[7] Third, companies need to assess whether investing in socially responsible business practices is intended to reduce the likelihood of being targeted by an activist group or whether it is intended to limit the damage in case of a controversy. Very well-known brands (such as McDonald's or Coca Cola) are likely to be targeted no matter how much they invest in socially responsible business practices, because targeting a well-known brand increases audience interest and thus improves the media environment for activists (see Figure 10.4 above).

An industry perspective

Up to this point, the strategic focus has been on individual firms and their competitive position, but corporate social responsibility can also play an important role in industry-wide strategies. This is illustrated in Figure 10.5.

So far we have focused on business unit strategies. As discussed in the previous section, CSR can play an important role both for benefit- and cost-driven value-creation propositions. To understand the importance for industry analysis it is again useful to rely on an established framework such as Porter's *Five Forces* (Porter 1985). Here, social concerns about a product can have both a direct effect and an indirect effect. An example of a direct effect is the environmental concern of some consumers over pollu-

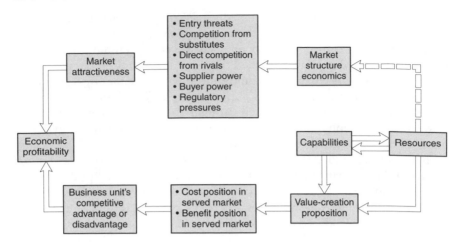

Figure 10.5 Strategy analysis framework

tion, which makes virgin materials overall less attractive than recycled or recyclable products. In such cases industry-wide strategies usually take the form of *image campaigns*. One such example is the campaign of the plastics industry that succeeded in changing the US public's perception of plastic as a landfill problem to plastic as an irreplaceable and useful material. By focusing on safety and health-care applications, the industry was able to shift the typical association of plastic with an empty water bottle to one where consumers associated plastic with a child's bicycle helmet. To be credible, such image campaigns need to be accompanied by industry-wide self-regulation, for example, with respect to environmental standards. Furthermore, such standards need to be self-enforcing.

The far more important effect of corporate social responsibility is indirect, through the political and regulatory environment. Industry characteristics, whether summarized by the *Five Forces* or any other theory, are not constant but shaped by the political, legal and regulatory environment. These *rules of the game* are themselves not fixed. Socially responsible strategies can play a critical role in this context as they may improve an industry's overall reputation in the eyes of the public, which then makes regulation less likely. Conversely, damage to an industry's reputation may make political and regulatory change more likely.[8]

One such example is the concept of self-regulation in the *shadow of public regulation*. The idea is that the adoption of industry-wide standards of socially responsible behaviour may help an industry prevent or at least delay public regulation. Good examples are the MPAA rating systems for violence and sexual content in movies or voluntary TV advertising restrictions by the spirits industry. Self-regulation has the advantage that the industry has complete control over the design and execution of the regulatory framework. The disadvantage is that effective self-regulation relies on the compliance of its members. Since courts or regulators usually cannot effectively enforce compliance, self-regulation must be self-enforcing to be effective. Whether industries will be able to overcome the associated collective action problems will depend, among other things, on the size of the industry, the magnitude of the political threat and so on.

These problems may in some cases make public regulation preferable, either to forestall more far-reaching regulation or to improve the market conditions of an industry. A good example of the first case is the support from the US tobacco industry for the 1965 Federal Cigarette Labelling and Advertising Act that mandated warning labels such as *Caution: Cigarette Smoking May Be Hazardous to Your Health*. The legislation was supported by the tobacco industry because it prevented both the states and the Federal Trade Commission from putting more restrictive labelling policies in place, a very real concern for the industry after the publication of the US Surgeon General's 1964 report on the dangers of smoking (Derthick 2002).

A good example of the second motivation is the support by domestic industries for import restrictions because of environmental or other social concerns. In these cases, activists groups and domestic producers may share the same goal, i.e. to limit imports that do not satisfy social or environmental standards, even though their motivations are different. Again the reasons for companies to support such standards are heavily dependent on the specifics of competition in the industry such as the degree of the competitive threat by a foreign supplier, constituency concerns for the social issue in question, and the ability to frame an issue to generate favourable media coverage.

Afterthought – shareholder values

So far, I have followed the convenient assumption of shareholder value maximization as the motivation for firms. This has had two advantages. First, it has allowed me to discuss corporate social responsibility as a *strategy*, i.e. as a plan of action to achieve a given goal. Second, it has allowed me to rely on some standard concepts from strategic management to illustrate some the challenges of pursuing socially responsible practices.

However, once we consider competition for capital and talent, this assumption becomes highly questionable. Consider first the competition over capital. Both the growth in social responsible investment funds and the social and political activism of some institutional investors ranging from TIAA-CREF to various pension funds suggest that companies competing for capital increasingly will need to pay more attention in the future to issues of social responsibility.

Indeed, the decision by socially responsible investors whether to purchase stock in a given company parallels the decision by consumers discussed above. It is also driven by concerns other than pure profit maximization. In some cases such concerns are formulated as *screens*. That is, a fund will not invest if the company has a presence in a certain industry (e.g. tobacco). All else equal, this will raise the cost of capital for the targeted industry. In other cases, socially responsible investors will try to use the investment decision to have influence over the business practices of the firm's management. For example, at a recent shareholder meeting of Caterpillar, various activists and socially responsible investors voiced concerns over Caterpillar's policy of supplying the Israeli military with bulldozers to destroy homes in the Occupied Territories. In this case, the investor relationship was used as a tool of social activism.

So if the owners of a company care about values other than long-term profit maximization, managers need to respond to these demands just as they respond to consumer preferences. Note also that we now have a value conflict between different groups of shareholders. Consider again the case of Caterpillar. As one would expect in such a controversial context, US based supporters of the Israeli government are now trying to use the very same process (i.e. shareholder resolutions) to put pressure on management to continue selling to the Israeli military. In sum, just as in the case of competition of customers, companies increasingly need to navigate environments of conflicting values as they compete for capital. This suggests the need to integrate issues of social responsibility into a theory of capital markets, a topic that goes beyond the scope of this essay.

The same argument applies to issues of human resource management, e.g. how to design compensation schemes where employees not only care about their remuneration, but also have fairness concerns. Recent research by the experimental economist Ernst Fehr and collaborators (e.g. Fehr and Schmidt 2002) has highlighted the importance of these issues. In various public goods and trust experiments they showed not only that groups of anonymous subjects tended to collaborate even if the monetary incentives suggested *selfish* behaviour, but that such collaborative behaviour tended to disappear as the experimenters introduced individualistic rewards, as suggested by any economic textbook. These and other experiments provide solid empirical foundations not only for the widely shared intuition among executives that a value-based culture helps improve overall performance, but also that a switch to incentive-based approaches may destroy such a culture, leading to a significant performance decline in the organization.

Conclusion: from ethics to strategy

After discussing corporate social responsibility from a strategic management perspective it may be worth revisiting the two alternative positions introduced above: the literature linked to Friedman's (1970) *the social responsibility of business is to increase its profit*s thesis and the *doing well by doing good* literature. As the essay has argued, both are misoriented and such misorientation inhibits the development of conceptual frameworks for leading in a environment characterized by competing value orientations.

The problem with Friedman's assertion is empirical. What does it mean that firms ought to maximize profits in all circumstances if both owners/shareholders and relevant customer segments are motivated by values other than profit maximization? If corporate leadership ignores such orientation, they are either not maximizing profits or not acting in the interests of shareholders. To be consistent, Friedman's argument needs to rely on an empirical premise: that all economic agents primarily care about material gains. But this hypothesis is not supported by empirical data.

Let's consider the *doing well by doing good* hypothesis. From a strategic management perspective, this is an odd research programme. As discussed above, whether socially responsible strategies are advisable or not depends on the behaviour of other firms, on consumer preferences, industry factors and so forth. Asking whether *being responsible* pays is a little like whether television advertising pays or whether cost-position strategies are better than benefit positioning strategies. In all cases, we need to analyze the strategic situation in more detail. Only then can we provide meaningful advice to leaders on how to manage in an environment of competing values.

Both Friedman's approach and the *doing well by doing good* approach tried to dispense with the challenges of value-oriented management. But Friedman's argument is based on a false empirical premise, while the *doing well by doing good* hypothesis is methodologically flawed. Without easy answers at their disposal, leaders will need to tackle such value conflicts directly. The solutions will be company- and industry-specific, and they will vary depending on the issue at hand. In such complicated decision contexts a strategic orientation is particularly useful. It helps to evaluate a given situation not just from one's own context, but from the context of other stakeholders. Understanding and anticipating such competing value-orientation is an essential step to responsible leadership.

Questions

1 Is the pursuit of socially responsible business practices always consistent with ethical principles? What should managers do when they encounter such conflict?
2 In the essay we discussed the significance of moral values in the competition over customers, capital and talent. For what other forms of competition could a strategic CSR perspective be relevant?
3 What are the consequences of ethically motivated shareholders for our understanding of competition for capital?
4 What are the methodological problems with an empirical analysis that tries to assess whether adopting sustainable business practices have positive or negative effects on a company's stock price?

5   What are the consequences for designing compensation plans if employees are also motivated by fairness concerns?

Notes

1   This type of competition can be modeled as a non-cooperative game with stable outcomes corresponding to Nash equilibria. See e.g. Tirole (2002) for details.
2   Fixing this methodological problem in empirical studies requires more advanced statistical techniques, such as structural estimation based on an underlying game-theoretic model of non-price competition.
3   For discussion of whether the use of socially responsible brands for competitive positioning improves social welfare, see e.g. Feddersen and Gilligan (2001) and Bagnoli and Watts (2003).
4   As far as I know, there is no exact data on the relative size of these customer segments.
5   I am not aware of a quantitative study that has tried to measure the financial impact on reputational damage, though both companies and activists clearly believe that such a linkage exists. The Rainforest Action Network (RAN), for example, typically targets a company's reputation rather than its sales directly (e.g. Baron 2006).
6   Note that there may be other reasons to adopt socially responsible practices, e.g. to improve a company's changes to win lawsuits or to have more influence in the regulatory and political environment. This appears to be the main reason for Philip Morris' recent attempt to position itself as the socially responsible tobacco company. In a rare coalition with anti-smoking advocates, Philip Morris tried to lobby for legislation in the US Congress that would give the Food and Drug Administration jurisdiction to regulate tobacco products. The strategy failed in the autumn of 2004 when the proposed amendment was not adopted by the US Congress.
7   Disney has since severed its ties with Miramax.
8   The focus in this section is on industry-wide strategies, but public regulation can also improve the competitive position of a specific company. This was the case in Philip Morris' support of FDA oversight on tobacco products, since passing such regulation would have made it easier for Philip Morris to effectively 'lock in' its dominant market position.

Bibliography

Bagnoli, M. and Watts, S.G. (2003) 'Selling to socially responsible consumers: competition and the private provision of public goods', *Journal of Economics and Management Strategy*, 12(3): 419–445.

Baron, D.P. (2001) 'Private politics, corporate social responsibility, and integrated strategy', *Journal of Economics and Management Strategy*, 10(1): 7–45.

Baron, D.P. (2006) *Business and its Environment*, 5th edn, New York: Prentice-Hall.

Crook, C. (2005) 'The good company', *The Economist*, 22–28 January.

Derthick, M. (2002) *Up in Smoke – From Legislation to Litigation in Tobacco Politics*, Washington, DC: CQ Press.

Diermeier, D. (1996) 'Shell and Greenpeace', Harvard Business School Case P19, 1 September 1996. Reprinted in D.P. Baron (2006) *Business and its Environment*, 5th edn, New York: Prentice-Hall.

Dowell, G., Hart, S. and Yeung, B. (2000) 'Do corporate global environmental standards create or destroy market value?', *Management Science*, 46: 1059–74.

Feddersen, T.J. and Gilligan, T.W. (2001) 'Saints and markets: activists and the supply of credence goods', *Journal of Economics and Management Strategy*, 10(1): 149–71.

Fehr, E. and Schmidt, K. (2002) 'Theories of fairness and reciprocity – evidence and economic applications', in M. Dewatripont, L. Hansen and St. Turnovsky (eds) *Advances in Economics and Econometrics – 8th World Congress, Econometric Society Monographs*, Cambridge: Cambridge University Press.

Friedman, M. (1970) 'The social responsibility of business is to increase its profits', *The New York Times Magazine*, 13 September, 32–3, 122–6.

Inglehart, R. (1990) *Culture Shift in Advanced Industrial Society*, Princeton, NJ: Princeton University Press.

Inglehart, R. (1997) *Modernization and Postmodernization: cultural, economic, and political change in 43 societies*, Princeton, NJ: Princeton University Press.

Margolis, J.D. and Walsh, J.P. (2003) 'Misery loves companies: rethinking social initiatives by business', *Administrative Science Quarterly*, 48 (June): 268–305.

Maslow, A.H. (1943) 'A theory of human motivation', *Psychological Review*, 50: 370–96.

Porter, M.E. (1985) *Competitive Advantage*, New York: Free Press.

Porter, M.E. and van der Linde, C. (1995) 'Green and competitive', *Harvard Business Review*, September–October: 120–34, 196.

Tirole, J. (2002) *The Theory of Industrial Organization*, Cambridge, MA: MIT Press.

Welzel, C., Inglehart, R. and Klingemann, H.-D. (2003) 'The theory of human development: a cross-cultural analysis', *European Journal of Political Research*, 42(2): 341–80.

11 Responsible leadership at ABN AMRO Real

The case of Fabio Barbosa

Erik van de Loo

Introduction

This chapter explores responsible leadership from the angle of an individual leader who managed to mobilize people and organizations along the path of corporate social responsibility. The leader is *Fabio Barbosa*, CEO of the Brazilian subsidiary of ABN AMRO Bank. After a short description of the organizational context, I will attempt to interpret the meaning of responsible leadership at ABN AMRO Real in Brazil. I use a psychological approach to leadership (Van de Loo 2000, Kets de Vries 2004), analyzing the dynamic interplay between rational and non-rational, visible and non-visible, business and personal factors over the life of Fabio Barbosa in the context of both his family- and career-history. In line with this so-called clinical approach to leadership, observations and in-depth interviews form the major source of data. The findings will be presented by answering the following questions: What is Fabio Barbosa's vision on banking and responsible leadership? How did he translate his vision into leadership strategies and behaviour in order to mobilize people and the ABN AMRO Real organization in Brazil for corporate social responsibility? What are the origins of his vision and how has he developed himself as a leader? Finally, what are the lessons learned for developing responsible leadership in business?

The research base for this case study consists of interviews, observations and published material (ABN AMRO REAL 2003a, Britto and Wever 2002, *Carta Capital* 2003 and 2004, Motta 2003, Dinheiro 2004, Mano 2004). I had the opportunity to observe Fabio Barbosa as a leader in action when he shared his vision on sustainability and responsible leadership with a group of young leaders in a global leadership development programme, which took place in Brazil in 2004. Over the last six years, I have spoken in depth with about thirty people about their observations and experiences of Fabio Barbosa's leadership – including Brazilians as well as non-Brazilians, and people from various levels, roles and positions within ABN AMRO Real. Finally, in February 2005, I interviewed Fabio Barbosa by phone about the origins and essence of his leadership.

ABN AMRO Real and corporate social responsibility

ABN AMRO is a large international bank with over 3,000 branches operating in almost 60 countries across the globe, employing about 100,000 people (ABN AMRO 2004). It was created in 1991 in the Netherlands when ABN Bank and Amro Bank merged. ABN AMRO serves clients in three distinct segments, which represent its Strategic Business Units (SBU): Consumer and Commercial Clients, Wholesale Clients and Private Clients. One of the countries where ABN AMRO is very active and has a significant presence is Brazil. In fact, aside from the Netherlands and the Midwest in the United States, Brazil is one of only three domestic markets where ABN AMRO operates a significant retail banking business serving consumer and commercial clients. The breakthrough came in 1998 when ABN AMRO bought Banco Real, one of the largest privately owned banks in the country. With the acquisition of Banco Sudameris in 2003 ABN AMRO reinforced its position significantly becoming 'the fourth largest privately-owned Brazilian bank by deposits and loans, and the fifth largest by assets' (ABN AMRO 2004: 39). By the end of 2004 its distribution network in Brazil consisted of 1,890 branches and mini-branches. During this phase ABN AMRO Real has managed to combine growth with becoming one of the most admired companies in Brazil. It moved in the overall rankings of most admired companies from 153rd place in 2003, to 15th place in 2004. In the retail bank segment ABN AMRO Real moved to second place (*Carta Capital* 2004). Organizational climate surveys indicate that 93 per cent of its 23,000 employees are proud to work for this bank and that 88 per cent identify with the values it promotes and acts upon (ABN AMRO Real 2003b).

The ABN AMRO Group has adopted four global corporate values: *integrity, teamwork, respect* and *professionalism*. Linked to these values the Group has formulated a series of business principles. They encompass among others a focus on creating long-term value for stakeholders, respecting human rights and the interests of the environment and to behave as a good corporate citizen. It is widely acknowledged by people from both inside and outside the bank that the social responsible approach of ABN AMRO Real in Brazil is strongly related to the role of the leader at ABN AMRO Real, Fabio Barbosa. In what follows, I will focus on how an individual leader like Fabio Barbosa can make a difference in helping an organization like ABN AMRO Real choose the path of corporate social responsibility. Although this chapter limits itself to describing Fabio Barbosa's achievements within ABN AMRO Real in Brazil, Fabio Barbosa is also well-known as a thought leader and role model in the area of corporate social responsibility within the worldwide ABN AMRO Group. He does not claim that this work is completed. It is work in progress, although much has already been achieved and initiated. To mention a few examples: an ethical fund called ABN AMRO Ethical FIA was created, which is in fact Brazil's first fund, which invests only in stocks from companies recognized for good practices in social, environmental and corporate governance actions (ABN AMRO 2005); special credit-lines were developed to finance socio-environmental projects such as forestry, basic sanitation and education; and in July 2002 Real Microcrédito was set up by ABN AMRO Real and ACCION as a for-profit microlending subsidiary in Brazil, specifically helping micro-entrepeneurs who otherwise encounter difficulties getting credit through the traditional financial system (ABN AMRO Real 2003a, ACCION International 2005). All these activities were already initiated when the *Equator Principles*[1] were voluntarily adopted by the worldwide ABN AMRO Group in June 2003.

Fabio Barbosa on banking and responsible leadership

Fabio Barbosa seems to be driven by a series of values and strong beliefs about what the role of a bank in society is and what it should be. Key words he often uses are: sustainability, client focus and corporate social and environmental responsibility. He frequently uses statements like: 'being successful is doing the right things right' and when he concludes a speech: 'we are at the site of our dreams, so dream big'. As a responsible leader he is not interested in just creating short-term financial success. As stated above, this approach is perfectly in line with the global corporate values and business principles of the ABN AMRO Group. Within the Group Fabio Barbosa seems to be the first senior executive with such an articulated and consistent view. In that sense he represents a strong source of inspiration for the rest of the Group with his *work in progress* at ABN AMRO Real. Sustainable success for a bank requires in his perception a relentless focus on clients. What are the clients' needs, values, concerns, ambitions and dreams? What is their position and role in society? And how are these related to financial needs and services? If a company misses out on these aspects it potentially alienates itself from the client-base and ultimately society at large. This would go against the ambition to create a sustainable successful financial institution.

For example, consumer awareness studies by the Ethos Institute (ABN AMRO Real 2003a) indicate that 70 per cent of Brazilians want companies to work towards the development of society. They reject issues like forced labour, racism, hazardous working conditions and give priority to environmental protection. An organization has to take these aspects into account in order to behave in a socially responsible way. It is about developing long-term relationships with clients and society. In doing so an organization is capable of adding value to both clients and society in a variety of ways. First, this added value may be related to specific financial services like micro-credit and providing loans which promote sustainability. These financial products and services are no charity. In order to be sustainable they have to be profitable. Second, however, on top of the bank's business products there are various forms of civic engagement which create value added, such as *The Escola Brasil* Institute. This institute is a non-profit organization initiated by volunteers from ABN AMRO Real with the mission to improve the school system in Brazil. The National Institute for Educational Study and Research reports that the government has increased the availability of public schools, but it is said that about four out of ten students will drop out before finishing high school (ABN AMRO Real 2003a). The Escola Brasil attempts to improve this situation. Since the launch of this initiative, more than a hundred public schools throughout Brazil have been adopted by 3,500 ABN AMRO Real volunteers. The volunteers help to improve the school infrastructure and encourage the introduction of various sports and cultural activities. These initiatives reinforce active social citizenship of employees.

Another sign of developing corporate social responsibility is the bank's diversity programme. The ambition here is to create employment opportunities for all kind of minority groups usually discriminated against on the job market. The bank openly and honestly states that on many diversity dimensions there still exists a situation of imbalance, for example, regarding the under-representation of women and Afro-descendants in the Brazilian workforce. This also underlines the significance of one of the questions frequently raised by Fabio Barbosa: 'How to be a successful bank in a non-successful society?'

For Fabio Barbosa, social responsibility is a stance that is part of everything you do. It impacts the relationships with all stakeholders involved, such as shareholders, clients, employees, suppliers as well as society at large. Suppliers and corporate clients are expected to adhere to environmental and labour standards too. If the bank identifies an issue in this context, it will apply an inclusive approach. The bank will try to help the supplier or client to develop their own way of operating up to required standards instead of rejecting or ending the working relationship.

Responsible leadership is based on key values like integrity and respect. Fabio Barbosa highlights the importance of 'doing the right things the right way'. Doing business is about achieving high standards of working, hard work and competition. It may be a *tough game*, but it should always be fair play: 'play always the ball, never the legs of your opponent'. No dirty tricks are allowed. Respect is required and expected. In business practice this implies accountability and reliability, for example, taking care always to be on time when you have appointments with colleagues, employees, clients and other stakeholders.

This view of responsible leadership has led Fabio Barbosa to conclude that social responsibility and making money are perfectly compatible. Corporate success and social responsibility are linked and leverage one another. His vision on banking and corporate social responsibility is well summarized in the mission statement adopted by ABN AMRO Real and displayed at all their facilities throughout Brazil:

> Our Mission: To satisfy the client, to create value for shareholders, employees and the community, to maintain the highest standards of ethics and to differentiate ourselves by the quality of our products and services and, most importantly, through our exemplary client service.

The mission reflects principles and attitudes which cannot be delegated to a department: it will only work if all employees share this attitude and make it the starting point of their actions. This is why ABN AMRO Real 'wishes to attract those who share our values, for only skilled, committed people can contribute to the organization and to society' (ABN AMRO Real 2003a). As a result, the majority of its employees identify with the vision of a bank in actively supporting a just and transparent society.

Fabio Barbosa advocates that in order to create a just society the whole financial system needs to change. As a chair of the committee for social responsibility of Febraban, the Brazilian Federation of Banks, he has fostered the debate and reflection on the role of financial institutions in society. Febraban's message is that a sound, ethical and efficient financial system is a pre-condition for the country's social and economic development (Febraban 2003).

How to inspire and mobilize people and organizations?

As seen from the preceding description, Fabio Barbosa has clearly-articulated views on banking and corporate social responsibility. Moreover, he has been effective in communicating them and translating them into strategies and behaviour, mobilizing many others inside and outside his organization. How did he manage to do this? From the interviews with Fabio Barbosa as well as with people who have worked with him and have been exposed to his leadership emerges a picture about his approach. The following combination of ingredients seems to be critical for his approach to inspire and mobilize people and organizations like ABN AMRO Real, clients, suppliers, the Federation of Banks in Brazil as well as the ABN AMRO Group.

It all starts with having personally articulated and identified with the above-mentioned values and convictions. Barbosa is deeply convinced that this is the way to go forward. This conviction comes across strongly as it is based on a deep, personal belief. This makes him, for many who meet him, an inspirational and even charismatic leader. This is reinforced by the fact that Fabio Barbosa's behaviour is aligned with the ideas he promotes. In his private life too, he cares, for example, about environmental issues. Not only does he ask others to be disciplined with time and resources and to behave respectfully towards others, he also applies these principles on a daily basis and in a visible way himself.

Next to that he tends to talk on a continuous base with people around him about these values and beliefs. It is said that he never misses out on an opportunity to share his views, repeating the same message over and over again. In almost every lecture and presentation he makes, he will refer to the above mentioned basic values and vision. By being repetitive, he is also extremely consistent and persistent in delivering this basic message. People acknowledge that it is in fact a very simple message too. Fabio Barbosa does not communicate in complicated philosophical or ideological terms. He uses understandable phrases like 'let us not play dirty games', or 'play the ball, not the legs of your opponent'. The message is often transferred in the form of questions that appeal both to the hearts and to the minds of people. For example: how to be a successful bank in a non-successful society? With these questions he manages to tap the level of ideals, values and (search for) meaning in others. It turns out that the questions Fabio Barbosa raises and the answers he proposes resonate strongly in others, at least in the Brazilian context.

In order to share his views Fabio Barbosa invests a large amount of his time in engaging with others – in fact, with all stakeholders inside and outside his organization. To give an example, one of his former direct reports said that Fabio Barbosa expected his team to get together every Tuesday morning for three hours. Even when there were no obvious issues to discuss, he urged them to attend these meetings. In hindsight, the manager acknowledged that exactly this has been a very valuable and effective strategy in staying connected and working through key issues and dilemmas in continuity. This is very much linked to Fabio Barbosa's notion of how to create lasting change. Leading an organization into the direction of sustainability and social responsibility cannot be the result of top-down decision making; employees at all levels need to become aware of the issues and dilemma's themselves, and to discuss or disagree with them in order to be able to identify with them. There should be no escape from scepticism, resistance and challenging and dissenting opinions and everyone ought to have the openness to confront the real issues and acknowledge that one does not have all the answers and solutions oneself. Accordingly, Fabio Barbosa tends to open his regular meetings with large groups of staff by telling them, 'I have a lot of questions and just a few answers for you'.

Fabio Barbosa promotes radical changes by reviewing and rethinking the role of financial institutions in and towards society. In fact, he wants to reinvent them. He proposes a radical and fundamental but not an abrupt change. As a leader he is convinced, consistent and resilient, but also very patient as lasting change comes step by step. It is a change from the inside to the outside. That is why Fabio Barbosa at a certain point in time did not follow the advice to organize large-scale meetings with hundreds of employees at the same time. He feels that one cannot speed up the change process by going from the outside in. It should be the other way round, and that asks for more time and smaller size meetings.

Moreover, he understands that you have to be as transparent as you can in trying to get there. Therefore, he has stimulated employees to monitor the progress they make and to be open and honest about the issues they face and the difficulty to make the changes. An example is the booklet that was published about the ambitions, the efforts and the results of trying to match human and economic values (ABN AMRO Real 2003a). The booklet reports statistics about various sustainability indicators in areas like diversity, micro-credit and environmental affairs. It opens with a dialogue between Fabio Barbosa and a critical customer who challenges the ambition and possibility of making capitalism more humane and inclusive.

Fabio Barbosa understands that to create sustainable change he needs to involve all stakeholders: shareholders, clients, employees, suppliers, local communities and society at large. Each of these interest groups needs to be engaged and he has put a lot of effort into doing that. ABN AMRO Real tries to inspire each stakeholder to become an ally in sustainability and justice. Yet again, he is well aware that this is a step-by-step approach. It starts with a meeting with the client or an NGO to share ideas and explore options on how to adhere for example to better labour standards and environmental conditions. In doing so, an inclusive approach is followed. For example, when an existing or potential client company damages the environment, the first step is to try to help this company to develop a better practice in this area. Only when they do not want to go that road, will ABN AMRO Real refuse to do business with that client. Fabio Barbosa is convinced that an organization has to be willing to turn down business opportunities if they conflict with its core values and vision. This is a question of organizational integrity. Values do count and as Fabio Barbosa points out, 'you don't forget your values in bad weather conditions'.

Another key ingredient has been the creation of a business model, integrating and visualizing the interests of all the stakeholders involved. At the heart of this model is the totally satisfied client. The client can only be satisfied when the organization has a real focus on the client, when the staff is committed and qualified, works with competitive tools, products and services and shares the right set of corporate values. Satisfied clients will generate good results. These results enable to add value for shareholders, employees and the community.

Fabio Barbosa has also created a small team of key people around him who are fully committed to make it happen. He has established an organizational structure, for example, a department for education and sustainable development and selected Maria Luiza Pinto, a native Brazilian, to head this department. Her experience as a senior global human resources executive at headquarters in Amsterdam coupled with her strong commitment for social responsibility made her the ideal candidate for this position. Once the values and vision will have been internalized and matched with and translated in core business practices, part of these designated structures will be dissolved.

The combination and systematic application of these various elements have so far proven to be very effective and inspiring for ABN AMRO Real.

I assume this is the result of consistently promoting social values, the capacity to align them with a business approach, translating them in actual behaviours and business decisions and involving all stakeholders in the process.

Developing as a leader, developing oneself

After outlining the vision of Fabio Barbosa on corporate social responsibility and describing how he has translated this vision into leadership behaviour and change strategies, I now would like to raise the question about aspects of the origin of his leadership. How did he manage to develop himself into the leader he actually is?

Listening to Fabio Barbosa, one realizes that his story started unfolding early in life. As a young boy, growing up in an upper middle class Brazilian family, he picked up some of the values and motivations that later turned out to be at the heart of his leadership style. His father held very strict values, for example, being respectful to others yet strict with money, paying on time and being on time. Fabio Barbosa describes himself as a young boy as 'already strong in terms of values'. Another role model for Fabio was his grandfather, the father of his mother, who lived only two houses away from the Barbosa family. He pictures his grandfather as a very diligent, humble and strict man, somebody for whom honesty and integrity represented important values. Fabio had a special bond with his grandfather who was a role model for him and who 'lectured' him about meaningful things in life; like 'treat others with respect' and 'never do things in your life that you will regret'. At school, Fabio was disciplined, always doing his homework. He wanted to achieve, get results, without over-performing. His performance at school was good but not outstanding, usually placing between fifth and seventh in his class. Fabio was aware of the fact that he was perhaps a bit more disciplined and achievement- and performance-oriented than his peers. It created an awareness of being different in these aspects. As a child, he seemed self-confident and self-aware, while believing that he was no better or worse than anyone else.

Fabio completed high school and studied Business Administration at the Getulio Vargas Foundation in Brazil between 1973 and 1976. In 1974 he joined Nestlé as a part-time intern. He worked for Nestlé in Brazil from 1976 until 1978 and left to obtain an MBA at IMD in Switzerland in 1979. In 1980 he was back at Nestlé and operated in finance and controlling functions, in Brazil, in Stamford (Connecticut, USA) and at Headquarters in Switzerland. In 1986 he returned to Brazil and worked six years for Citibank and two years for the Long Term Credit bank of Japan, also in Brazil. Thereafter he joined ABN AMRO Bank in Brazil.

These experiences made him even more aware of and respectful towards differences related to national and organizational cultures. They helped him to develop the ability to adapt his style and language according to the specific context he is in. Both his stay at IMD and the experience of his first job at Nestlé had a liberating and reinforcing impact on him. He discovered that characteristics like being disciplined, performance-driven, straightforward and on time were in these new environments highly appreciated. Even more, he experienced that the values and characteristics he had acquired in his childhood in Brazil could be applied and enable him in his career.

One might describe this as the first developmental phase of Fabio Barbosa's leadership. Some of the significant precursors were in his childhood where he was socially educated on the level of values, in particular by his father and his grandfather. This finding is in line with the general finding of the impact of family upbringing on leadership. Families are among the major factors in the shaping of one's personality and the values one adopts. The clinical approach to leadership provides us with a lot of findings and insights in this context (Kets de Vries 2001, 2004, Coutu 2004). In the case of Fabio Barbosa it is clear that the key values driving his leadership are deeply rooted in his personality. During childhood, these values were planted in him like seeds, allowing him later on in the first phase of his career to use and live them in the work environment.

In a second phase of his leadership career, Fabio Barbosa decided to return to his native Brazil. He felt that, with his education and experience, he wanted to make a contribution in his home country. He was now looking beyond the boundaries of his own career and self-interest. He started to combine working for Citibank in Brazil with teaching finance at a local university. He soon became aware that there was a need not only to teach finance, but also to link it to ethics and ask the question of 'why and for what purposes do you use financial expertise and products?' One might argue that in this phase Fabio Barbosa really elaborated and developed his thinking about finance and its role in society.

A new and third leadership phase started when he actually stepped into a leadership role as chief executive. First, in 1996, as president of ABN AMRO Bank in Brazil. Later on, after the acquisition of Banco Real, as president of ABN AMRO Banco Real. Fabio Barbosa discovered that his own thinking and his own opinions on banking and society resonated strongly in others. This reinforced his ambition to make a difference in this field: 'I was mature enough to bring the message, so I should spell it out.' But he also acknowledges that he was influenced and educated by key people around him. Osório dos Santos, for instance, was head of Consumer Finance at ABN AMRO. Seeing how he interacted with people, Fabio Barbosa felt encouraged to express his feelings and not be ashamed to relate to people on a more human level. In doing so, Fabio discovered not only his gift in relating to people but that it was also very rewarding. A similar role model was Flammarion Josué Nunes, who was a member of the Board of Banco Real and joined Fabio Barbosa on the board of ABN AMRO Real. Fabio observed how Flammarion was able to speak 'straight from the heart', even to large groups of people. A third person of influence was Ricardo Guimarães, an external consultant. Fabio once had a discussion with Ricardo about people who had inspired him with great ideas. Ricardo responded by telling Fabio: 'You have these ideas yourself, don't keep them to yourself'. I think that this shows that, even in this third phase and already in a senior leadership role, Fabio Barbosa was still in the process of developing himself. Slightly shy as a person, he trained himself to open up to other people and to large audiences to talk about his beliefs, values and vision. He dared to use what was at the core of his person.

Therefore, what had an impact on the way he took up his leadership role were not only his values and beliefs, but also the process of self-development. Fabio Barbosa's own path of development has progressed from lessons early on in life to self-awareness, and finally to the capacity to translate awareness into behaviour. It is a process from the inside to the outside that has taken many years. One might argue that Fabio Barbosa used his own experience as a frame of reference and a benchmark for how to understand and approach the processes required to create sustainable change: to increase awareness, to create role models and be a role model himself for other people, engage them in dialogues and allow and facilitate a process to unfold from the inside out.

An interesting facet of Fabio Barbosa's leadership is that he is not only sensitive to and aware of the processes needed and the longer time horizon involved, he also combines it with being disciplined and results-oriented. He understands the necessity of clarity in decision making, planning, organizing, defining targets and milestones, as well as measuring and following up on them – also with respect to sustainability and corporate social responsibility. The source of these leadership and behavioural qualities are, as described, also rooted in the early phases of his life.

Conclusion

What can we learn from Fabio Barbosa and his leadership role at ABN AMRO Real? What kind of learning does it contain for other companies and leaders who would like to develop responsible leaders?

First, it highlights that an individual leader can indeed make a difference. Fabio Barbosa has so far had a huge impact in this domain. Second, his impact is probably the result of a combination of factors: a configuration of values, competencies and qualities which make him both quite unique and effective. He is a person of strong values, who has the capacity to articulate and communicate them, who demonstrates persistence, discipline, respect, self-confidence, self-awareness, not to mention autonomy in his way of thinking. Thirdly, these qualities are not innate but developed through social education, learning from role models over his lifetime and career. Fourthly, it has taken him a long time to get to where he is now – that is, to develop the potential he had in order to become the person he is. This personal core, as well as the way he has learnt and allowed himself to use this core as a significant source of motivation, is the foundation of his charisma as a leader. Fabio Barbosa tends to say that leadership development is in essence about becoming a better, more complete human being. In this context, Fabio Barbosa likes to tell the story of a painter who almost every day destroys the painting he has just painted. A wise man asks him why he always destroys his paintings. The painter answers: 'because the painting is not perfect'. 'Oh', the wise man responds, 'become first a better person yourself and your paintings will emerge naturally'.

Questions

1   As the chapter illustrates part of one's self is based on values and beliefs acquired early in life. How does this statement apply to you?
2   Fabio Barbosa was inspired and influenced by a few key persons both in the family context and work environment. Are there people who have also had a deep influence on you? Who are they? How did they achieve this?
3   Fabio Barbosa said that to become a better leader, you first needed to become a better, more complete human being. What is your opinion of this statement?
4   If companies would ask your help on how to develop responsible leaders, how would you advise them?
5   One of the key messages of Fabio Barbosa is that developing corporate social responsibility in organizations should unfold from the inside out and that this undertaking is a time consuming process. Do you think that this applies to most organizations and cultures? Do you know countries or contexts in which it might be better to adopt the opposite approach – to approach the issues from the outside in, in order to speed up the process?

Note

1   The Equator Principles are a set of guidelines developed by ten leading banks from seven countries for managing social and environmental risks related to the financing of projects. They are based on the policies and guidelines of the World Bank and the International Finance Corporation. The institutions that adopt these principles seek to ensure that the projects they finance 'are developed in an manner that is socially responsible and reflect sound environmental management practices' (The Equator Principles 2003: 1).

Bibliography

ABN AMRO REAL (2003a) *Human and Economic Values, Together*, Sao Paulo: ABN AMRO Real.
ABN AMRO Real (2003b) 'Respeito é bom e dá lucro', interview with Fabio Barbosa, DVD.

ABN AMRO (2004) *Making More Possible,* Annual Report 2004, ABN AMRO Holding N.V. Online. Available HTTP: http://www.abnamro.com/com/about/ar2004en.pdf (accessed 26 April 2005).

ABN AMRO (2005) *Sustainable Development: SRI funds.* Online. Available HTTP: http://www.abnamro.com/com/about/sd/sd_sri.jsp (accessed 26 April 2005).

ACCION International (2005) *Real Microcrédito.* Online. Available HTTP: http://www.accion.org/about_where_we_work_program.asp_Q_T_E_24 (accessed 26 April 2005).

Britto, F. and Wever, L. (2002) *Vivendo Appredendo & Ensinando* (Living, Learning and Teaching), Rio de Janeiro/Sao Paolo: Negócio.

Carta Capital (2003) 'All for one', interview with Fabio Barbosa, 14 May: 44–6.

Carta Capital (2004) 'Who came close: Brazil's most admired companies', 13 September: 46–8.

Coutu, D.L. (2004) 'Putting leaders on the couch: a conversation with Manfred F.R. Kets de Vries', *Harvard Business Review,* 82(1): 64–71.

Dinheiro (2004) 'There are no shortcuts in the economy', interview with Fabio Barbosa, *Isto é magazine,* 5 October: 20–22.

Febraban (2003) *Febraban, CNF and Related Entities.* Online. Available HTTP: http://www.febraban.org.br/Arquivo/Quemsomos/english.asp (accessed 26 April 2005).

Kets de Vries, M.F.R. (2001) *The Leadership Mystique: a user's manual for the human enterprise,* London: Financial Times Prentice Hall.

Kets de Vries, M.F.R. (2004) 'Organizations on the couch: a clinical perspective on organizational dynamics', *European Management Journal,* 22(2): 183–200.

Mano, C. (2004) 'Values of merit', interview given by Fabio Barbosa, Magazine *Exame,* 4 February: 64–7.

Motta, A. (2003) 'Society has the solutions', interview with Fabio Barbosa, Newspaper *O Globo,* 5 July: 4–5.

The Equator Principles (2003) 'The Equator Principles: an industry approach for financial institutions in determining, assessing and managing environmental and social risk in project financing'. Online. Availabe HTTP: http://www.equator-principles.com/documents/Equator_Principles.pdf (accessed 26 April 2005).

Van de Loo, E. (2000) 'The clinical paradigm: Manfred Kets de Vries's reflections on organizational therapy', *European Management Journal,* 18(1): 2–22.

Part III

How to develop responsible leadership in business?

12 Principled-based leadership
Lessons from the Caux Round Table

Stephen B. Young

Introduction

The socio-economic problems in the world cannot be tackled by governments or civil society alone. The Caux Round Table (CRT) believes that the world business community should play an important role in improving economic and social conditions. In this chapter I show how a group of committed senior business leaders across countries and cultures has bundled their energy in the CRT network to define principles for responsible business (*Principles for Business*), to promote them and to start a change process in business towards corporate responsibility. Based on the experience over the past 20 years of intensive work and dialogues with senior business executives participating in Caux Round Table dialogues, I derive five leadership lessons: *first, the need for principles*; second, *what gets managed, gets accomplished*; third, *interests must be addressed*; fourth, *culture counts*; and fifth, *the fish rots from the head*.

The Caux Round Table

The Caux Round Table is an international network of senior business executives principally from Japan, Europe and the United States working to promote 'moral capitalism' (Young 2003). A fundamental belief is that the world business community should play an important role in improving economic and social conditions in the world. Therefore, the organization is committed to activating business and industries to become agents of innovative global change for the better. In 1986, the Round Table was founded by Olivier Giscard d'Estaing, Vice-Chairman of INSEAD and Frederik Philips, former President of Philips Electronics. Initially the focus was on reducing escalating trade tensions. Over time the network has broadened its view on global corporate responsibility to include focusing on reducing economic and social threats to foster stability and peace in the world. In this context the Round Table recognizes the importance of principle-based and shared leadership for a revitalized and harmonious world and emphasizes 'the development of continuing friendships, understanding and cooperation, based on a common respect for the highest moral values and on responsible action by individuals in their own spheres of influence' (Caux Round Table 2005).

The idea of principled business leadership was introduced by the members of the CRT network. There was firstly the belief among members, based on their personal experience in business, that success in business requires more than fidelity to the short-term bottom line of reported profits and losses. This belief triggered a broader discussion, a series of dialogues and a collaborative process among network members from Europe, Japan and the United States, resulting in 1994 in the definition and publication of a set of ethical business principles for decision making. These so- called CRT Principles for Business consist of seven general principles and then specify certain responsibilities towards six stakeholder groups: customers, employees, owners/investors, suppliers, competitors and communities.[1] This collaborative process of defining a statement of responsible business practice by business leaders, for business leaders is in fact an expression of leadership by example. CRT members were leaders in the sense that firstly, their position was based on moral values and ideals, secondly, they took a position based on their ideals and values, and thirdly, they dared to speak truth to power. This action by members of the Caux Round Table network demonstrates an implicit theory of leadership – *action based on principle*. This leadership stance is rooted in values and resists the pressures of pragmatism and the temptations of power.

In fact, it is the information about and the implementation of these Principles for Business both on a global scale and at the company level that represents a key priority of the work of the Caux Round Table. On a global scale the Round Table promotes better outcomes for globalization. In order to do that, CRT members are for instance working to raise the level of awareness of senior business leaders, thought leaders and opinion leaders worldwide about new opportunities to alleviate global poverty. At the company level CRT campaigns for the implementation of the CRT Principles for Business as a cornerstone of principled business leadership.

Lessons from the Caux Round Table

The experience of senior business executives participating in Caux Round Table dialogues over the past 20 years affirms that leadership is more than management. Their experience also supports five lessons for those who would be leaders: first, application of principles separates leadership from management (the *big picture*); second, principles must be implemented through management systems and benchmarks (the *little picture*); third, leadership must address the interests and needs of people as well as their values and aspirations; fourthly, culture counts in defining how people will respond to principles; and fifthly, dysfunction in corporate cultures centers on the decision making of the most senior leaders and managers. In the following, I will discuss these lessons in more detail.

Lesson number one: the need for principles

The first lesson to be taken from the Caux Round Table experience is cross-cultural affirmation of an old truth: leadership is far more than management. Leadership rises above the status quo. It is steering the *Titanic*, not rearranging its deckchairs or playing music as the ship sinks beneath the cold waters of the North Atlantic.

According to Kotter's (1996) distinction between leadership and management, managers have to ensure that the work gets done and that short-term results expected by different stakeholders (clients, shareholders) are delivered. Therefore, they need to produce a certain degree of predictability and order through a systematic process of *planning and budgeting*, a structured approach to *organizing and staffing* as well as thorough *controlling and problem solving*. While managers are accountable for the administration of work on the deck of the ship, leaders are responsible for steering the ship so that it does not run aground and sink. Leaders are responsible for *establishing direction* by developing a clear vision of the future, for *aligning people* both inside and outside the corporation and for *motivating and inspiring* employees. Having the bigger picture in mind they need to be able to make changes, to redirect the firm and to adjust the course of the ship not only in the face of an iceberg, but as soon as a responsible and farsighted evaluation calls for it.

The experience of publishing the Caux Round Table Principles for Business taught us that leadership and ethics share a common core. You can't really have one without the other. Leaders must stand for something. They serve ends and purposes higher than themselves. They lead from the realm of ethics and enter into the world of deeds guided by their values, principles and aspirations. However, as we know from history not all values, principles and aspirations of humans are good or noble. Hitler, Stalin, Mao Tse-tung and Pol Pot were all leaders and each was intensely and sincerely committed to a purpose and driven by certain values, principles and aspirations that, as we know today, were ill-spirited. They originated from a bad and misguided values-base and created terrible tragedies. The realm of business is also not safe from the consequences of misguided principles and values. When leaders are too much concerned with their own power, prestige or financial reward, 'they act less and less as good stewards for the interests of stakeholders' (Baukol 2002: 5). Purely individualistic and materialistic values coupled with hunger for power and grandiosity as well as greed for money and personal profits can produce leaders like Ken Lay, Jeffrey Skilling and Andrew Fastow at Enron or Bernie Ebbers at WorldCom. These leaders are responsible for the collapse of whole organizations, destroying economic and social value and severely affecting the life and work of thousands of stakeholders. As tragic as these examples of 'bad leadership' (Kellerman 2004) may be, they highlight the importance and responsibility we have to look into the values-base and the principles that guide leaders' action. The calling of a leader must necessarily call into question the substance of the principles he or she lives by. Not every principle that guides a leader is one that we would want to follow.

In contrast to traditional leadership research, which postulates that leadership is value-free, our practical experience tells another story. Much of leadership constitutes normative work, choosing and articulating norms in social settings. As culture workers, leaders need to be good communicators, storytellers, networkers and relationship managers, aligning the energies of others behind a common, collective endeavour. In this sense, leaders are also builders of community; they are part of the distinctive human capacity to be intentional in changing our life circumstances – finding food, defending homes, punishing errant behaviour. Leadership could not happen if humans had no conscience. The human capacity for socialization and reciprocity calls for leaders to coordinate the ends and purposes of the collective activity. Leaders appeal to the capacity of others for commitment and self-mastery. Leaders can bring us out of chaos. But, in my judgement, to which end they lead us is always open to question and debate. If leadership rests on values and application of principle, those notions of right (or wrong in some cases) lend themselves to discussion and personal affirmation.

Leaders who act in a global, complex and uncertain environment are confronted with a multitude of challenges ranging from interacting with a plurality of stakeholders, who often have different and conflicting interests and values (see Maak and Pless 2006; Pless and Schneider 2006) in dealing with complex ethical dilemmas. Often they face decision-making situations where there is no clear right or wrong to an ethical dilemma. They have to decide based on good judgement and moral principles. To help leaders navigate responsibly in an uncertain and complex environment, the Caux Round Table formulated a set of principles that provides leaders with orientation. The CRT encourages business leaders to incorporate these principles and guiding values into their strategic thinking, problem solving and decision making.

Lesson number two: what gets managed, gets accomplished

The experience of publishing the Principles of Business in 1994 taught the Caux Round Table a lesson that has since had great applicability – that publishing principles doesn't do much to change the world. To have any effect, principles must be implemented. Principles without a supporting management process are little more than decorations, a thin veneer of good intentions that cannot endure the often corrosive effects of experience. Karl Marx, in his thesis on Feuerbach, made a similar point when he criticized philosophers: 'Up to now philosophers have only interpreted the world. The point, however, is to change it.'

The arena of praxis tests the skills of leaders. Implementing norms, coordinating efforts to realize an objective and applying standards in practical situations all test the ability of leaders to be relevant in the world. At the suggestion of Professor Kenneth Goodpaster of the University of St Thomas in Minnesota and rapporteur for many Caux Round Table Global Dialogues, the Caux Round Table has adopted a mission slogan of 'From Aspiration to Action'. This slogan embodies the CRT's belief that the Principles for Business must be broken down to more specific standards and benchmarks before they can be applied sensibly to the facts.

One area in which we have seen principles being put into action is the quality movement in the United States. Each year, the President and the Department of Commerce present the Malcolm Baldridge National Quality Award to a selected number of firms that have demonstrated quality and organizational performance excellence. To assess the firms, the principles of quality had to be analyzed and broken down into more specific components such as reject rate or customer satisfaction. The precedent of the quality movement recommended itself to a working group of Caux Round Table participants. Based on the understanding that implementing a comprehensive improvement process will bring a company more and more into effective alignment with the Principles for Business the CRT has applied a similar approach and developed a self-assessment framework for companies. This *self-assessment and improvement process* evaluates companies on 49 areas drawn form the CRT Principles of Business as they impact the six stakeholder constituencies. In each area of concern, specific questions were posed; each question served as a point of measurement as well as a benchmark for possible improvement. In all, some 275 individual points of assessment were devised (Goodpaster 2003).

As experience shows the contribution of a management support process to effective leadership lies in several areas. First, the process of assessing what is lacking and consulting others as to what should be done generates support from many individuals for the effort. It is difficult for an individual, subject to opposition or resistance from co-workers, to undertake change in isolation. The principle-centred concerns of the leadership must penetrate the beliefs and motivations of those who deliver the results. Second, effective management minimizes friction and maximizes the impact of the total effort contributed to the enterprise. Third, effective management allows individual incentives to be aligned with the goals of the enterprise. If the troops refuse to follow, the general can't win the battle.

Lesson number three: interests must be addressed

In seeking support for the Principles for Business and adoption of the implementation process, Caux Round Table participants learned a third lesson. In business enterprise, at least, leadership must confront the desire of individuals for their interests to be attended to. People are not in business to save the world or engage in charity. They want to make money. If they perceive that a set of principles or a set of management tasks will divert them from making money or will only tangentially help them make more money, they show little interest. Moralists conclude from this that greed and self-interest within the world of business prevent business from ever rising to the level of responsible, principled behaviour. One could take that common point of view, of course. But then one is left somewhat dumbfounded to explain how to create private wealth for individual empowerment through market exchanges of goods and services. If the moral standard for everyone is to be saintly selfless, then the dynamics of enterprise will be hard to come by and society will lose as a result. Thus a case must be made that principled business leadership is good for business. How can such a case be credibly made? Isn't it true that ethics and business are like oil and water and never mix?

The recommended approach, based upon the obligations and responsibilities contained in the Caux Round Table Principles for Business, is to consider the importance to a business of various capital accounts – financial, physical, human, reputational and social. Paying a return on each of these different kind of capital accounts keeps capital flowing into the business and supports its continued profitability. Not paying a return on capital condemns the business to failure.

Payment for the use of finance and physical capital is straightforward. Money is transferred from the business to the owner of capital in the form of dividends, interest, rent or lease payments, or for some plant and equipment, in a cash purchase price. Paying a return for the use of human capital is more novel: it consists of salaries and working conditions to attract the talent necessary for the business to prosper. Payment for goodwill or reputational capital usually comes about as a result of quality in goods and service, good customer relations, an *equity brand* value in the goods and services provided, and dealing truthfully and fairly with all concerned including suppliers. Paying for the social capital of a good business climate with adequate physical, intangible and institutional infrastructures comes in the form of taxes, charitable contributions, care of the environment, volunteerism in the community, and so on.

Note that many aspects of paying a sufficient return on these forms of capital causes a company to be wise and responsible in its relationships with key stakeholders: customers, employees, owners and investors, suppliers, competitors and communities. As a consequence, the business is both principled and profitable. There is no conflict between the financial demands of making money and the responsibilities expected from a corporate citizen. Each activity supports the other: more profit permits greater care in responding to stakeholders and well-treated stakeholders contribute more readily to business success. The firm adds to its goodwill and, therefore, to its market power.

The management process of implementing the Caux Round Table Principles for Business adds not only to the reputational, human and social capital accounts of a business, but to its bottom line as well. The case is made that senior managers of enterprise should not hesitate to adopt enhanced *quality* management procedures.

Lesson number four: culture counts

In its global work, Caux Round Table participants have discovered that business leadership is culturally embedded. Fundamental to the articulation of the Caux Round Table Principles for Business was the Japanese concept of *Kyosei*, brought to the deliberations of participants by Mr Ryazaburo Kaku, then Chairman of Canon Inc. The Japanese concept of *kyosei* means living and working together for the common good, and enabling cooperation and mutual prosperity to co-exist with healthy and fair competition. It advocates the concept that successful companies are not hard-shelled pods, cut off from customers and employees. Rather, as Mr Kaku told the Caux Round Table, a successful company's outer membrane is permeable. The company's sense of self extends outwards to customers and downwards to employees. By taking their needs into account, the business functions symbiotically – helping itself grow while serving others.

Then, European participants, responding to Mr Kaku's formula for success, explained that in Europe, business is rewarded best when it is respectful of norms of human dignity. Human dignity as a conecpt is rooted in Christian religion. It refers to the sacredness or value of each person as an end, not simply a means to the fulfilment of others' purposes or even majority prescription. A business that respects the human dignity of its customers, communities and workers, as opposed to one that practises a super-adversarial American model of cowboy capitalism, gains support from unions and governments.

Caux Round Table participants, seeking to find common ground for an ethic of business responsibility that would foster principled business leadership, blended core requirements of *Kyosei* with the aspirations of *human dignity* to shape a set of principles. In this experience the value of cultural norms became apparent. To impose Japanese sensibilities on Europeans or vice versa would fail; no ethical framework would then embrace a single global business community. So the key question that arose was how business principles as universal global norms are linked to particular value patterns of discrete and actual cultures. Due to the fact that religions often have a formative influence on the values system of the culture of a country or a region (i.e. Buddhism in Asia, Christianity in Europe and North America, Islam in the Arab world) the Caux Round Table decided to compare the Principles of Business with eleven significant religious and spiritual traditions[2] resulting in a paper 'Essays on world religions: grounding the Caux Round Table Principles for Business on fundamental ethical teachings' (Young 2002).

Due to the limited space available in this chapter the nexus between the CRT Principles and selected religious traditions cannot be reproduced here. However, the matrix shown in Table 12.1 summarizes where the general CRT principles as well as the stakeholder principles resonate in the thinking and writing of the respective religious and spiritual traditions. Though, it provides only reference points, not fully elaborated theological dogma. To this extent, then it oversimplifies the ethical possibilities contained within a religious tradition. Yet, the interested reader will find a detailed introduction in and discussion of the respective religious traditions in the above mentioned paper.

The purpose of the matrix (see Table 12.1) is not only to invite a conversation about values/ethics within a religious tradition as higher norms are applied to business activity, but, more importantly, to demonstrate that within each of the eleven religious and spiritual traditions such a conversation is possible. Religions and the deep cultural structures they perpetuate from generation to generation are not obstacles to finding a universal and moral legitimate approach to business. In fact, as this analysis showed, the CRT Principles for Business catch commitment from different religious perspectives. As such they can be a stimulating starting point for intercultural dialogue on the possibility of principled business leadership across cultures.

Actually, an implication of the matrix for leadership is that in those cultures referring to these religious and spiritual traditions normative demands can be made of those who lead and act. Principled leadership regularly appears in human community. As such it is a relational phenomenon (Maak and Pless 2006). It may even be that principled leadership is necessary for the success of community as it may constitute the principal social glue binding individuals firmly to joint endeavours. The common theme threading its way through every cell of the matrix evokes self-restraint and concern for others. Often, but not always, both qualities go hand in hand. Both are important qualities in interactions with stakeholders and thus for the CRT stakeholder principles. Table 12.2 gives specific examples for the notion of *concern for others* as they appear in different religious traditions.

As in the native Meso-American, Mayan perspective, the virtue of avoiding self-magnification would seem to apply very aptly to the hubris shown by Kenneth Lay, Jeffrey Skilling and Andrew Fastow as they set Enron up for a huge fall into bankruptcy.

Perhaps the classic demonstration of the role of religious and spiritual traditions for business linked Calvinist Protestant beliefs with the creation of capitalism in sixteenth-century Holland and, later, in England and the English colonies in North America. Max Weber's famous work *The Protestant Ethic and the Spirit of Capitalism* (1930) drew attention to the role of values and beliefs in building business cultures of delayed gratification, savings, interpersonal trust and joint ventures. While Weber's precise exposition of how Protestant values fostered modern capitalist enterprise has not fully survived critical examination over the years, his assertion of a

Religious foundation	Principle 1: The responsibilities of business	Principle 2: The economic and social impact of business	Principle 3: business behavior	Principle 4: Respect for rules	Principle 5: Support for multilateral trade	Principle 6: Respect for the environment	Principle 7: Avoidance of illicit operations	Stakeholder principles: customers	Stakeholder principles: employees	Stakeholder principles: owners: investors	Stakeholder principles: suppliers	Stakeholder principles: competitors	Stakeholder principles: community
Foundational Judeo-Christian Old Testament visions of social justice	Noahide Covenant: 'Be fruitful and multiply on the earth'; see also 1Kings 4:24; Leviticus 19:5–10	Noahide Covenant; Isaiah 3:14–15	Proverbs 20:17; 10:9; 12:2; 16:8 Leviticus 33:35	Leviticus 26: 3–5; 2 Samuel 22: 21–3	Exodus 21:23; 23:9; Leviticus 19:33	Leviticus 25:1; Genesis 1:22; Isaiah 5:8	Exodus 21:33; 22: 1–14; Deuteronomy 16:18	Leviticus 19:13; proverbs 20:17; 11:1	Deuteronomy 24:14–15; 24:6	Avoid fraud; Leviticus 19:13	Deuteronomy 24:14–15; Proverbs 20:23	Eat the fruit of your own labor; Psalm 128: 1–2	Isaiah 3:14–15
Canonical Protestant moral authorities	Luke 12:30; 12:24–8; Matthew 3:31–3; to whom much is given, much is required. Luke 12:48	To whom much is given, much is required. Luke 12:48	Man does not live by bread alone. Luke 4:4; Mark 8:36; Matthew 16:26; love of money root of all evil 1 Timothy 6:10; Golden Rule. Matthew 5	Romans 13:4	Parable of the Good Samaritan. Luke 10:30–7	Calling of ministry. Mark 10:43–5	Romans 13:4	Golden Rule. Matthew 5; Matthew 25:32–46	Golden Rule. Matthew 5	Parable of the faithful servant. Matthew 25:14–30; John 10:13; Luke 16	Parable of the debtor. Matthew 18: 23–34	Lay not up treasures upon earth. Matthew 6:19–20	Parable of the Good Samaritan. Luke 10:30–7; stewardship. Matthew 5:13–14
Papal teachings on business responsibility	The call to work as co-creator. Laborem Exercens	The call to work as co-creator. Laborem Exercens	Respect for the human person. Laborem Exercens	Respect for the human person. Laborem Exercens Avoid excessive Self-Love. Centissimus Annus	Co-creator with God. Centissimus Annus	Co-creator with God. Centissimus Annus	Respect for the human person. Laborem Exercens	Respect for the human person. Laborem Exercens Avoid excessive self-love Centissimus Annus	Respect for the human person. Laborem Exercens	Avoid excessive self-love. Centissimus Annus	Avoid excessive self-love. Centissimus Annus	Avoid excessive self-love. Centissimus Annus	Avoid excessive self-love. Centissimus Annus
Ethical vision of the Koran	Create wealth for others. Koran 4:36; 6:165; 16:16	Create wealth for others. Koran 4:36; 6:165; 16:16	Keep promises. Koran 2:174; 23:1	Do not transgress. Koran 5:87	Promote trade. Koran 4:26	Do not transgress the balance. Koran 55:1	No unjust acquisition of property. Koran 2:188; 30:38	Just weight and full measure. Koran 6:149; preserve self from greed. Koran 64:12	No oppression. Koran 42:35; 16:90	Seek bounty. Koran16:16	Treat fairly. Koran 83:1	Preserve self from greed. Koran 64:12	No pride or injustice. Koran 42:35; 46:19
Thai Theravada Buddhist teachings	Virtues of *danam* and *tapem; purna* actions	Virtues of *maddavam* and *tapam; purna* actions	Virtues of *pariccagam* and *ajjavam*	Virtues of *silam* and *pariccagam*	Virtues of *akkodham* and *avihimsa*	Virtues of *pariccagam* and *avirodhanam*	Virtue of *silam*	Eightfold way; right livelihood	Eightfold way; right speech; right action	Wealth to benefit others	Eightfold way; right livelihood	No attachment; no clinging to wealth	Promote community well-being; *purna* actions

Table 12.1 Continued

Religious foundation	Principle 1: The responsibilities of business	Principle 2: The economic and social impact of business	Principle 3: business behavior	Principle 4: Respect for rules	Principle 5: Support for multilateral trade	Principle 6: Respect for the environment	Principle 7: Avoidance of illicit operations	Stakeholder principles: customers	Stakeholder principles: employees	Stakeholder principles: owners investors	Stakeholder principles: suppliers	Stakeholder principles: competitors	Stakeholder principles: community
Mahayana Buddhist teachings	*Karuna* (compassion); Sila (*moral virtue*); dependent co-arising	*Karuna* (compassion); Sila (*moral virtue*); dependent co-arising	Sila (*moral virtue*); *dependent co-arising*	Sila (*moral virtue*)	*Karuna* (no discrimination based on otherness); dependent co-arising	*Karuna* (compassion); dependent co-arising	Sila	Eightfold Way: right livelihood; wise discernment	Eightfold Way: right speech, right action; wise discernment	*Karuna* (compassion); sila (moral virtue)	Eightfold Way: right livelihood	Dependent co-arising	*Karuna* (compassion); wise discernment
Expression of Original Confucian Morality	Analects Bk XIII, Ch IX, 3; Bk XIII, Ch XVI, 1; Mencius, Bk IV, Pt 1, Ch IX, 1	Analects, Bk XIII, Ch IX, 3; Bk XIII, Ch XVI, 1; Mencius Bk IV, Pt 1, Ch IX,1	Analects: Bk I, Ch VIII, 2 and Bk IX, Ch XXIV; Mencius, Bk IV, Pt 1, Ch I, 3	Analects Bk X, Ch X	Mencius, Bk VII, Pt 1, Ch XXIII, 1; Bk I, Pt 2, Ch V, 3; Bk II, Pt 1, Ch V, 2	Mencius, Bk 1, Ch III, 3; Analects, Bk VII, Ch XXVI	Analects, Bk XII, Ch I, 1, 2 and Bk, IV, Ch V, 1	Analects, Bk X, Ch	Analects, Bk X; Bk XV, Ch XX	Analects, Bk XVI, Ch X; Bk I, Ch VIII, 2; Bk II, Ch XIII	Analects, Bk XV, Ch XXI; Bk XV, Ch XX	Analects, Bk IV, Ch X; Bk IV, Ch V, 1	Mencius, Bk IV, Pt 1, Ch III, 3; Bk I, Pt 1, Ch IV, 4, 5
Hindu Varnas as expressed in the *Law of Manu* text	Manu Ch 2, 2–4, 224; Ch 8, 3–6; Ch 9, 325–332; Ch 3, 118; Ch 9	Manu, Ch 2, 2–4; 224, Ch 3, 118; Ch 4, 32; Ch 9.	Manu, Ch 4, 156, 176; Ch 4, 237, 256; Ch 8, 111, 165	Manu, Ch 1, 108, 109; Ch 4, 176; Ch 8, 3–6	Manu, Ch 8, 339	Manu, Ch 4 on harm to earth and animals	Manu, Ch 7, 49, 124	Manu, Ch 2, 93; Ch 7, 3; Ch n7, 49	Manu, Ch 2, 93; Ch 7, 3; Ch 9	Manu, Ch 2, 93; Ch 8, 3-6, 151-153; Ch 7, 3; Ch 7, 49; Ch 9	Manu, Ch 2, 93; Ch 7, 3; Ch 7, 49; Ch 9	Manu 7, 49	Manu 11, 10; Ch 7, 3
African spiritual understandings	Positive creative force; let life forces thrive	Positive creative force; let life forces thrive	Reciprocity; do not diminish the life-force of another; moral norm of community; act with diligence and faithfulness	Moral norm of community; do not diminish life force of another	Use positive creative forces; benefit from pluralism; multiple expressions of creation; respect community; do not emulate lower orders of creation	Respect for creative forces	Do not diminish the life force of another; act with responsibility and faithfulness	Reciprocity; do not diminish life force of another	Reciprocity; do not diminish life force of another	Reciprocity	Reciprocity	Multiple expressions of creation	Moral norm of community; gaining a good life demands building community; those with greater force have greater responsibilities
Way of the Japanese *Kami*	Do not obstruct the *Kami*; bring forth bounty; life sustaining activity	Do not obstruct the *Kami*; bring forth bounty; life sustaining activity	Upright and honest heart	Sincere and pure; no unruly self-assertion	Do not obstruct *Kami*; bring forth bounty	Sincere and pure; do not obstruct natural forces	Upright and honest heart; sincere and pure	Upright and honest heart; strategic thinking	Upright and honest heart; strategic thinking	Upright and honest heart; strategic thinking	Life sustaining activities	Life sustaining activities	Flourishing people and community
Meso-American indigenous theology	Generativity; provide for; nurture	Generativity; provide for; nurture	Don't be a trickster; don't deceive	Give respect; no self-magnification; keep on the green road	Give respect; no self-magnification	Give respect; show appreciation; no self-magnification	No self-magnification; don't be a trickster	No self-magnification; no deception	Respect contributions of others	Provide for; no self-magnification; don't be a trickster	Respect contributions of others	No self-magnification	Provide for; nurture; keep on the green road; cargo system

* The virtues Thai Theravada Buddhist Teachings are and mean the following: *ajjavam* (honesty and freedom from pretence); *akkodham* (freedom from anger); *avihimsa* (freedom from malice); *avirodhanam* (an avoidance of wrong doing); *danam* (giving); *khanti* (patience); *maddavam* (gentleness and humility); *silam* (right conduct); *tapam* (concentration of effort).

Table 12.2 Examples of *concern for others* in different religious traditions[3]

Judeo-Christian Old Testament of the Bible

The poor are to be provided for and not oppressed (Exodus 22:22; 22:25; 23:6). 'When you reap the harvest of your land, do not reap to the very edges of your field or gather the gleanings of your harvest. Do not go over your vineyard a second time or pick the grapes that have fallen. Leave them for the poor and the alien' (Leviticus 19:9–10).

Protestant Christian New Testament of the Bible

In Matthew 25 Jesus teaches that the kingdom of God will be open to those who give of themselves and of their goods. Those who accumulate only earthly riches will gain for themselves everlasting punishment while the righteous, those who care for others, will gain life eternal (Matthew 25:32–46). Specifically, the righteous are those willing to feed the hungry, give drink to the thirsty, receive strangers, clothe the naked, visit those in prison. This teaching runs parallel in meaning to the famous story told by Jesus of the Samaritan who, rather than the ritually correct Levite, took care of a man beaten by robbers (Luke 10:30–7).

Islam and the Koran

The Surah says that 'those that preserve themselves from their own greed will surely prosper' (Surah 64:12). Those with wealth are enjoined by The Koran to provide for others in society, for the beggar and the deprived (Surah 70:22).

Thai Theravada Buddhist teachings

In Thai Buddhism the following virtues which are related to *self-restraint* and *concern for others* play an important role: personal sacrifice - material as well as spiritual (*pariccagam*), gentleness and humility (*maddavam*), giving (*danam*). The acquisition of wealth is acceptable if, at the same time, it promotes the well-being of a community or society (Rjavaramuni 1990, Reynolds 1990).

Mahayana Buddhist teachings

In the Mahayana tradition compassion (*karuna*) – regard for others – plays an important role on the path to perfect Buddhahood (Bodhisattva ideal). It can be understood as an internal motivation. The spirit of karuna is caught in these lines: 'May I be the doctor and the medicine and may I be the nurse for all sick beings in the world until everyone is healed ... May I be a protector for those without one, and a guide to all travelers on the way; may I be a bridge, a boat and a ship for all those who wish to cross ...' (Harvey 2000, 124).

Hindu teachings (Law of Manu)

'A householder must give as much food as he is able to spare to those who do not cook for themselves, and to all being one must distribute food without detriment to one's own interest' (Manu, Chapter 4, 32).

Shintoism and Kami

Shintoism is a Japanese religion that worships *Kami*. Kami are various deities of heaven and earth that can appear in the form of natural forces, mountains, lakes, rivers, birds, beast, human beings and their spirits. The spiritual practice of living on good terms with the Kami follows principles such as sincerity, awareness of one's participation in the life-forces of others, a refusal to harm the life-forces of others and concern for others.

African spiritual understandings

'Concern for others' is an underlying principle of African spirituality (i.e. the 'concept of forces') and community. Community is built up from individuals, but ranked in a hierarchy of reciprocal relationships. The 'concept of forces' places certain responsibilities for others on those who are higher in the hierarchy. For instance, those possessing great forces like ancestors, deities, chiefs and those with power and means. They are expected to augment the life force of those beneath them in the hierarchy. And community has the duty to help or let individuals share in the wealth generated within the groups of which they are integral parts.

Note: These examples and the corresponding citations are taken from the study of Young (2002). For a list of references please refer to this text.

link between the values as a partial cause and enterprise as a result has gained credibility (Landes 1999).

On the other hand, the matrix does not make reference to every normative stance in a tradition, only those that provide a basis for living by the behaviours recommended by the Caux Round Table Principles for Business. As is well known, some traditions contain values inimical to good business behaviour. Take the case of traditional Mexican values, for example. Under the influence of aristocratic Spanish mores, carried to the Americas by domineering conquistadors bent on personal aggrandizement, Mexican business practices have been more concerned with assuring the social status and powers of dominion of its owners than with promoting general economic development. The principles at stake in this system ratify the autonomy of powerful families and subordinate public concerns to their status needs. They are placed in the fortunate position of being able to pass on to others in society the costs of their behaviour in the form of low wages, weak civil institutions, limited public health and educational facilities, pollution of the environment, etc. The head of a family enterprise is better seen as a Don with quasi-feudal rights of seigniorism than as a steward of a social enterprise serving stakeholders.

For the Caux Round Table Principles of Business, a different value scheme than social superiority and one drawn from Catholic social teachings can be found. It is the norm of 'human dignity' that is articulated in several Papal Encyclicals. *Human dignity*, along with *Kyosei*, was one of the formative frameworks of the Principles for Business as they were being drafted in 1993 and 1994 by participants in the Caux Round Table network. 'Human dignity' sets a standard of recognition of the other, subordinating selfish conceits to more communal concerns. As one's human dignity gives one a claim on others, so too does their equivalent moral nature give them a claim to benefit from one's thoughtful solicitude of their needs and point of view. Acting out of concern for human dignity affects leadership and produces virtuous conduct in leaders vis-à-vis customers, employees, owners, investors, suppliers, competitors and communities – the key stakeholders entwined with every business enterprise and leadership action.

In Japan, a traditional estimation of the state of interpersonal security and well-being known to Japanese as *Ninjo* justifies the business practices that support the *Keiretsu* structure of company groups with interlocking financing and boards of directors. Many Japanese, it seems, prefer to subordinate their abilities and individual interests to the demands of the group in order to obtain the benefits of Ninjo psychological well-being that come with fidelity to others in the reciprocal relationships providing Ninjo support.

Japanese companies can accordingly thrive on low levels of equity capital and low profit margins that would cripple companies in European economies and in the United States. Here is another example of how culture drives business behaviours, though in this case not in accordance with the Caux Round Table vision of principled business leadership. The different institutional arrangements for organizing corporate enterprise in Japan and Europe/America produced different accounting standards. Currently, an attempt is underway to narrow the gap between the conceptual categories used in the different business environments. The Accounting Standards Board of Japan agreed to work with the International Accounting Standards Board on convergence between the two approaches. But at the heart of the matter were two very different perspectives on the goal implied by the English word convergence. For the Japanese it meant mutual acceptance of standards that were similar but not necessarily identical. For the international body convergence meant arriving at identical standards. For the Japanese, standards that matched the realities of different business cultures provided the most effective means for presenting business performance in those different environments. 'There is no right or wrong answer', said a Japanese. 'It's like religion, Christianity or Buddhism' (Financial Times 2005).

To support the case for reform in Japan, which would take the form of an evolution away from the Keiretsu company group structure, the Caux Round Table has suggested placing emphasis on a different set of still very Japanese values. First, there is the ethic of Kyosei, a form of interpersonal interdependence that provides an embrace of more outsiders than do the rules of Ninjo. With Kyosei there is more open and acknowledged sharing of concerns with those who only touch one's life for business in less intense ways, such as customers or communities. Under Ninjo arrangements, the circle of those whom we let penetrate our concerns is very small in its social diameter; it embraces only long standing and committed members of the company group, leaving out customers, communities and the generality of others.

As shown in the above matrix, Mahayana Buddhism offers an ethical perspective supporting Kyosei and the Caux Round Table Principles for Business. Similarly, the sincerity sought for in *Shinto* practices subordinates the selfish ego to an open-mindedness that can easily include the interests of others. Shinto and Mahayana teachings, therefore, offer Japanese an ethical platform for innovation of their business culture and corporate institutions.

Lesson number five: the fish rots from the head

Most Caux Round Table participants have run companies and most have been chairman of corporate boards as well. The American participants largely ended their business careers at the top of the typical American corporate hierarchy combining the positions of board chair and chief executive officer. But what all participants agreed upon is the necessity for board leadership.

The board, not the CEO, has the fundamental responsibility to manage and direct the affairs of the corporation. The CEO should support and assist the board and attend to execution of the strategies and policies set by the board. The buck stops with the board, however, when the mission and purpose of the enterprise is at stake. Sadly many corporate boards do not live up to their responsibilities. Many of the American corporate scandals of the late 1990s and opening years of the twenty-first century could have been forestalled or minimized by alert and proactive boards of directors.

The work of setting policy and strategy, of defining mission and choosing priorities as well as clarifying values and principles, determines the culture of a company. Creating a culture for the firm is the executive function of the board. The board, therefore, has the power and the responsibility to create the ethos in which the company will seek to become and remain profitable. The board must find an ethic for the company. If it fails to do so, by default others will create one and implement it, often through manipulative dysfunction (known as *office politics* and acidly displayed in the Dilbert cartoons) and more often to the detriment of owners and employees. An uncommitted, irresponsible and ignorant board raises risks of enterprise collapse and certainly leads to abuse of power within the organization. The proper study of board members is, therefore, a necessary prerequisite and should be in the interest of stakeholders of a corporation. In conclusion, principled business leadership at the board level is imperative for guiding a corporation to successful accomplishment of their business and societal responsibilities and should be the desired norm.

Conclusion

These five lessons: the need for principles; what gets managed, gets accomplished; interests must be addressed; culture counts; and, the fish rots from the head pass on the collective experience of many Caux Round Table participants. Anecdotally many participants demonstrated in their careers reliance on inner convictions, a deep structure of belief, as the source of their leadership potential. Leadership draws on faith for its moral courage and its power of persuasion. Short-term results and immediate gains may serve to manipulate the fear and greed of others, but they have no power to stay the course or inspire the significant advance in technology or business method.

During the American Revolution, in the midst of despair in the Valley Forge winter camp, Thomas Paine (1995) wrote disparagingly of 'summer soldiers and sunshine patriots'. We also have the advice to: 'Make no small plans; they have no power to fire the minds of men'. Leadership needs resources of ethics and virtue from which to outlast the trials and tribulations that come and go with fortune's tides and from which to think greatly. Leaders without a deep sense of conviction risk becoming only temporary managers of circumstance, flotsam and jetsam floating on the waves of life.

Considering the challenges of poverty, HIV/AIDS, environmental destruction, social imbalance between developed and developing world there is a moral obligation to those with wealth and power. The Caux Round Table is convinced that to whom much is given, much is expected. Those business leaders with the ability to make a difference should act with a view, not to their own advantage, but out of concern for those not well served by current economic and political institutions of wealth creation and distribution.

Questions

1   The CRT's moral position is that the business community should play an important role in improving economic and social conditions in the world. What other positions are discussed in the CSR dialogue? What is your position with respect to corporate responsibility? And on what values is your position based?

2   What is the role and sphere of influence of business leaders to contribute to the betterment of economic, social and environmental conditions for people in the world? Why is principled business leadership specifically important at board level?

3   How can the case be made that principled business leadership is not only good for society but also important for business?

4   To what extent can the CRT Principles for Business be applied in different cultural and religious contexts?

5   As said, publishing principles doesn't do much to change the world. What has the CRT done so far to diffuse and implement its principles in the business world? What else could be done? What are your suggestions?

Notes

1   The Caux Round Table *Principles for Business* are outlined in a document consisting of three sections: In the first section which is the *Preamble*, members specify that these principles are intended as a foundation for dialogue and action by leaders in search of business responsibility. In the following two sections the 'General Principles' and the 'Stakeholder Principles' are defined. The following paragraph is an excerpt of the CRT principles. (For full text, see Caux Round Table 1994.)

   The *General Principles* contain the following six principles:

   Principle 1.   The responsibilities of businesses: beyond shareholders toward stakeholders;

   Principle 2.   The Economic and social impact of business: toward Innovation, justice and world community;

Principle 3.   Business behavior: beyond the letter of law toward a spirit of trust;
Principle 4.   Respect for rules;
Principle 5.   Support for multilateral trade;
Principle 6.   Respect for the environment;
Principle 7.   Avoidance of illicit operations.

The Stakeholder Principles define an ethical approach toward different stakeholder groups:

Customers: We believe in treating all customers with dignity, irrespective of whether they purchase our products and services directly from us or otherwise acquire them in the market.
Employees: We believe in the dignity of every employee and in taking employee interests seriously.
Owners/Investors: We believe in honouring the trust our investors place in us.
Suppliers: Our relationship with suppliers and subcontractors must be based on mutual respect.
Competitors: We believe that fair economic competition is one of the basic requirements for increasing the wealth of nations and ultimately for making possible the just distribution of goods and services.
Communities: We believe that as global corporate citizens we can contribute to such forces of reform and human rights as are at work in the communities in which we operate.

2   Additional consideration is underway regarding other traditions such as the Jewish Talmudic learning and practice, the many texts of Hindu learning and insight, the special practices of Eastern Orthodox Christianity and the moral and spiritual traditions of Native Americans and African communities.
3   The descriptions and citations in the table are taken from Young's study (2002), where also the relevant bibliographical information can be found.

Bibiliography

Baukol, R. (2002) 'Corporate Governance and Social Responsibility', paper presented at the Tokyo Stock Exchange, Tokyo, April 2002, Online. Available HTTP: http://www.cauxroundtable.org/BankolJapanPresentation4–19–02.doc (accessed 7 April 2005).

Caux Round Table (1994) *Principles for Business*, Online. Available HTTP: http://www.cauxroundtable.org/documents/Principles%20for%20Business.pdf (accessed 7 April 2005).

Caux Round Table (2005) *Caux Round Table: Principles For Business*, University of Minnesota Human Rights Library. Available HTTP: http://www1.umn.edu/humanrts/instree/cauxrndtbl.htm (accessed 6 April 2005).

Financial Times (2005) 'Accounting Teams Struggle to sing a similar tune', 9 March: 2005: 14

Goodpaster, K.E. (2003) 'Moving from aspiration to action', paper presented at practitioner-scholar pre-conference session of Society for Business Ethics conference, Seattle, July 2003. Online. Available HTTP: http://www.cauxroundtable.org/documents/Kgoodpaster.ppt (accessed 15 April 2005).

Harvey, P. (2000) *An Introduction to Buddhist Ethics: foundations, values and issues*, Cambridge: Cambridge University Press.

Kellerman, B. (2004) *Bad Leadership: what it is, how it happens, why it matters*, Boston, MA: Harvard Business School Press.

Kotter, J.P. (1996) *Leading Change*, Boston, MA: Harvard Business School Press.

Landes, D. (1999) *The Wealth and Poverty of Nations*, New York: Norton.

Maak, T. and Pless, N.M. (2006) 'Responsible leadership: a relational approach', in T. Maak and N.M. Pless (eds) *Responsible Leadership*, London, New York: Routledge.

Pless, N.M. and Schneider, R. (2006) 'Towards developing responsible global leaders: the Ulysses Experience', in T. Maak and N.M. Pless (eds) *Responsible Leadership*, London, New York: Routledge.

Paine, T. (1995) 'The American Crisis', in E. Foner (ed.) *Thomas Paine: collected writings*, New York: Library of America.

Rajavaramuni, P. (1990) 'Foundations of Buddhist social ethic', in Russell F. Sizemore and Donald K. Swearer (eds) *Ethics, Wealth and Salvation: a study in Buddhist social ethics*, Columbia, SC: University of South Carolina Press, 35–43.

Reynolds, F.E, (1990) 'Ethics and wealth in Theravada Buddhism', in Russell F. Sizemore and Donald K. Swearer (eds) *Ethics, Wealth and Salvation: a study in Buddhist social ethics*, Columbia, SC: University of South Carolina Press, 59–76.

Weber, M. (1930) *The Protestant Ethic and the Spirit of Capitalism*, trans. T. Parsons, London: G. Allen and Unwin.

Young, S.B. (2003) *Moral Capitalism: reconciling private interest with the public good*, San Francisco,CA: Berrett-Koehler.

Young, S.B. (2002) *CRT Principles for Business and Great Religious Traditions. Essays on World Religions.* Online. Available HTTP: http://www.cauxroundtable.org/CRTPrinciplesandReligiousTraditions08–03.doc (accessed 7 April 2005).

13 Leadership through social purpose partnering

James E. Austin

Introduction

The complexity and magnitude of socio-economic problems confronting societies throughout the world transcend the capacities of any single sector – business, government or civic. Dealing with them effectively calls for creative collaboration across sectors. Such partnering has begun to emerge and holds significant potential as a powerful organizational modality for contributing to societal well-being. Cross-sectoral collaboration will become a primary transformational vehicle in this century. Creating such alliances requires significant leadership. This chapter will explore and illustrate why and how business leaders and their companies are forging social purpose partnerships.

Why engage in social purpose partnering?

The underlying motivations of businesses to allocate resources for social betterment are varied and multiple. One can conceive of these as falling somewhere on a spectrum with altruism at one end and utilitarianism at the other (Austin *et al.* 2004). The former is the desire to help others without any self-gain while the latter is helping others with the expectation of also generating benefits to oneself. There are examples at both extremes but most seem to fall in between as blends of charity and self-interest.

One can reasonably ask, do motives matter? Those arguing yes may contend that charity should be purely altruistic and that it is immoral to benefit from it, citing norms present in most religions' credos. Those arguing no may assert that what really counts is that actions produce social benefits for others regardless of the benefactor's motives or benefits it received. Another useful window onto this debate is the concept of sustainability, in the sense of how durable are the actions producing the benefits for society. What will make businesses' engagement in social purpose undertakings more sustainable? Actions rooted deeply in a leader's or a company's core values may lead them to continue to engage in social activity in spite of not accruing self-gain or even incurring significant economic burden because 'it is the right thing to do'. However, if these activities are perceived as just being 'nice things to do' but not critical to the sustainability of the business, they become readily disposable. In contrast, if the social investments are seen as simultaneously producing significant practical or strategic benefits for the company, then they will more likely be sustained even when a company might encounter financial difficulties. Experiences reveal that there are significant win–win engagement opportunities, which is what we shall explore in this paper.

But the question posed above was not just why companies should engage in social betterment, but also why do it by partnering with others. Certainly companies can, should and do carry out many actions and activities individually that are socially beneficial. Partnering is an added form that enables companies to accomplish more than they can alone. Civic groups, variously called non-profit, non-governmental or civil society organizations, are one important set of partners and governmental entities are the other. Entities from each of the three sectors possess distinctive resources and competencies that are complementary and all relevant to the solution of many societal problems. Collaboration across these sectors can capture the synergies of resource complementarity, generate economies of scale and scope, and create innovative solutions to tenacious social problems. Cross-sector collaboration is not new, but distinct, more robust forms are emerging.

Emerging partnering paradigms

Corporations have traditionally been charitable benefactors of non-profit organizations. Corporate giving in the United States was over $13.4 billion in 2003 (AAFRC 2004). What is significant, however, are the changes in how companies are approaching their relations with the non-profits. There appears to be a collaboration continuum encompassing three different types of relationships or stages, beginning with the traditional *philanthropic* stage in which the company is the benefactor and the non-profit the grateful beneficiary of a gift. In oversimplified terms, it tends to be a relatively passive cheque writing relationship of peripheral strategic importance to the business, but often quite valuable to the non-profit recipients. Over the past decade many companies have moved into a second *transactional* stage relationship with the non-profits, which involves an increased and two-way value flow using both organizations' key people and resources beyond money and focused on clearly defined activities or projects. Cause-related marketing, event sponsorships and employee volunteer programs are examples of this type of relationship, which is more engaging and more significant to the partnering organizations. A smaller but growing number of firms have evolved their relationship into an *integrative* stage, in which the partners' missions, strategies and values become aligned in strategically important ways. The collaboration generates significantly greater value for the partners and society. Figure 13.1 depicts the characteristics of the partnering relationships across the collaboration continuum.

While the foregoing was derived from studies of partnerships between businesses and non-profits, many aspects appear to also hold for collaborations between businesses and governments. Cross-sector partnerships become stronger the closer their missions, values and strategy are aligned with the collaboration. Leaders are value generators and social purpose partnerships are all about creating value for the collaborators and for society. Value creation is greater when partners deploy their core competencies and combine them in innovative and synergistic ways. We will now provide examples of collaborations that illustrate different dimensions and degrees of alignment and value generation.

Values-driven collaborations

A survey by the author of 400 *Fortune 500* firms revealed that about one-third have embedded in their mission statements or credos values aimed explicitly at contributing to the social betterment of society. For some firms, these often altruistic values are primary drivers of their collaborations.

HEB, one of the leading supermarket chains in the US is owned by the Butts family (Lozano *et al.* 2003). It grew from a single store in Texas to a major retailing force in the south-west. The founders have always believed in giving back to the communities that they serve. These values have materialized in the form of partnerships with local food banks. Instead of selling the food products that have been cosmetically damaged in the

	Stage I	Stage II	Stage III
Nature of relationship	Philanthropic ———→	Transitional ———→	Integrative
Level of engagement	*Low*	——————————→	*High*
Importance to mission	*Peripheral*	——————————→	*Central*
Magnitude of resources	*Small*	——————————→	*Big*
Scope of activities	*Narrow*	——————————→	*Broad*
Interaction level	*Infrequent*	——————————→	*Intensive*
Trust	*Modest*	——————————→	*Deep*
Managerial complexity	*Simple*	——————————→	*Complex*
Strategic value	*Minor*	——————————→	*Major*

Figure 13.1 The collaboration continuum

Source: adapted from Austin 2000: 35.

secondary market, HEB donates these. Whenever the company opens a store in a new community it also forms an alliance with the local food bank, so when it went international by setting up a supermarket in Monterrey, Mexico, it established a partnership with the Monterrey Food Bank run by Caritas. This evolved beyond a simple philanthropic relationship involving the donation of merchandise. The company helped the Bank open new warehousing facilities and capture the knowhow from HEB's partnerships with US food banks. Over time, the Monterrey Food Bank in turn helped HEB to improve upon its food logistics system and to open food banks in other Mexican cities where the company had opened new stores. They found additional joint social purpose activities that involved many employees from both entities. The organizations became closely linked and an HEB manager joined the board of the Monterrey Food Bank. While HEB stressed that this engagement was not done as a way to increase sales, the association did create a positive reputation that was helpful to the company in attracting talent away from competitor supermarkets and in dealing with government authorities issuing store location permits.

At the other end of the continent in Argentina, the country's largest newspaper *La Nación* formulated a set core values that included promoting *solidarity* among the citizenry to foster mutual assistance for those in need (Berger *et al.* 2003). This value led it into a partnership with a social entrepreneur who had created a 'Solidarity Network' that identified families in need and also people willing to help. The collaboration with *La Nación* converted these shared values into a jointly produced section of the newspaper that described people's needs as well as offers of help that helped link philanthropic supply and demand, in effect creating a solidarity marketplace. This was only possible by fusing the core competencies of the company (publishing) and the non-profit (research on philanthropic needs and supporters). The activity was very satisfying for the company's employees and gave concrete meaning to the firm's value statement. While the positive reception by readers of this new section of the newspaper created the opportunity for the company to differentiate itself and create a competitive advantage, the firm's altruistic motivations led it to in fact foster the adoption of the approach by other newspapers.

Merck, one of the world's leading pharmaceutical companies, developed in the 1980s a drug, Mectizan, that could contribute greatly to the alleviation of river blindness, an affliction that caused enormous suffering in large parts of Africa (Austin *et al.* 2001a). After finishing the human trials that confirmed that Mectizan was far superior to any other existing treatment, the company discovered that there was no one to pay for it. The ultimate consumers were too poor and international aid agencies indicated that they did not have the resources to subsidize the operation. In effect, there was market failure. The need existed but the market forces to meet it did not. CEO and Chairman Roy Vagelos stated, 'Distribution to the people in need was the final responsibility of our company', thus rooting the decision in corporate values. By 2002, the Mectizan donation programme was reaching 25 million people annually. Vagelos' successor Raymond Gilmartin elaborated further on the company's approach:

> George W. Merck, the son of our founder ... and the architect of the modern-day Merck (stated), 'Medicine is for the people, it is not for the profits'. That may sound surprising for the chief executive of a private-sector company to say – and cynics may be sceptical. But I'll tell you what he said next: 'The profits follow, and if we have remembered that, they have never failed to appear. The better we have remembered it, the larger they have been.' He went on to say that 'we cannot rest until the way has been found, with our help, to bring our finest achievements to everyone'. His vision helped firmly establish Merck tradition and values – a commitment to making medicines available without immediate concern for profits.
>
> (Remarks by Raymond V. Gilmartin to the
> Committee for Economic Development,
> New York, Helmsley Hotel, 16 October, 2000)

Although Merck stepped forward to produce and donate the drug free in increasingly higher quantities, it could not carry out the programme alone. It needed to partner non-profit organizations and governments in the recipient countries that took charge of the in-country logistics and administration of the treatment, activities in which Merck did not have competence. The partnering approach continued when Merck decided to address the analogous but even larger problem of AIDS in Africa (Austin *et al.* 2001b). It joined forces with the Gates Foundation with each donating $50 million plus retroviral drugs in partnership with the government of Botswana, where a third of the adult population is afflicted with the disease. In addition to the money and retroviral drugs, the company is also providing its management expertise in working with the government, multilateral agencies, NGOs and companies to create an effective nationwide system of treatment and prevention. The project, begun in 2000, was deemed to be a five-year pilot. Given its significant progress, Merck, Gates and the Government of Botswana agreed to extend the project for another five years. The company's actions have been values-driven and they believe that living up to those values gives the company an advantage in recruiting top talent.

Similarly, another values-driven corporation is Timberland, the boot and outdoor apparel company (Austin and Elias 1996, Austin and Leonard 2004). Under the mantra of 'Boots, Brand, Beliefs', it holds as a core value the belief that the company and its employees should make a positive difference in their communities. Its CEO, Jeffrey Swartz, considers community service to be an integral part of the company's strategy. Timberland provides employees with 40 hours of paid time per year to engage in community activities. It has brought this value to life by partnering with the non-profit City Year, which is dedicated to promoting community service through its cadres of youth corps members. While this relationship started out as traditional philanthropy with the donation of some boots for the City Year Corps Members, it has developed into a strategic alliance permeating all aspects of the company's operations. The company is similarly deeply integrated into City Year, providing the Corps Members' entire uniform, helping the organization scale up nationally and to obtain other corporate partners, and having the company's CEO serve as chairman of the City Year board. This very successful company does not consider this partnership to be philanthropy or cause-related marketing. Rather, the corporate leaders see it as an investment in a relationship that is integral to its model of attracting, motivating, developing and retaining highly committed employees who do not have to separate who they are outside and inside of work.

Strategic alignment and fusing core competences

Whereas the foregoing examples emphasized core values as the key energizer of the alliances, additional power comes when the strategies of the partners become aligned and they find ways to combine their core competencies to fuel that strategic alignment (Porter and Kramer 2002). Starbucks, the global leader in served coffee, certainly is a values-driven company and that has led it into several alliances with non-profits (Austin and Reavis 2002). One of these that has taken on extra power because of strong strategy fit is the collaboration with Conservation International (CI), a leading environmental NGO. Environmental preservation is one of Starbucks' stated values, so it was receptive to CI's proposal to join forces in southern Mexico to promote shade grown coffee cultivation techniques that would provide richer habitat and help protect an endangered rainforest biosphere reserve. Starbucks could have simply made a donation to CI to support their conservation work, but instead the company saw a strategic alignment between environmental preservation and the creation of a sustainable coffee supply system. Environmental degradation and plummeting world coffee prices were causing producers to stop harvesting and caring for their coffee cultivations. This posed a structural threat to the sustainability of Starbucks' global strategy of rapid expansion (opening three new stores every day).

Consequently, CI combined its expertise in training small producers in environmental and quality control techniques and management of farmer cooperatives with Starbucks' market knowledge and purchasing and distribution capabilities to develop a new supplier system for shade grown organic coffee. This resulted in a successful addition to Starbucks' product line, higher incomes for the farmers and greater preservation of the biosphere reserve. It also lead to the creation by Starbucks and a set of environmental non-profits of an entirely new set of procurement standards aimed at promoting and incentivizing a supplier system that was economically, environmentally and socially sustainable. Starbucks was not keeping this as its proprietary system but rather promoting its adoption as an industry standard. Starbucks' CEO Orin Smith expressed their philosophy this way: 'Aligning self-interest to social responsibility is the most powerful way to sustaining a company's success.'

The search for strategic sustainability gave birth to another seemingly incongruous partnership between two organizations, both of whom had just experienced changes in CEOs who provided fresh looks at their previous strategies (Austin 2000). The Nature Conservancy (TNC), one of the leading environmental conservationists, concluded that its strategy of buying land was not a sustainable approach to preserving biodiversity because it would never have sufficient resources to buy enough land, given that ecosystems did not recognize property lines. Georgia-Pacific (GP), one of the major forest products companies, concluded that its strategy of fending off environmentalists and regulators was not sustainable, especially given the growing green preferences of consumers. TNC decided it needed to figure out how to deal with commercially used natural resources, and GP decided it needed to figure out how to become a good environmental steward. From these strategy reformulations emerged the collaboration opportunity. They entered into dialogue and agreed to manage jointly a GP forest property to enable timber extraction in environmentally acceptable ways. They discovered that combining TNC's expertise in environmental science with GP's expertise in forestry created new and more effective ways for environmental stewardship of commercially worked timber land.

Brazil's leading cosmetics firm, Natura, had strong values about contributing to community and preserving the environment and had several activities to promote both (Fischer and Casado 2003). However, a new business idea created strategic centrality. They decided to create a new product line entirely derived from natural ingredients found in indigenous communities in the country's remote rainforest areas. To make this idea a reality the company needed to create alliances with the communities, with an ingredient processor, and with an NGO that would certify that the operation with the community was economically, environmentally and socially beneficial. The new Ekos product line has proven very successful and beneficial to all of the parties involved. In this case the collaboration is clearly an integrative relationship where the business and social purposes and strategies are congruent and all partners are combining their core competencies.

A similar congruency was manifested in the alliance between the Peruvian eco-tourism company Rain Forest Expeditions and an indigenous community in a rainforest preserve (Revilla and Peres 2003). The company and the community shared common goals of environmental preservation and complementary assets: the company had management skills and access to potential eco-tourists; the community owned the preserve and knew it intimately. They created a joint venture, Posada Amazonas that built lodges and ran eco-tours. The company created a 50–50 joint venture and agreed to train the local community with the goal of their developing the skills to self-manage and fully own the operation in the future. This joint ownership differentiated the company from other eco-tourism firms and gave it a competitive advantage in attracting clients. The company's CEO stated, 'Corporate Social Responsibility is my competitive advantage'.

Leadership challenges of social purpose partnering

While the foregoing examples reveal the richness of social purpose partnering, crafting such strategic alliances is enormously challenging for business leaders. Cross-sector collaborations confront multiple barriers. Overcoming them requires various leadership capacities.

Organizational culture

Businesses, non-profits and government entities generally have very different organizational cultures. Their language, decision making processes, time frames, governance systems, management styles and operating procedures are often quite distinct. A business leader needs to have cultural openness, flexibility, empathy and patience to interact effectively with leaders from the social or public sectors. These are akin to the capabilities one needs to operate successfully in a foreign country.

Alignment

Alliances are most powerful when partners' missions, values and strategies are closely aligned, but achieving this across sectors is relatively new terrain. It requires leaders to broaden their mindsets as to corporate purpose and have a more robust definition of stakeholders that encompasses the broader community with its non-profit and governmental institutions. These groups need to be seen as constituencies to be benefited but also as resource contributors to the company's success.

Value generation

Traditionally, businesses have tended to look at interactions with non-profits or government organizations as costs. Leaders need to make a paradigm shift and view these engagements as investments that are sources of value generation, social and economic. This first requires the leader's rethinking corporate philanthropy so as to move it from simply doling out cash to good causes to creating a strategic focus that is integrated into and contributes importantly to the overall corporate strategy. Next, it requires a fresh and broader look at how the company can mobilize its core competencies and assets – skills, infrastructure, technology, networks, reputation, client base, etc. – to generate social value and economic value simultaneously. In this search for new value generators, the leader should seek out complementary sets of competencies from potential or existing non-profit or public sector partners.

Capabilities

One of the impediments to moving to a higher level of joint value creation is the absence of adequate capabilities of either the company or the non-profit to undertake powerful social investments collaboratively. Business leaders must be willing to ratchet up their personnel and organizational capacity to undertake a new level of activity. They are generally more able to do this than their potential non-profit or public partners. Consequently, it may be necessary for the business to also invest in strengthening the partner institution so that it can deliver fully on the value proposition of the collaboration.

Control

By definition, collaboration implies ceding some degree of control. Collaborative leaders have to be willing to share power. In business alliances this often involves arrangements between near equals; there is a certain built-in balance of power. In cross-sector collaborations, this balance is often missing, with the business often having a much larger economic and organizational resource base. Consequently, business leaders need to have a sensitivity to exercising undue influence made possible by this imbalance.

Communication

Poor communication often can hinder the full development of a collaboration. As previously stated, a business leader first needs to have an understanding of the partner's organizational culture and language. Frequency and clarity of communication among the partners is also important. One business proceeded to invest a great deal of time and resources planning an event that they would sponsor for their non-profit partner, only to find out subsequently that such an event would actually not be very helpful. Communicating intentions and listening to needs prior to taking action is highly desirable. A leader's communication also plays a vital signalling role within the company. The leader's statements (and actions) about the importance of a cross-sector collaboration create an authorizing environment that unleashes the personnel's energies and efforts.

Building strategic collaborations across sectors is clearly a daunting task fraught with risks and complications. Leaders need to have the courage to venture into these less charted waters, and they are often propelled forward by a vision of these alliances being powerful transformers.

Collaborations as a transformative force

Great leaders make a difference in the world, and collaborations are powerful vehicles for business to realize its full potential as a transformative force. Strategic cross-sector collaborations create multiple transformations. The partners themselves are transformed because the interactions of people and resources enrich each other in a multitude of ways, including lateral learning, touching their institutional values and attitudes and strengthening their capabilities so as to achieve more effectively their respective missions. Strategic partners indelibly imprint one another. Collaboration tends to breed more collaboration, not only with the same partners but with others. Learning how to partner and seeing the benefits from it build confidence to seek out other opportunities. Furthermore, there is a demonstration effect that attracts previous non-cooperators into the collaboration arena. Society is transformed not only by the positive effects on the many problems being addressed by partners combining their core competencies in innovative ways, but also by the additional social capital formed by distinct actors creating deep new relationships. Transformative cooperation calls for structural change. Leadership through cross-sector collaborations are redrawing the boundaries and creating new institutional configurations for achieving that change.

Questions

Social purpose partnering is a relatively new dimension of leadership. The following questions are offered for reflection by leaders as they move forward in the collaboration journey:

1   Have I integrated the social dimension into my company's strategy as a full contributor to our success?
2   Are my core competencies being fully utilized to generate social value synergistically with economic value?
3   What does my current collaboration portfolio look like and what should it become to capture the full benefits of social purpose partnerships?
4   What do I have to strengthen personally and organizationally to become a world class cross-sector collaborator?
5   How do I want my collaborations to transform the world?

Bibliography

AAFRC American Association of Fundraising Counsel (2004) *Giving USA 2004*, annual report on philanthropy, Bloomington, IN. Available HTTP: http://www.aafrc.org (accessed 14 April 2005).

Austin, J.E. (2000) *The Collaboration Challenge*, San Francisco, CA: Jossey-Bass.

Austin, J.E. and Elias, J. (1996) *Timberland and Community Involvement*, Harvard Business School Case, 796–156, 12 May, Boston, MA: Harvard Business School.

Austin, J.E. and Leonard, H.B. (2004) *Timberland: Commerce and Justice*, Harvard Business School Case, 305–002, 19 July, Boston, MA: Harvard Business School.

Austin, J.E. and Reavis, C. (2002) *Starbucks and Conservation International*, Harvard Business School Case, 303–055, 2 October, Boston, MA: Harvard Business School.

Austin, J.E., Barrett, D. and Weber, J.B. (2001a) *Merck Global Health Initiatives (A)*, Harvard Business School Case, 301–088, 26 January, Boston, MA: Harvard Business School.

Austin, J.E., Barrett, D. and Weber, J.B. (2001b) *Merck Global Health Initiatives (B): Botswana*, Harvard Business School Case, 301–089, 26 January, Boston, MA: Harvard Business School.

Austin, J.E., Reficco, E. and Berger, G. (2004) *Social Partnering in Latin America*, Cambridge, MA: Harvard University Press.

Berger, G., Roitter, M. and Rena, C. (2003) *La Nación Newspaper and the Red Solidaria*, Harvard Business School Cases, SKE-012, 24 July, Boston, MA: Harvard Business School.

Fischer, R.M. and Casado, T. (2003) *Natura Ekos: From the Forest to Cajamar*, Harvard Business School Case, SKE-016, 29 July, Boston, MA: Harvard Business School.

Lozano, G., Romero, C. and Serrano, L. (2003) *HEB International Supermarkets and the Banco de Alimentos de Caritas de Monterrey*, Harvard Business School Case, SKE-004, 25 February, Boston, MA: Harvard Business School.

Porter, M.E. and Kramer, M.R. (2002) 'The competitive advantage of corporate philanthropy', *Harvard Business Review*, 80(12): 56–69.

Revilla, J. and Perez, F. (2003) *Posada Amazonas*, Harvard Business School Case, SK002, 17 July, Boston, MA: Harvard Business School.

14 Towards developing responsible global leaders

The Ulysses experience

Nicola M. Pless and Ralf Schneider

Introduction

The ability to develop a next generation of leaders capable and willing to take on the complex challenges of global business in an emerging global stakeholder society has become a key concern for forward-looking companies. The recent crashes of once-respected global players like Enron, WorldCom, Parmalat and other companies have highlighted the importance of good business conduct and put responsible leadership and corporate governance firmly on the business agenda. What business can learn from these examples is that, in order to avoid those fatal events and create instead sustainable businesses for the future, we need to go beyond traditional leadership models, both on the strategic as well as normative level. In fact, this means that we need leaders who think and act with integrity, with responsibility and with foresight. Some corporations have already started to move into the direction of a new leadership model and reshape the way in which they groom their future leaders.

In this chapter, we present the unique approach of Pricewaterhouse-Coopers (PwC),[1] a leading global professional services organization, towards developing their future leaders in the so-called Ulysses programme. PwC as an organization acknowledges and stresses the need for values and trust in business (DiPiazza and Eccles 2002). Ulysses translates this thinking into a development journey that attempts to support high potential partners to develop into future leaders with a global and responsible mindset.

We start by framing the context of the organization and outlining the leadership challenges that the firm has identified. Against this background we introduce the programme by first showing how its objectives are linked to the firm's long-term leadership objectives; second, by presenting the learning philosophy as a developmental frame of experiential learning; and third, by outlining the phases of the programme. The specific feature of the programme are the aid projects with cross-sector partners in developing countries. We show that these projects create an action learning context of *business in society*, that mirrors the reality of global leadership challenges.

Finally, we illuminate some of the success factors for developing future leaders through social projects in cross-sector partnerships.

The context of the organization and the leadership challenges

PricewaterhouseCoopers is the world's largest professional services firm. It was created in 1998 from a worldwide merger of two well-known firms (Price Waterhouse and Coopers and Lybrand), each of them with historical roots going back some 150 years. As a knowledge-based firm it provides industry-focused assurance, tax and advisory services for public and private sector clients.

Leading within network structures: The structure of the firm mirrors the *complexity* of the global business environment within which it operates and the diversity of clients and markets it serves. PwC is a global network of local member firms (so-called country practices) located in 144 countries with offices in 769 cities. The firm's structure is that of a three-dimensional matrix consisting of territories and regions, lines of services (assurance, tax and advisory services) and industries (Consumer and Industrial Products and Services, Financial Services and Technology, InfoComm, and Entertainment). Each of the national practices operates as a legally and economically autonomous partnership. These partnerships are all linked together as member firms of the PwC network. This creates an organization of considerable complexity requiring leaders to keep a global perspective (helicopter view) while operating within a networked environment characterized by a high degree of decentralization. Within such structures the traditional top down management approach fails. It needs to be replaced by a horizontal leadership style which is based on relationships and trust, connecting people and thinking across boundaries. The mentality of *power over* subordinates is replaced by *power through* others requiring leaders to mobilize people and release energy through purpose and meaning, good reasoning and addressing the collective imagination.

Leading a diverse workforce: PwC employs more than 122,000 people who work in 144 countries creating a melting pot of talents, cultures, nationalities, styles and professional backgrounds. Its challenge is to integrate people with such diverse backgrounds across organizational boundaries, countries and cultures, to create an organizational environment where people feel respected, recognized and heard; where they can grow and evolve to their full potential and where they can operate effectively in global teams. A 'culture of inclusion' (Pless and Maak 2004: 129) based on solid moral grounds provides not only a fertile basis for connecting and unleashing the wealth of knowledge, experience and potential for creativity inherent in a diverse workforce; it also contributes to the identification of people from different backgrounds with the firm (pride in being part of a global family), which helps retain valued employees and in turn fosters the delivery of innovative products and solutions to clients.

Leading in a stakeholder environment: PwC leaders know that an organization's licence to operate stems from society and that such a licence depends on a business's ability to build public trust (DiPiazza and Eccles 2002) – not only with the business and financial communities, but with society at large. In light of the scandals that have shaken the global business world over past years, leadership at PwC feels assured of its mission to build public trust and enhance value for clients and their stakeholders by setting a standard for business and leading the profession. Doing so does not just mean providing quality service of the highest professional standards, it also requires 'assessing the impact of decisions on all parties over the short and long term' and 'considering the ethical dimensions of our actions' (PwC 2004: 9). The understanding is that trust is based on improved 'relationships built on quality and integrity' (PwC 2003: 5) both in the organization and towards external stakeholders. It is also assumed that this can be achieved by connecting people internally and externally and combining business excellence ('enhance value for clients and their stakeholders', PwC 2003: 5) and exemplary business conduct ('set a standard for business and lead the profession', PwC 2003: 5) with corporate citizen engagement (connect 'with the communities where we live and work', PwC 2003: 3). This of course requires current and future leaders to understand the changing role of business in society and the demands this places on them. It requires them to redefine the way they look at their role and responsibility as business leaders – to act with perspective, empathy, integrity and responsibility, to build and sustain relationships with different stakeholders and to cope competently with dilemmas and conflicts.

The Ulysses programme emerged as an early response to these challenges and the ambition to find concrete answers to three related questions:

- What is the leadership model that will help identify and develop the leaders needed to succeed in a networked knowledge environment and a global stakeholder society?
- How can these leaders become a conduit to reconcile and harness the richness of diversity across a global knowledge network and lead it to its full potential?
- How can organizational talent development contribute to transform public trust into a long-term competitive advantage by developing responsible leaders who think and act in a broader, connected way?

The Ulysses journey started as a grassroots initiative in late 1999, when a small group of PwC visionaries came together and invented Ulysses as a quest for finding answers to these questions by experimenting with new ways of learning. Supported by top management, the first programme was developed in late 2000 and run as a pilot in the summer of 2001. It soon became clear that Ulysses had the potential to develop qualities required of the firm's future leaders – qualities of being able to strive in a complex, global, diverse and connected environment. As such, it could act as a catalyst to realize some of PwC's strategic anchors of its business, namely to connect people and thinking, to foster and leverage diversity, to be engaged in the community, to live a more responsible and sustainable business model and to build public trust (DiPiazza and Eccles 2002). Since then Ulysses has become a cornerstone of PwC's Key Talent Programmes.

Ulysses: a global leadership development programme for responsibility

A core assumption underlying the Ulysses programme is that it will contribute to the better understanding and tackling of the global challenges that PwC as an organization faces, which in turn determine the roles and relationships of the business in society. It is assumed that the future performance of the organization will be determined by principled and values-conscious actions starting with future leaders that contribute to a high-integrity culture. Hence, there is a perceived need for leaders who act with integrity, who are able to build sustainable and flourishing relationships with different stakeholders (subordinates, peers, clients etc.) and contribute to PwC's sustainable business success by cultivating a high performance and high diversity culture that, respectively, enables innovative service solutions and shapes good corporate citizenship. Therefore, the leadership development programme is built around the following strategic dimensions: diversity, sustainability and leadership.

In order to prepare the next generation of global leaders for the challenges of the future, Ulysses targets high potential partners at PricewaterhouseCoopers, who have been identified by their territories to take on senior leadership responsibilities at national and international level within the next five to ten years. The programme is designed as a three-month full-time programme, where participants attend a one-week residential module, take part in a five-month coaching process and a ten-week project assignment. They are sent in multicultural teams of three to four people to developing countries. There they work with social entrepreneurs, non-governmental and international organizations on aid projects such as capacity building in Moldova, landmine mitigation in Eritrea, strengthening coordination in the fight against HIV/AIDS in Uganda or child help line support in India, to name but a few. While the project partners profit from the business acumen of PwC professionals, participants on the other hand receive a unique developmental opportunity which not only helps them to grow personally, but also to build a strong peer network among current and future leaders. Every year, 20–25 participants have the opportunity to participate in the programme. While the absolute number of participants is still relatively small, the systemic effect of Ulysses on the organization is already observable and reflected in numerous community actions driven by former programme participants. In fact, the programme's intention is not big numbers, but to initiate sustainable change for innovation, high performance and responsible business by creating a *butterfly-effect* in the organization, through leadership development as a form of systemic intervention.

Functions and objectives of the Ulysses programme

Ulysses as a leadership development programme has different functions. First, it has a *personal development function* focused on self-awareness and self-development with respect to intra- and interpersonal leadership skills (e.g. coaching) and values (e.g. respect, integrity). Second, it has an *integration function*: the programme brings together people from different parts in the world and creates a global network based on shared experiences and learning; it initiates an ongoing dialogue among leaders on corporate values and a shared vision in a connected stakeholder environment. And third, it has a *strategic function* by providing a context to experience and anticipate developments in the future and translating them into shared commitment for sustainable change. These functions are closely related to the programme's objectives, which are tightly linked to the firm's vision, mission and strategy as we will see in the following.

Connecting leaders

PwC is a global network of local practices requiring ongoing integration work. An integrative goal of Ulysses is to connect current and future leaders across borders of businesses, countries and cultures and to build a network among them. Therefore, the programme brings together a diverse group of participants who have three things in common: their affiliation with PwC, their belonging to a group of potential future leaders as well as a deep learning experience that connects their thinking, their feeling and their acting as future leaders across the organization. The programme also connects these potential leaders with the current global leadership team, thus fostering exchange and connection between the leadership generations.

Coping with complexity

Working in a global and complex environment, interacting with multiple stakeholders with different values, interests and demands requires leaders who are able to cope with complexity, neutralize tension, keep perspective and are able to give guidance also under uncertainty. Consequently, one of the Ulysses learning goals is to prepare leaders to guide the firm in a global world of ambiguity and tension between diverse interests and stakeholder groups.

Leveraging organizational diversity

Despite the fact that PwC is a multicultural organization it is recognized that the firm has not yet been leveraging its global presence and composition to its full potential. Thus, a crucial learning goal is to further develop interpersonal and intercultural competence of participants (by working in multicultural groups) that help them better work in and more effectively lead multicultural teams thereby unleashing their inherent potential for innovation and creativity.

Developing a values-based leadership understanding

Guiding and retaining highly intelligent knowledge workers is rarely achieved through *command and control*. Instead it requires from leaders a different set of qualities like, for instance, the ability to connect to a diversity of followers; to influence them without using authority but through acquiring their commitment and trust; to help them achieve objectives by empowering and coaching them and to help them grow; and ultimately to create and cultivate an organizational environment where people feel recognized, respected and heard regardless of nationality, gender, age, etc. They also need to be moral leaders: preserving the values of the organization, leading with integrity and by example, being trustworthy and accountable, knowing what is right and what is wrong, applying it in decision making situations and passing it on to followers, and also being able to cope with ethical dilemma situations and finding a proper solution. Hence, a further objective of the programme is to help participants rethink leadership and develop a more values-based, reflective, balanced and people-oriented approach that considers the impact of action on the self and others.

Developing a corporate citizen mindset

As said, leadership recognizes the responsibilities of business in society and understands business excellence, exemplary business conduct and corporate citizenship engagement as an important approach to build public trust. On that ground, the programme firstly aspires to raise awareness among the participants for the challenges in the global world, like poverty, environmental pollution and human disease. Secondly it aims to develop an understanding for the responsibilities of business leaders in society. Thirdly it strives to foster community engagement through experiential learning in cross-sector partnerships as well as stakeholder dialogue as an active approach towards responsible leadership and sustainable business.

The learning philosophy

The Ulysses programme is designed as an experiential action learning opportunity for future leaders based on international project assignments. What distinguishes these assignments from traditional ones is, first, the fact that participants work in developing countries with cross-sector partners and, second, the use of a developmental framework in which the assignments are embedded, combining challenging projects with individual assessment and support throughout the programme. In fact, the Center for Creative Leadership considers assessment, challenge and support as crucial elements for effective leadership development experiences (Van Velsor *et al.* 1998). Assessment can be understood as the starting point that tells participants where they currently stand: what their current strengths and developmental areas are, what their ideal self-image of a good leader might be and how to develop in that direction. Challenge is a feature of the developmental experience, which provides a chance to experiment, to practise and to grow while working with others and being exposed to different perspectives and unfamiliar settings. Jay Conger and Beth Benjamin (1999) stress that job experiences containing significant challenges, often adverse ones, are fertile ground for leadership development with the potential to open up a whole new learning universe for current and future leaders. As we will see below, the project assignments selected for the Ulysses journey have the quality to stretch and challenge people. Challenging experiences are important to trigger learning by forcing people out of their comfort zone and stimulating them to find ways to adapt to new situations, to develop interpersonal and intercultural skills, to understand different viewpoints and see things from different angles, to acquire new insights and broaden their perspectives.

The programme also recognizes that it is crucial to keep the balance and not over-stretch its participants, which would hinder new learning. Therefore, support is an indispensable element in the development process. It involves helping people cope with the struggle and pain of developing and bear the weight of the experience. Support is needed 'to help them maintain a positive view of themselves as people capable of dealing with challenges, who can learn and grow, who are worthy and valuable. Seeing that others place a positive value on their efforts to change and grow is a key factor for people to stay on course with development goals' (Van Velsor *et al.* 1998: 15).

Executive coaching is a form of learning support that is provided in the Ulysses programme to help and enable participants in their psychological development on the individual as well as the team level. The coaching approach applied makes use of various models, such as Heron's six category intervention model (Heron 2001), which triggers reflection and 'shift' in participants. According to the executive coaches Lisa Garvey-Williams and Hermann Fischer, the idea is to create a holistic coaching experience stimulating self-reflection on the cognitive and spiritual level (head and mind), developing awareness for one's own and others' emotions and feelings (heart) and the ability to transfer this understanding into behavioural change (hand). Ultimately the objective is, as Lisa Garvey-Williams points out, 'to help participants to become excellent coaches enabling themselves and others to reach a new level of potential'.

Another form of support for transforming experience into learning and in fact complementing the coaching process is action research (AR). The action researchers provide learning interventions during the residential modules and conduct narrative interviews throughout the programme starting in the preparation phase and continuing to the networking phase. They facilitate a systematic and appreciative dialogue on the intellectual and normative level along the three learning dimensions – diversity, sustainability and leadership, both on the individual and the team level.

Apart from assessment, challenge and support the Ulysses philosophy promotes learning through dialogue. Therefore, a dialogue methodology called 'dialogarchitecture' (Frank 2004) is an integral and integrating part of the programme throughout its phases. It provides a visual frame for dialogue connecting people, content and experiences via visual images. The dialogarchitect® Hans-Jürgen Frank creates a visual space by translating verbal contributions of plenary discussions, team coaching sessions as well as facilitators' contributions into shared images, which appear on storyboards capturing a profound part of the Ulysses journey. These storyboards are used as a shared communicative surface and programme memory, which not only allow participants to go back to, recapitulate and reflect on former presentations, sessions and discussions, but also to identify shared patterns of learning. Furthermore, it helps facilitate an ongoing learning dialogue throughout the programme and to foster storytelling based on key images (for examples of such images see www.dialogarchitect.com).

The programme phases

Ulysses consists of five integrative development phases – selection, preparation, field assignment, debriefing and networking, in which assessment, challenge, support and dialogue are thoroughly balanced and present throughout.

Selection phase

In the first *selection phase*, the PwC country organizations identify high potential future leaders for participation in the programme. Each country can usually send only one person into the programme per year. The identification process is decentralized and conducted in the respective country. Therefore, different identification processes are used: some countries shortlist potential participants and then select them via interviews, other countries have an open application process and select the participant via assessment centres. Regardless of the selection process, the final candidate is nominated by senior management.

Preparation phase

In the second *preparation phase*, selected participants are prepared to embark on the journey. At this stage, they are individually briefed on the programme by the programme managers, they receive instructions to collect their 360 degree feedback data from different feedback givers (e.g. supervisors, peers in the workplace, employees, customers, etc.) and conduct a first conference call with their coach. Then participants come together from all over the world to meet for the first time physically in the foundation week. The purpose of this week is to prepare participants for a holistic learning experience (head, hand and heart) on the individual, interpersonal and group level.

On the *individual level*, participants work with their coaches on their 360 degree assessment data that gives them an understanding of where they currently stand as leader (strengths and development needs). With the action researchers they explore their underlying, often hidden values base as individuals and as leaders through narrative dialogue. Coaching and action research together stimulate self-reflection and self-evaluation on the emotional and normative level. This is of utmost importance, because people with lack of self-awareness can jeopardize multicultural team projects by contributing to sub-optimal individual and group performance, by creating increased stress and anxiety in others and hindering the emergence of a productive team environment (Day 2001, Dotlich and Noel 1998). In the coaching process the assessment data is used to define with the coachee the learning objectives, to work on the development plan and to start their personal leadership story. On a daily basis participants also receive an introduction into yoga and meditation. Lisa Garvey-Williams, who is also a yoga instructor, stresses that:

> through the yoga and meditation experience, which is evident throughout the programme, participants learn how to better nurture their interior condition as leaders physically, emotionally and mentally. This can result in a better balance of body, mind and spirit as well as improved belief in oneself, strength, courage, an opening of the heart, and a realization of the connectedness in the world around us.

At the *team level*, participants work with their team coaches on defining team objectives, building a team culture as well as developing their coaching skills with the goal of enabling each team member to coach his or her peers in the field. Furthermore, most teams have the chance to meet a representative of the partner organization who joins them for two days during the foundation week. Together with them they discuss and launch their project plan.

At the *group level*, participants develop a common understanding of the *Ulysses journey*. They get input from distinguished speakers on topics along the learning dimensions. In addition, they are familiarized with the overall vision of the Ulysses learning experience in the context of PwC's strategy and have the opportunity to meet and talk to members of the global leadership team who come in as faculty.

Assignment phase

In the third *assignment phase*, participants spread out in their intercultural teams into the developing world to work with their hosting partner organizations on human, social and environmental aid projects. The actual projects are challenging in many respects. They require participants not only to live and work for two months in developing countries, in a different culture far away from home, but also to step out of their comfort zone of the Western style of living and doing business. They need to learn to do a new job in a complex and uncertain environment and use a new skill set. They need to cooperate with partners from different sectors and interact with local communities, non-governmental organizations and/or social entrepreneurs, who often have a different mindset and value system. And last but not least, they live and work in multicultural teams and need to create a cohesive working team culture to accomplish their projects.

Evidently, the aim of these project assignments is to provide a truly holistic and challenging experience across boundaries of countries, continents, cultures, sectors, work and life, that stretch participants on different levels. Throughout this phase team participants go through individual adjustment periods (culture shock), through demanding relationship building phases with the project partners as well as through dynamic team identity building stages. In order to avoid participants becoming over-challenged and losing their productive learning mode, participants are encouraged to practice yoga and meditation. They also receive coaching support on an ongoing basis: on the one hand through team mates themselves who were instructed in coaching each other, and on the other hand through regular phone calls with and through an onsite visit by their coach. Finally, there is the Ulysses learning platform available which is frequently used to exchange photos, stories, opinions, experiences among teams and to get input and feedback from other teams which are dispersed around the world.

Debriefing phase

After a short re-entry phase of two to three weeks to allow participants to reconnect briefly with their families and home offices, the whole Ulysses group reconvenes in the review week. During this week the field experiences are debriefed individually, in teams and in the larger group (sense-making process), systematically reflected with respect to the Ulysses learning dimensions and transformed into knowledge and stories. After an initial sharing of experiences and stories in the large group, each team further reflects and develops its story during the week in interaction with coaches, action researchers, facilitators and the dialogarchitect®.

This process helps participants on the one hand in reflecting on their own learning through dialogue on the intellectual, emotional, normative and practical level; on the other hand it supports them for sharing their stories and discussing their learning with the board; and furthermore, it prepares them for transferring their experience and learning back into the organization via storytelling. The unique approach is to facilitate debriefing at different levels: firstly, the content dimensions of the programme, secondly, on the group, team and the individual level and thirdly, on the visual, intellectual, the intra- and interpersonal and last but not least the normative level. In fact, with respect to the development of responsible leaders, the debrief on the values base becomes crucial. Therefore, the action researchers engage the participants in deep narrative interviews that inquire into the relational and normative dimension of their experience as individuals, as team members and as project partners and systematically debrief the field experience along the diversity, sustainability and leadership dimension. This helps participants, as researcher Thomas Maak points out, in both making sense of their experiences along the learning dimensions and in understanding their values base for actualizing *ethical intelligence* (Pless and Maak 2005).

Networking phase

The last phase is about transferring the learning back into the workspace and into the broader PwC network. It is about sharing the experiences, applying learning (also overcoming possible resistance and barriers to change) to become a better leader with clients, people and the firm, evoking interest for sustainable development and community engagement, kickstarting some new initiatives in the spirit of the Ulysses programme, thereby further fostering organizational learning, contributing to a sustainable business model and to building public trust. This phase is also about growing and cultivating the Ulysses network as a network with a responsibility to drive positive change across the organization. In the networking spirit many participants stay in touch with programme management, coaches and researchers. As part of the research process the latter conduct follow-up interviews with the participants after 18 to 24 months and by that further stimulate reflection, dialogue and networking. Organized by the Ulysses programme management team, the first official alumni event took place in June 2005 and reunited alumni from three programmes. According to Alina Stefan, Ulysess programme team member, these alumni events are crucial to keep the Ulysses spirit and the momentum going:

> They give alumni not only the opportunity to reconnect with their experience and to network with other Ulysses fellows from other classes, but also to share the progress on their learning journey and to continue their dialogue with PwC's global leadership team.

Success factors of leadership development in cross-sector-partnerships

The Ulysses programme is a unique development programme in the sense that it opens up new vistas on talent and leadership development. However, it also places new challenges on the management of such learning interventions. The success of leadership development in cross-sector partnerships depends on a couple of factors. So far, the following three factors have been identified.

Selecting the right partner organization

Inquisitiveness, willingness and ability to learn as well as emotional and interpersonal qualities are necessary prerequisites for learning success on the participants' level. However, equally important is the selection of the partner organization. Therefore, partner organizations are systematically screened and evaluated by the project management team. Elena Artal, programme manager of Ulysses, points out that the selection of partner organizations is based on criteria such as reputation and track record, community impact and community involvement, as well as innovative solutions to development problems. 'We strive to represent different organizations working on the development arena, from intergovernmental organizations such as UN agencies, to non-governmental organizations working on different areas of development, like poverty alleviation, economic development and HIV/AIDS among others.'

Defining the right projects

A further success factor is the selection of the right projects. Projects provided by the partner organizations need to be challenging on the one hand. On the other hand the skill base required to work on these projects needs to reflect participants' expertise, so that the knowledge and skills can be optimally leveraged to benefit the aid project and the partner organization. Furthermore, the projects need to open up learning areas where people can gain new insights and develop new competencies. An example would be a project that requires a tax auditor to leverage her professional expertise in accounting and additionally involves this person in a new area of competence like designing and delivering strategy workshops for the partner organization and its stakeholders.

Team composition for diversity learning

The Ulysses programme is also about creating a multicultural learning space among the PwC participants and establishing closer network ties. Therefore, it is important to compose diverse project teams in terms of national, cultural and geographic representation as well as gender and seniority. A Ulysses team can get as diverse as the following example shows: a woman from Australia working with three men from Romania, Thailand and the UK on a capacity building project with a local training centre in Zambia. While participants can express their preferences for which projects and in which countries they want to work, it is the programme management that, while considering participants' wishes, ultimately decides on the composition of the teams with respect to their diversity.

Conclusion: developing responsible leaders for sustainable business

In this chapter we presented the Ulysses programme as a case example for developing future leaders for the challenges of *business in society* through cross-sector partnerships. Combining the objective of developing leaders and contributing to the common good, the programme creates a true win–win situation for all people and stakeholders involved. On the one hand, not-for-profit organizations and communities in developing countries receive expertise and knowledge that they can usually not afford. They also get attention which can create enormous hope (especially in neglected areas) and mobilize new energy and resources for the betterment of the situation. On the other hand, reaching out and engaging in social projects around the world sharpens the consciousness and awareness of future business leaders for the social disparities in the world as well as for the responsibilities of business in a global economy. Ulysses is only the beginning of a journey towards responsible leadership at the individual, the corporate and the business level. Nonetheless, it has proven that even a small group of people can make an impact. Hopefully, other organizations too will join this journey.

> Never doubt that a small group of thoughtful committed citizens can change the world; in fact, it is the only thing that ever has.
>
> (Margaret Mead)

Questions

1 How does the Ulysses programme prepare future leaders for the challenges of business in society?

2　What are the learning objectives of the programme and how are they linked to the firm's vision, mission, strategy?

3　What kind of challenges does the experiential learning approach in cross-sector partnerships offer and how are they linked to the learning dimensions?

4　How do you assess the benefits of cross-sector partnerships for PwC, its partner organizations and the communities in developing countries?

5　What do you think is the impact of this programme on PwC and the business world?

Note

1　PricewaterhouseCoopers refers to the member firms of the worldwide PricewaterhouseCoopers organization.

Bibliography

Conger, J.A. and Benjamin, B. (1999) *Building Leaders: how successful companies develop the next generation*, San Francisco, CA: Jossey-Bass.

Day, D.V. (2001) 'Leadership development: a review in context', *Leadership Quarterly*, 11: 581–613.

DiPiazza Jr, S.A. and Eccles, R.G. (2002) *Building Public Trust: the future of corporate reporting*, New York: John Wiley.

Dotlich, D.L. and Noel, J.L. (1998) *Action Learning: how the world's top companies are re-creating their leaders and themselves*, San Francisco, CA: Jossey-Bass.

Frank, H.J. (2004) *Ideen zeichnen* (drawing ideas), Weinheim, Basel: Beltz.

Heron, J. (2001) *Helping the Client: a creative practical guide*, 5th edn, London: Sage.

Pless, N.M. and Maak, T. (2004) 'Building an inclusive diversity culture: principles, processes and practice', *Journal of Business Ethics*, 54: 129–47.

Pless, N.M. and Maak, T. (2005) 'Relational intelligence for leading responsibly in a connected world', in K.M. Weaver (ed.) *Proceedings of the Sixty-fifth Annual Meeting of the Academy of Management*.

PricewaterhouseCoopers (2003) **connectedthinking*, PricewaterhouseCoopers 2003 Global Annual Review. Online. Available HTTP: http://www.pwc.com/images/2003AR/BW.html (accessed 27 March 2005).

PricewaterhouseCoopers (2004) *what matters**, PricewaterhouseCoopers 2003 Global Annual Review. Online. Available HTTP: http://www.pwc.com/extweb/aboutus.nsf/docid/F5844C8D23D911EB85256F4A004EFBOE/$file/PWC_Global_Annual_Review_2004.pdf (accessed 27 March 2005).

Van Velsor, E., McCauley, C.D. and Moxley, R.S. (1998) 'Our view of leadership development', in C.D. McCauley, R.S. Moxley and E. Van Velsor (eds) *The Center for Creative Leadership Handbook of Leadership Development*, San Francisco, CA: Jossey-Bass.

15 Developing leaders for sustainable business

Mark Wade

> A leader has to be both practical and visionary to command respect
> (Jeroen van der Veer, CEO, Royal Dutch/Shell Group)[1]

Introduction

In business, it is not enough to possess the qualities of a leader – one must be able to apply them within the context of the world today; a world where companies are expected to be accountable not only to shareholders for financial performance, but to stakeholders for their wider economic, environmental and societal impacts. In the face of such scrutiny, successful leaders will embody both a high value system and an external mindset, sensitive to the wider world in which they operate. To this end, sustainable development represents an excellent values-based framework for viewing the world, identifying risks and opportunities, and improving decision making.

In practice, this means looking at every business decision through a *sustainable development lens* – understanding and managing your environmental and social impacts and managing them as part of normal operations. It also means meeting short-term priorities with full consideration of longer-term needs, and seeking out the views of others *before* taking decisions. At Shell, we learnt this the hard way, when events of the 1990s called our behaviour unexpectedly into question. As a consequence, we realized that we needed a new way of thinking and communicating and doing.

But embedding sustainable development within your organization is not simply a matter of establishing systems and processes. You have to win hearts and minds. This means convincing people of the business case and making it relevant in their daily lives. In Shell, this has resulted in the development of a broad programme of tailored learning.

It also means making the most of both internal and external expertise. Above all, it requires a willingness to learn from mistakes and a passion to succeed along with an acceptance that, as an organization, you are in it for the long haul.

Leadership and sustainable development

What is a successful leader?

Every business needs leaders. In Shell, we not only look for leadership qual-ities in those we recruit, we nurture and develop people throughout their careers – from those on first assignment, through to the few who achieve senior executive positions. This is because we see people as the most impor-tant part of our organization. Indeed, attracting, developing and retaining top talent is essential for success. It is a view that will resonate with many blue-chip companies today, along with the nine leadership competences defined by Shell:

- builds shared vision;
- champions customer focus;
- maximizes business opportunities;
- demonstrates professional mastery;
- displays personal effectiveness;
- demonstrates courage;
- motivates, coaches and develops;
- values differences;
- delivers results.

The question is, how can these competencies be deployed in the most effec-tive way? Against what challenges and expectations will successful leaders be measured? To answer this, we need to look at the world in which they operate – a very different world from that of 20 or even 10 years ago. It is a world of intense competition, where change is a constant, globalization a fact and corporate accountability demanded. It is a world in which society is increasingly concerned about the long-term social and environmental *sustainability* of today's economic development. People are worried about climate change, erosion of eco-systems, issues of health, extremes of poverty and wealth, and unsustainable levels of consumption. With the global population set to rise by 50 per cent and energy demand expected to double or even triple by 2050, there is a real sense of urgency and alarm at the prospects for the planet and future generations. This raises questions about the role and behaviour of business in society and especially for vital, high profile industries such as energy.

In this world, companies are exposed to unprecedented levels of risk, scrutiny and challenge. We are expected to satisfy not only investors on financial performance, but a wide range of other parties on environmental and social performance. It is a world of no hiding places. The demand is: show more; deliver more ever faster and more responsibly. How companies and their leaders live up to these expectations now determines their future; and failure to meet them can have stark consequences, as highlighted by a number of high profile corporate scandals. These have resulted in boycotts, damaged reputations, and in some cases, liquidation. Shell has experienced the downside of this over the events of Brent Spar and Nigeria in the mid 1990s and, more recently, the re-categorization of oil and gas reserves. But, conversely, there are also great opportunities. For an increasing number of top companies, adopting sustainable development (SD) is seen as a way of not only embracing this agenda, but delivering long-term success; and it is not difficult to see why.[2]

The broad benefits of SD-thinking

Sustainable development is both a value and a broad framework of thinking. It encourages an inclusive, outward-looking and values-based approach to business. SD-thinking therefore offers companies an excellent reference point for defining and applying their vision and values – their *corporate magnetic north*.

Where there is a strong culture of integrity, they are also more likely to go beyond compliance and innovate to achieve market differentiation. Certainly, we in Shell see a *strong commitment to business principles and sustainable development* as a fundamental part of our competitive edge. It is highly consistent with addressing our short- and long-term needs and in helping to meet the energy challenges of the societies we serve. We know that how well we match up to these challenges – as a Group and as individuals – will be a defining factor in our continued success. In practice, it means looking at every business decision – large and small – through a sustainable development lens. This encourages people to identify the environmental and social impacts of their decisions and to manage them as part of normal operations. It helps them address short-term priorities with consideration of longer-term needs, encouraging them to seek out and value the views of others *before* taking decisions. Put simply, it means acting with greater honesty and sensitivity to one's operating environment. Leaders do not even need to use the term *sustainable development* to exemplify the behaviours that are consistent with it.

So how does all this fit with the nine leadership competencies? Simply, a corporate commitment to contribute to sustainable development gives them a context and a value system in which they can be applied, providing relevance and purpose. Leaders who embody this way of thinking are then better equipped to steer a course through the complex dilemmas that any values-based organization will face. They will be able to:

- build relationships;
- identify trends and opportunities;
- avoid risk;
- optimize the strategic value growth of their enterprise.

In short, SD-thinking not only helps them secure a *licence to operate* but, more crucially, a *licence to grow*. So how did Shell come to this way of thinking?

The emergence of the sustainable development paradigm

The catalyst for Shell

Shell has always been a values-driven company. Our core values of honesty, integrity and respect for people are the foundations of our *General Business Principles*, first codified in 1976. Having set that framework, we prided ourselves on operating to what we felt were the highest business standards. So it came as a shock in 1995 when two events – the disposal of the Brent Spar and the tragic events in Nigeria – catapulted Shell into the international headlines and called into question our behaviour. The Group found itself ill-equipped to deal with the public criticism and was badly shaken by these events. At every level, people were asking how could it be that Shell's behaviour is seen to be falling so far short of society's expectations? We believed we had acted responsibly and ethically in both cases, but what we learnt was that doing it right is not the same as getting it right; and as a principled organization, it was completely unacceptable for us to be seen to be not living up to people's expectations.

There was an urgent desire by senior leaders to find out what had gone wrong and why. In 1996, Shell therefore embarked on one of the largest stakeholder engagement exercises ever conducted in the energy sector. It included non-governmental organizations, government officials, academics, labour representatives and community leaders in 14 countries who were engaged in around 20 roundtable discussions. Gradually, through the process, Shell learnt to *bite its tongue*, stop defending itself and listen. The roundtables were followed by a global survey of 10,000 people. The results showed that a significant minority had serious concerns on what they perceived as Shell's lack of regard for the environment and human rights. What was clear was that having values is not enough. The way values are expressed, as behaviour, needs to be constantly refreshed to reflect changing public expectations. Society has shifted from an acceptance of a 'trust me' approach, to a 'show me' mindset and now, increasingly, to an 'involve me' imperative. Clearly, we needed to reconnect with our stakeholders.

Responding to the challenge

The true test of leadership is how well one copes with challenges of this scale; how to transfer the negative energy into the positive transformation of an organization. Shell's first response to these findings was the acceptance by senior leadership that they were important. The second was to face up to the fact that this would require significant changes to the way the business operated. The first, in 1997, was to update the Shell General

Business Principles to include specific commitments to support fundamental human rights and to contribute to sustainable development. We also greatly strengthened our health, safety and environment policy and procedures; and put processes in place to ensure leaders worldwide took these measures seriously. Furthermore, a renewable energy business was set up in solar, wind and other forms of alternative energy and a Hydrogen business was established. Minimum environmental standards were also set, based on norms in OECD countries, to be applied wherever Shell operates. In addition, a number of Group targets were established. These included reducing greenhouse gas emissions to 10 per cent below 1990 levels by 2003, ending venting of gas by 2003; while on the people side, we set targets for the number of women in senior positions.

Hardwiring: creating a solid foundation

But this was just the start. It is one thing to make the headline changes, quite another to understand what making a commitment to contributing to sustainable development truly means on a daily basis; and how to integrate it into your organization. Indeed, it is meaningless unless there is the capacity to apply this approach and add value to both your business and the societies you serve. Ultimately, the aim is for a cultural change, where it becomes second nature for people to look through the SD lens when making any business decision. In the meantime, a consistent, structured approach needs to be instilled. This means progressively *hardwiring* SD considerations into policies, standards and governance; strategy and portfolio evolution; targets, systems and processes; reporting and assurance.

It is a process Shell is continuously developing and refining; and as our understanding grows, so does the awareness of how much more can be achieved. Nevertheless, we have made progress. For example, as part of the submission when competing for internal funding, all new investment proposals must now include:

- integrated social, health and environmental impact assessments;
- stakeholder engagement plans;
- the future costs of emitting carbon, with concrete actions taken to minimize them;
- meeting all Shell environmental standards;
- consideration of all aspects of the Shell sustainable development principles.

Increasingly *must do's* are being prescribed for particular roles and activities. For example, refinery managers are required to have in place:

- social performance plans to maintain an open dialogue with stakeholders, generate jobs and other benefits for neighbouring communities; and minimize unwanted social impacts;

- energy efficiency improvement targets, including running an Energise™ energy review and conservation programme by 2008 to meet business and Group targets.

Likewise, oil and gas projects leaders must:

- complete integrated environmental, social and health impact assessments, demonstrating they have the plans and resources to engage with key stakeholders, protect the environment and manage impacts on communities;
- not explore or drill for oil and gas in natural World Heritage sites and follow our biodiversity standard when operating in other environmentally sensitive areas.

Another important example of hardwiring is the inclusion of sustainable development as a measure in the Group scorecard, now comprising 20 per cent of the total score in 2005. This reinforces the importance of SD performance, as it impacts the pay of all Shell people.

Softwiring: winning hearts and minds

> Outstanding leaders appeal to the hearts of their following – not just their minds.
>
> Anonymous

It is one thing to write the manual in terms of rules and processes to be followed. But if that is all that happens, the manual will simply sit on the shelf. At best, a culture of minimum compliance will be achieved; at worst, one of avoidance. What is also needed is to touch the *hearts and minds of people*, so that they feel it is the right way to do business and can see how business value can be derived. However, care must be taken not to whip up a mere froth of enthusiasm. Without giving people the tools and supporting systems, it will soon evaporate. Hardwiring and softwiring need to go hand in hand.

There will always be enthusiastic people who happily embrace the SD concept and strive to apply it in their daily work because it resonates with their personal values. Others, however, will need more convincing. Resistance should not be underestimated. With pressure already on costs, timescales and human resources, there will be little appetite for additional initiatives or activities that do not have clear links to value creation. Misconceptions that have to be overcome include the belief that sustainable development is:

- costly, with the *inevitable trade-offs* greater than the potential for value creation or win–win solutions;

- additional, rather than integral, to normal business activities;
- just another corporate initiative that will burden all staff;
- just social investment;
- just PR;
- just being nice to the bunny huggers;
- a dangerous distraction from meeting the needs of shareholders.

It is therefore vital that people at all levels are convinced of the strength of the business case and the practicality of your approach. In reality, this means translating sustainable development into something that is tangible and relevant to both business teams and individuals. No mean undertaking – especially within a large multinational organization like Shell.

So, given the scale of challenge, where do you begin? As with hard-wiring, a clear structure for softwiring sustainable development is essential. In Shell, this is the job for SD Learning. As Dennis Baltzley, Head of Leadership Development, Shell, points out SD Learning plays an important role in developing leaders:

> We have a clear point of view on how our leaders learn. We want both powerful leadership skill-building that leaves people changed, and mind stretching topics that make people question existing mental models, all within a framework of solving real world issues. Addressing sustainable development does all of that.

The role of SD Learning

In 2003, SD Learning was set up to provide a concerted approach across the Shell businesses. Our objective: to achieve a step change in SD aware-ness, understanding and capacity of Shell people to apply SD-thinking in their everyday decisions.

While our aims were ambitious, our approach was subtle. Our strategy was to operate *beneath the radar* so as not to give the impression of intro-ducing a new and costly initiative. This meant making the most of current resources – utilizing existing delivery mechanisms and maximizing the cross-business sharing of tools and approaches. It also meant developing new tools only where needed and deploying them on a demand-led basis.

The SD Learning team drives the programme. It comprises the SD Advisers from each of the businesses, the Corporate Centre, the Shell Learning organization, Shell Global Solutions (an internal consultancy) and functional experts from different areas and departments such as Contracting and Procurement, Health, Safety and Environment (HSE) and Social Performance Management. The team's activities form part of the broader work programme of the SD/HSE planning committee, chaired by Chief Executive, Jeroen van de Veer. This committee is charged with embedding sustainable development into the way Shell operates – both the hard and the softwiring.

The team aimed to instill in Shell people:

- basic SD awareness;
- the understanding that sustainable development is integral to the Group's strategic direction and competitive edge;
- the capacity to innovate based on SD-thinking, with a mindset attuned and responsive to their environment;
- basic SD-related competencies, tailored to priority audiences.

As the size of the undertaking was daunting, an SD Learning framework was developed (see Figure 15.1). This enabled the exercise to be broken down into bite-sized chunks that could be progressed in a systematic way. It also provides a shared vision of common purpose and clarity on roles and tasks.

The team focuses its efforts on collective actions of common value across the organization. Individual members are primarily responsible for progressing their own SD Learning activities in direct support of their business or function. The team and the framework therefore serve as a common reference point, avoiding duplication of development effort and providing a ready conduit for the exchange of best practice and ideas. All that is described below is the sum of the individual and team efforts across the organization. Activities are structured under three main headings:

Objective	Activity	Medium	Agent
Awareness and understanding	**Communicating** • Key messages • Latest updates • Best practice examples	• SD e-portal • Newsletters, e-letters • Shell report • Resource library	• Corporate centre • Businesses • Functions
Working knowledge Skilled	**Training/learning** • SD presentation packs • SD case studies • SD best practice guides • SD modules/events • SD e-learning tools	• SD workshops • SD master classes • Chronos (e-learning) • Leadership assessment and development • Training/coaching interventions	• SD advisers • Subject experts • Self-directed • Programme managers
Mastery and advocacy	**Beyond training** • Active learning • Experienced people • Functional leadership • Competency profiling	• SD networks • Cross-postings • Career planning • Competencies	• Businesses • HR planners • SD/HSE advisers • SD practitioners

NB: Content indicative, not comprehensive

Figure 15.1 The sustainable development learning framework

- Communications – raising basic awareness and understanding;
- Training and learning – developing working knowledge and skill;
- Beyond training – mastery and advocacy.

Communications – raising basic awareness and understanding

At the first level, our aim is to achieve a basic awareness and understanding of what sustainable development means in Shell and why it is important. To this end, a library of standard presentations and communications material – based on a set of common terms, core messages and best practices – was developed. Consistency of language and presentation is essential to avoid confusion. Examples include the SD lens, the seven principles of sustainable development and the seven elements of the business case (see Figures 15.2, 15.3, 15.4). These slides, and the associated *storyline*, were agreed at the very highest level and have become iconic in the way sustainable development is communicated within Shell.

The wealth of material is widely available through the SD Portal and related business SD websites on the Shell internal web. It is also promoted through a wide range of other media, such as the Shell Report, newsletters, magazines, speeches and web casts. This is carried out by both the Corporate Centre and the businesses. We have reached tens of thousands of people across Shell in this way, raising a basic level of awareness and understanding. But no matter how good the material, the impact of communications alone is usually low and short-lived and has to be constantly reinforced. To help people understand how SD-thinking is relevant to their daily jobs, you have to get more intimate!

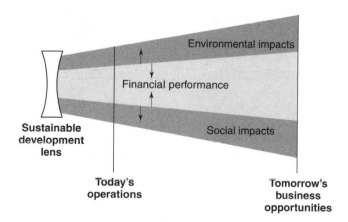

Figure 15.2 Looking through the sustainable development lens

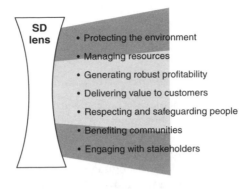

Figure 15.3 Shell's commitment to contributing to sustainable development

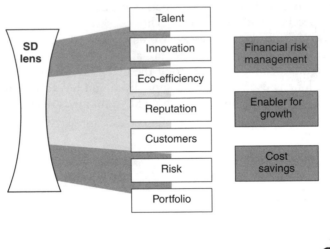

Figure 15.4 Sustainable development makes good business sense

Training and learning – developing working knowledge and skill

At the next level, we therefore aim to deepen the learning experience, tailoring it to a specific role or audience. Training and leadership development programmes are existing mechanisms for reaching people on an individual or small group basis and the ideal vehicle for communicating SD Learning:

Infuse or bolt-on to existing programmes

Sustainable development is being bolted-on and infused into an ever-increasing number of courses and leadership development programmes – for example, *Managing HSE*, Country Chair *Fast Track* and *Finance in the Business* courses. It is also being infused or bolted on to the leadership development portfolio of interventions, from graduate selection through to executive development. For example, exercises based on real Shell investment decisions are used to enable people to practise applying the SD lens and explore for themselves how business value can be generated. Stakeholder role-plays add a realistic dimension while learning how to engage with people of differing views. We find that the most effective route is to work with the managers of the programmes in order to understand their priorities and build in elements that serve their needs directly; and they always include relevant case studies illustrating the practical reality of contributing to sustainable development within Shell today.

Create new, dedicated SD modules and workshops

Challenging, interactive and business relevant, SD workshops are for those people who are inspired to learn more and become skilled in applying core, SD-related competencies. They run for anything from half a day to two days and are delivered not only by internal SD experts and facilitators, but external experts on subjects, such as climate change and social performance. They can also include third parties, such as *Forum for the Future*, a UK-based sustainable development charity (see http://www.forumforthe future.org.uk/).

SD Learning has developed three types of workshop, based on accelerated learning techniques. Module 1 is a two-day workshop designed to enable people to speak confidently and knowledgeably about sustainable development and help embed it in their part of the organization. It not only covers the values and business case, but explains Shell's position on issues such as climate change and biodiversity. It also gives special emphasis to social performance management and stakeholder engagement skills. As importantly, it provides a range of tools for embedding sustainable development into business processes and advice on where to go for specialist help. At the end of the workshop, participants receive a CD-Rom resource kit of reference material and tools. The workshop format has been popular wherever it has been run around the world. A series of events has served, for example, the Shell Country Chairs of Africa and their market and external affairs managers (a Country Chair is the legal representative of Shell in a country of operation; usually, they are also the General Manager of the main Shell business in that country). They have also attracted SD Advisers and change agents who have attended in a train-the-trainer capacity in order to learn how to deliver accelerated SD learning to their own colleagues in the line. Often, these workshops have stimulated the call for return events tailored to specific target audience needs. These are being satisfied by Module 2 type workshops.

Module 2 is a flexible template that can be tailored to specific audiences and business needs. Building on Module 1, it begins with a fast track refresher of the key messages on sustainable development and sets the context for the focused delivery of selected areas of competence development and business improvement. These could include social performance, stakeholder engagement, environmental and social impact assessment, climate change and contracting and procurement. It is designed to:

- help people make the link between sustainable development and their particular area of expertise;
- focus on groups with shared interests, e.g. project teams on a new development; refinery management teams; or those who have similar roles but in different businesses, e.g. a regional network of social performance advisers.

Module 3 is a day and half SD Masterclass developed and delivered in association with Forum for the Future. It is aimed specifically at the senior professional and junior executive level. Here, the emphasis is on integrated decision making. It is designed to:

- build personal awareness of global issues and their implications for business;
- build an understanding of how leaders can apply SD-thinking by using integrated decision making and systems thinking;
- engage participants' hearts, as well as minds, by experiential learning;
- build capacity to engage and innovate with SD-thinking.

The Masterclass has been successfully piloted in our Exploration and Production business, with more classes planned. A key ingredient of its success was the direct involvement of senior executive leadership, who attended sessions and engaged with participants in the strategic and operational challenges of applying SD-thinking. The Masterclass template is now available to other Shell businesses for adaptation.

All these workshops are run on a demand-led basis – either from individuals wishing to know more, or as requests from business or local operating company leaders. The response to date has been encouraging, with demand growing year on year, as word spreads.

E-learning – reach large audiences in an engaging way

Thousand of people are reached each year through SD modules on courses, leadership development events or SD workshops, but the numbers are small compared to the population. This is where Chronos comes in. Concise, motivational and easy to use, Chronos is a web-based tool for exploring and understanding sustainable development and making it meaningful and relevant to everyday life. Chronos was developed by the World Business Council for Sustainable Development (WBCSD), in partnership with the University of Cambridge Programme for Industry (CPI, see http://www.cpi.cam.ac.uk). It has been specially customized by the SD Learning team for use by Shell and our business partners: 10,000 licences have been bought by our businesses in order to reach deep and wide across the Shell world.

Chronos (*khronos*) is the Greek word for time. It was chosen as the name of this learning programme because long-term thinking is so important to sustainable development. For example, it helps people to:

- explore the values and the business case for sustainable development by seeking win-win solutions to difficult decisions in the workplace;
- bridge the gap between personal values and corporate action, testing their ability to make the case for sustainable development;
- embed sustainable development in both their business processes and the hearts and minds of those around them, utilizing a variety of tools and further reading from the Shell library of standard material.

In short, it offers all the benefits of a more intimate engagement, but with a much wider audience. Chronos is a powerful stand-alone tool for helping people on their personal journey, but its real strength will come from using it in combination with courses and other engagement events. Chronos is part of the on-boarding kit for all new joiners to Shell and is being used as pre-work before courses and events. We also encourage individuals to take a personal initiative in using it to improve their understanding of sustainable development.

Beyond training – mastery and advocacy

The classroom, real or virtual – no matter how good – is no substitute for practical experience, however; particularly if it is led by the vision and enthusiasm of individuals in the line committed to change. It is said that when a critical mass of early movers is achieved at around the 15 per cent level, then the rate of organizational change accelerates rapidly. It is therefore vital to make the most of these enthusiastic people, or change agents as they are sometimes called, who are already keen to embrace the concept of sustainable development. This is where *SD Networks* come in. Much effort has been devoted by the businesses to identifying and equipping networks of people who can:

- speak confidently and knowledgably about sustainable development;

- raise awareness and understanding of sustainable development with their colleagues;
- help embed sustainable development in their part of the organization.

These networks take many forms in Shell. Some have been created to represent the breadth and depth of a population – a diagonal slice, for example, through our Chemicals business. A network of 50 or so people from all levels and activities serve as focal points for bringing SD-thinking into their part of the business. They were brought together originally in a five-day induction workshop and are kept supplied with the latest tools and thinking for embedding and communicating sustainable development.

Networks of practitioners have also been set up to problem solve and share best practice around areas of common interest, e.g. bringing sustainable development to aspects of engineering. Other networks comprise people who have sustainable development in at least part of their job description. This is typical of the networks in our Exploration and Production, and Gas and Power businesses. These people have a clear role in bringing SD-thinking to national/regional, project or major site activities. *Specialist networks* are another example. Take our Oil Products business. Here, people can sign up to a *Climate Change network* whose purpose is to prepare the organization for a carbon constrained world. It helps them integrate the cost of carbon into investment proposals and master the intricacies of reporting and trading carbon emissions. It also provides practical advice on energy efficiency improvement. Similar networks focus on social performance management around operations. There is also a constantly growing network of people who have signed up to receive the latest information on sustainable development via business or Corporate Centre produced bi-monthly, SD e-newsletters. These provide people with news, resources and best practices, both in the Group and worldwide. Collectively, these networks represent thousands of people across the organization.

However, as Adrian Loader, Director Strategic Planning, Sustainable Development and External Affairs, underlines:

> The challenge is to move sustainable development out from the specialists and into the mainstream. It is vital that everyone has the chance to contribute – to understand why and how to make this the way we do business.

Leadership for sustainable development

The best leaders are those who have a true purpose, a passion for what they do and an ability to bring out the best in the people they lead. They will be keen to learn from their mistakes and the experiences of others. Above all, they will accept that there is a reason to change. In our complex and fast moving world, they will be the kind of people who find the time and space to reflect and practise what they have learned; who are humble and honest enough to accept that there is always room for improvement. As such, they become an example to others.

There are a number of visionary and impassioned leaders within Shell whose sensitivity to their local operating environment and dedication in applying the SD lens has had a powerful impact. Examples include leaders of major ventures, such as the gas-to-power project in Malampaya, the Philippines[3] and the Athabasca Oil Sands Project in Alberta, Canada.[4] By applying SD principles such as Minimize Environmental Impact, Working with Stakeholders, and Benefit Communities *early* in the planning process, issues were identified which could be mitigated as part of the project execution. Opportunities for increasing local wealth creation were also identified. The projects were completed within the timeframe and within budget, while greatly enhancing the reputation of Shell as a responsible operator in the Philippines and Canada. In both cases, leadership set up stakeholder panels to work closely with local management – examples of the *involve me world*.

People of this calibre exemplify the competences consistent with an SD mindset and are recognized as being suited to managing projects in sensitive areas. It means they have displayed a marked breadth of vision, external mindset and capacity to:

- seek out and identify key trends and influences of strategic significance to the business (economic, environmental and social) and use insights to optimize strategic value growth;
- address short-term priorities with full consideration of longer-term needs;
- integrate economic, environmental and social factors in strategic decision making and the management of daily operations;
- actively seek out and value the views of others through engagement with internal and external stakeholders, in order to identify short- and long-term risks and opportunities;
- show visible leadership in creating a culture of challenge and innovation; diversity and inclusiveness;
- ensure others have the information, resources and authority to carry out operations compliant with legal and company standards and values;
- build long-term relationships with a wide range of internal and external parties.

These capacities are being seen as increasingly important in resource planning and career progression. It is not only in major projects that leaders of this calibre are having an impact. They are bringing new perspectives to product and service innovation. Leaders with high levels of empowerment obviously have a greater opportunity to influence strategic thinking and effect lasting change. But that does not mean that you have to be senior to be a leader. In fact, you don't even have to hold a position in order to be a leader. Nor does it mean that SD-thinking is only something the boss needs to consider. Two examples in Shell illustrate this clearly.

Two part-time administrative assistants in the Shell UK head office were concerned about the amount of paper being thrown away without thought for where it went – mostly as mixed waste. So they approached their line manager for support in organizing waste paper collection for recycling, which was piloted on their floor. Thus *Conservers in Shell* was created. The scheme soon spread to the rest of the building, then across to the main London and Hague offices, where it is now firmly established. *Conservers in Shell* now work with building management teams to recycle plastic and batteries, and even more significantly, look at improving energy efficiency within the offices. The initiative has not only raised awareness of sustainable development and shown that everyone can contribute to it; it has also reduced costs significantly.

The second example is *Project Better World* (PBW). This initiative was started by a group of young Shell researchers in our Amsterdam laboratory six years ago. They developed the idea of providing opportunities for Shell staff to extend their appreciation of the wider world. To this end, they approached the Earthwatch Institute (see <http://www.earthwatch.org> to enable Shell employees to do voluntary work placements for biodiversity conservation and community development across the world. They brought the idea to senior management and it is now firmly established, with 40 people going on two-week placements each year. They also organize six month placements for people via the Voluntary Service Overseas (VSO) scheme. Involvement in PBW is a valuable way of developing an external mindset – a defining feature of responsible leaders. The scheme continues to be run by self-starters such as these.

So is the strategy working?

Just as we need continuously to measure and report progress in our economic, environmental and social performance (see Shell Report 2004 at http://www.shell.com), so too do we need to assess the level of SD awareness, understanding and competence across the business on a regular basis. Indeed, knowing whether you are winning or losing, where and why, is key to maximizing limited resources. An SD Learning survey has been deployed recently to assess just that. This diagnostic, web-based tool assessed the level of SD *knowledge* of individuals across Shell; their *attitude* (are they switched on or turned off?); and the *context* in which they are working (is it helping or hindering their ability to apply SD-thinking?). For example, results indicate that we have been successful in instilling a basic awareness of sustainable development across Shell. This has encouraged us to shift emphasis to building the skills of people in specific roles. We are now able to deploy for example Module 2 workshops with greater accuracy tailored to specific needs, e.g. project engineers, refinery teams. But it is also important to look outwards in order to learn and share expertise. At Shell, we do this firstly, by participating in SD learning laboratories with peer group companies, e.g. via the World Business Council for Sustainable Development (WBCSD), Cambridge Programme for Industry (CPI) and the Society for Organizational Learning (SOL) SD Consortium (see http://www.solonline.org); secondly, by cooperating with business schools and universities, e.g. through the European Academy of Business in Society (EABIS)(see http://www.eabis.org).

Conclusion: the challenge ahead

Embedding sustainable development in an organization is a leadership challenge and will always be a huge experiment in trial and error. It will probably take a generation of managers before it becomes a truly unconscious way of working and an intrinsic part of the business culture. A mark of success will be when we no longer have to use the term SD, it is simply how we do things.

At Shell, we are aware that we have a long journey ahead of us, as we continue to learn how best we may develop leaders for sustainable business. Nevertheless, there are encouraging signs that we are heading in the right direction – bringing not only value to our businesses, but real benefits to the societies we serve.

Questions

1   This chapter does not conceal the crisis Shell experienced in the aftermath of Brent Spar and the tragedy in Nigeria. How did Shell cope with the crisis? What was the key learning and what were the major steps in the change process?
2   How was sustainable development embedded within the organization? Why is it important to win the hearts and minds of people?
3   How does the sustainable development thinking resonate with the competences required of Shell leaders?
4   What is the role of the learning function in preparing leaders for the social, environmental and economic challenges in business?
5   What kind of activities and methods does Shell use to raise awareness and build understanding for sustainable development within the organization and to make it relevant to people in their daily roles?

Notes

1   The expression 'Shell' and 'Group' refers to the companies of the Royal Dutch/Shell Group of companies. Each of the companies that make up the Royal

Dutch/Shell Group of companies is an independent entity and has its own identity.
2 The World Business Council for Sustainable Development (WBCSD) comprises some 170 multinational companies, including Shell, committed to contributing to sustainable development. Together, they operate in almost every country in the world, reaching two billion customers a day and have a collective market capitalization of some US$3 trillion (see <http://www.wbcsd.org>).
3 The Malampaya Deep Water Gas-to-Power project led by Shell Philippines Exploration and Production is now producing gas offshore and transporting it by a 500 km pipeline to receiving facilities onshore. It represents the largest and most significant industrial investment in the history of the Philippines and is set to meet 30 per cent of the country's power generation requirements.
4 The Athabasca Oil Sands Project is a joint venture of Shell Canada Limited (60 per cent), Chevron Canada Limited (20 per cent) and Western Oil Sands L.P. (20 per cent). It is one of the world's largest construction projects of recent years and will supply the equivalent of 10 per cent of Canada's oil needs.

Index

Note: Page references in **bold** indicate figures or tables

ABN AMRO Group 171–2
ABN AMRO Real 171, 173–4, 176;
    see also Barbosa, Fabio
acceptability, zone of 65, **65**
accountability 7, 11, **38**, 95–107, **105**,
    110, 138
action research (AR) 220, 221
actions 112; based on dialogue 124,
    125; ethical analysis of 57–61;
    means and ends of 28; and
    production and leadership 120;
    virtue and 112–13; voluntary and
    involuntary 112
AIDS: partnerships to work against
    206
altruism 25–7, 202
AR (action research) 220, 221
architects, leaders as 47
Argentina: social purpose partnerships
    205
Aristotle 120; on character 116,
    116–17; on feelings 116; on habits
    112, 113, 114–15; on rhetoric 108,
    117, 118–19, **118**; on virtue 43, 108;
    on voluntary and in voluntary
    actions 113
Athabasca Oil Sands Project, Canada
    241, 244
Avolio, Bruce 25

bad leadership 17, 33, 42, 188
Badaracco, Joseph 95, 96, 98
banks: role in society 172–4
Barbosa, Fabio 170, 171; on banking
    and responsible leadership 172–4;
    development as a leader 177–9; his
    leadership approach 174–7
Baron, D. 161
Bass, B. 19, 29

behavioural paradigm 123
Ben & Jerry's 159
board leadership 197–8
Body Shop International 47–8, 88, 158
Botswana: partnership to combat AIDS
    206
BP 160
BrainLAB 127
Brent Spar oil platform 160, 162–3
bribes 140, 141
Brundtland Commission 80–1
BUPA (British United Provident
    Association) 144
Burke, James 48
Burns, James MacGregor 19, 27–9, 40,
    45, 48, 110
business case: for corporate
    responsibility 74–5; see also 'doing
    well by doing good' approach
business processes, internal 143;
    pressures of and responsibility 82–4;
    versus shareholders dilemma 145–7,
    145; versus society dilemma 144–5,
    144

capital accounts 190
care, caring, ethics of 11, **38**, **38**
Caterpillar 166
Caux Round Table (CRT) 185–6;
    lessons from 186–7; lesson one – the
    need for principles 187–8; lesson
    two – what gets managed, gets
    accomplished 188–9; lesson three –
    interests must be addressed 189–91;
    lesson four – culture counts 191–7,
    193–4, 195; lesson five – leadership
    from the board 197–8; Principles for
    Business 186, 199–200
Center for Creative Leadership 219

centre-driven decision making 64–6, **65**
challenges faced by leaders 188; in
  social purpose partnering 209–11; in
  a stakeholder society 34–9; to values
  and integrity 102, 102–4
Chand, Amber 82
change: leaders as change agents 48;
  and responsibility 82–4
character 43, 115–16; at odds with
  integrity 102; leaders' and rhetoric
  108, 119; of leaders of successful
  companies 103; traits 37–8, 124;
  virtue and 112, 116–17
charisma 2, 24, 29, 40–1, 111, 124,
  180; and transformational leadership
  29
charity 202, 203, 209–10
Chattopadhyay, A.K. 85–6
Chronos 239
CI (Conservation International) 207
City Year 207
coaches: and leader development
  219–20, 221, 222; leaders as 46–7
codes of conduct 56, 140
cognitive approach 123–4
collaborations: barriers to 209–11;
  collaboration continuum 203–4,
  204; strategic alignment and fusing
  core competencies 207–9; as a
  transformative force 211; values-
  driven 204–7; *see also* Ulysses
  programme
communication: Fabio Barbosa using
  174–5; leaders as storytellers 47–8;
  possible barrier to collaborations
  210; and responsibility 124
competitive analysis 62
competitive positioning 158–60, **159**,
  160
Confucius 56; on altruism 26; on
  leadership 44
Conger and Benjamin 219
consciousness, human 151
Conservation International (CI) 207
Conservers in Shell 242
Corporate Social Responsibility *see*
  CSR
corporations 54; corporate
  responsibility 72–3, 84; corporate
  values and other values 38–9;
  cultural context of 127–8; internal
  business processes 143, 144–7;
  obstacles to being responsible 79–89;
  perspectives on responsibility 73–9;

role in society 147, 218
cost–benefit analysis 62–4
costs: competing on 160; of
  reputational damage 161, 168
credence goods 160
critical thinking 43
cross-sector partnerships: success
  factors for leader development and
  224–5; *see also* social purpose
  partnerships; Ulysses programme
cross-sectoral collaboration 202;
  integrative approach 203,
  206–7; as transformative force 211
CRT *see* Caux Round Table
CSR (Corporate Social Responsibility)
  68, 72, 155, 166–7; ABN AMRO
  and 172–4; and competitive
  positioning 158–60; industry-wide
  163–5, **164**; and reputation
  management 160–3, **161**, **162**; and
  shareholder values 165–6; Ulysses
  programme and 218; value-based
  environment 156–8, **156**
cultures: concept of multiple 127–8;
  dynamic model of leading
  responsibly across 128–32, **129**;
  global cultural norms 191–7, **193–4**,
  195; managing by reconciling
  dilemmas 140; possible barrier to
  collaborations 209

decision making 54–5; blind spots and
  biases 62–4; centre-driven 64–6, **65**;
  compass 61, **62**, 65; ethical analysis
  and 55–7; and four modes of ethical
  analysis 57–61
DeGeorge, Richard 97, 98
deontology and ethics 23
d'Estaing, Olivier Giscard 185
dialogue: intrapersonal and
  responsibility 124, 125; learning
  through 220, 223
dilemmas 140, 142; internal
  organization versus shareholders
  145–7, **146**; multiple stakeholder
  142–4, **143**; reconciliation 140–2;
  reconciliation as a multi-step
  procedure 148–9; reconciling inner
  149, **150**; shareholders versus society
  147–8, **147**; society versus internal
  goals 144–5, **144**
distance and responsibility 81–2
diversity challenge to leadership 35–6;
  see also multicultural work context

'doing well by doing good' approach
155, 159, 167
dos Santos, Osório 178
dynamic model of leadership 125–7,
126; across cultures 128–32, **129**

effectiveness of leaders 22–3, 27, 33,
139; ethics and 21–2
ego: and leaders of successful
corporations 103; and responsibility
86–7
e-learning **234**, 238
emotional intelligence 151–2
emotions: and character 115–16;
rhetoric and 119
empathy 75
employees 142–3
Enron 33–4
Equator Principles 172, 180
Escola Brazil 173
ethical analysis 19–20, 57
ethical intelligence 43, 152
ethical leadership 111, 124–5
ethics 17; and altruism and self-interest
25–7; Aristotle on 112; challenge
faced by leaders 36; common core
with leadership 187; and decision
making 54–66, **62**; deontological
and teleological perspectives 23;
ethics/effectiveness continuum 21–3;
future of leadership ethics 30;
leaders' moral standards 24–5; and
leadership definitions 20–1;
leadership and personal ethics 110;
negative connotations 98; and
normative theories of leadership
27–30; responsible leadership and
124–5; treatment in leadership
studies 17–20; *see also* morality
ethos 108, 116
Excel Industries Pte. Ltd 70, 71
experience, integrity and 101
experiential learning 49; Ulysses
programme 219–24
Eziba Inc. 82

Fastow, Andrew 33, 34
fear, leading through 109–10
Federal Sentencing Guidelines 105
feelings: and character 115–16;
rhetoric and 119
followership 3, 29, 109, 110
formal reasoning 58
Frank, Hans-Jürgen 220

Friedman, Milton 74, 155, 167

Galvin, Bob 80
Garvey-Williams, Lisa 219, 220, 221
Gates Foundation 206
Georgia-Pacific (GP) 208
Ghandi, M. 151
gift-giving 140–1
globalization 122–3, 213; Ulysses
global leadership development
programme 213, 215–25
GLOBE Leadership Studies 124, 131
goals: agreement on leadership goals
109; analysis of 58
Golden Rule 26, 76
Goleman, David 151
Goodpaster, Kenneth 189
GP (Georgia-Pacific) 208
Graphtex Inc. 79
'great man' leadership theories 2, 41,
124
Greenleaf, Robert K. 29, 29–30, 45,
77, 111, 149
Greenpeace 160, 162–3
Grundfos 69–70, 70–1, 81
Guimaraes, Ricardo 179

habits 112, 113–14; and virtue 114–15
happiness 37–8
hardwiring 12, 231–33
Harman, Willis 90
harms and wrongs 64
heart quality 151
HEB 204–5
Heron model 219
Hesse, Herman: *Journey to the East*
(1956) 29, 45
Hilti AG 131
HIV/AIDS 224
Hofstede, G. 127
holistic approach: to leadership 34, **35**;
to responsibility 75–6
Hollander, E.P. 23
human dignity 196
humanist perspective on responsibility
75
humanness 149

I-dentity 86, 90
ideals 149–50
image campaigns 164
inner path, to responsible leadership
149–52
instinct and moral judgement 55

instrumental perspective on
    responsibility 74–5, 89–90
integrity 1, 95–6, 142; actions and 42;
    and business relations 105–6; can it
    be taught? 105; challenges to values
    and 102–4; contrasting views of
    96–9; culture 47; four dimensions of
    99–101; maintaining 105; and
    responsibility 75; special uses of
    101–2; virtue expressed as 112
interests and rights 64
internal business processes 143;
    pressures of and responsibility 82–4;
    versus shareholders dilemma 145–7,
    145; versus society dilemma 144–5,
    144
internationalization 122–3
interpersonal relationships: and
    intrapersonal dialogue 125;
    relational values 38

Japan 196–7
Jensen, Niels Due 69, 70–1, 81
Johnson & Johnson (J&J) 48, 145–6
Journey to the East (Hesse) 29, 45

Kaku, Ryazaburo 191
Kets de Vries, M. 150
Khan, H.I. 150
Kolind, Lars 83–4
Kyosei 191, 197

La Nación (Argentinean newspaper)
    205
leaders: character 103, 108;
    competences 228, 229; as a humane
    person 149; influence of individual
    179; made not born 48–9; moral
    standards of 24–5, 42–4; roles and
    responsibilities 44–8; values of 42,
    125, 187–8
leadership challenges 11, 33, 34–42
leadership: conceptions of 123–7, **126**;
    definitions of 20–1, 40, 109–11;
    definitions of responsible 1–2, 34,
    139–40; impact of family upbringing
    on 178; management versus 187
leadership: context, situation 2, 23, 35
leadership development 49; Ulysses
    programme 215–25
leadership research *see* research
leading/leadership across cultures 7,
    122–37, 192
learning 108; experiential 49, 219–20;

of integrity 105
Levi Strauss 43–4
Locke, Edwin 25

Maitra, Ashoke 86–7
Malampaya Deep Water Gas-to-Power
    Project, Philippines 241, 244
management: and leadership 1, 187;
    supporting principles 188–9
Mandela, N. 151
Maslow, A.H. 157
materialist values 157
media, reputation and 161–2, **161, 162**
Merck 205–6
Merriam, Dena 84–5
Michigan studies 22
Mill, John Stuart 23
modal values 28
Monterrey Food Bank 205
moral awareness 43
moral imagination 43–4
moral influence 110
moral insight 55–7
moral muteness 60
morality: integrity and 98–9, 99, 101,
    104; leader as a moral person 42–4;
    of leaders 17; moral sense and 97;
    moral standards for leaders 24–5;
    'transforming leadership' theory and
    28; *see also* ethics
motivation: fear and love as motivators
    110; importance of motives 202;
    motivational aspect of integrity 100
Motorola 80
multicultural work context 36–7,
    122–3, 127–8, 139–40; PwC
    214–15, 216, 218, 222, 225; *see also*
    cultures

Natura 208
Nature Conservancy, The (TNC) 208
networks: PwC Ulysses programme
    223–4; sustainable development at
    Shell 239–40
Ninjo 196, 197
NOCIL 86
non-profit organizations: partnerships
    with 203–4; *see also* social purpose
    partnerships
normative analysis 58
normative theories of leadership:
    servant leadership 29–30;
    transforming leadership 27–9
Nunes, Flammarion Josué 178

Ohio studies 22
Ollé, Ramon 81
organizations *see* corporations; non-profit organizations
Oticon 83–4

Paine, L.S. 99
partnering 203; *see also* social purpose partnerships
Patagonia 158
pathos 108, 116
people: ethical analysis of effect of actions on 59; main asset of an organization 142–3
personality, art of 150–1
persuasion 108, 118–19
philanthropy, corporate 202, 203, 209–10
Philip Morris 63, 168
Philips, Frederik 185
Pinto, Maria Luiza 176
Plato: on leadership 26, 41; on rhetoric 118
Porter, M. 155
Posadas Amazonas 209
post-materialist values 157
power: mode of ethical analysis 59–60
pragmatic analysis 57–8
PricewaterhouseCoopers (PwC) 213, 214–15; Ulysses programme 215–25
principles 43; and addressing other interests 189–91; CRT *Principles of Business* 186, 199–200; culture and response to 191–7, **193–4**, **195**; and ethical analysis 58–9; implementation of 188–9; integrity and 99–100, 101; and leadership 186–7; need for 187–8; senior management and 197–8; statements of business principles 56; *see also* values
product differentiation 158–9
production (*poieisis*) 120
Project Better World (PBW) 242
prudence 120
purpose: mode of ethical analysis 57–8
PwC *see* PricewaterhouseCoopers

quality movement, USA 189
questions and moral insight 56–7

Rain Forest Expeditions 208–9
Raman, Ananth 78–9
rational perspective on responsibility

74–5, 89–90
Rawls, John 96–7
reason 117
reflective practitioners 43
regulation, of industry 164–5
relational intelligence 152
relationships 34; centre of leadership 39–42, 50, 109; importance of 39; leadership as a moral relationship 110; relational values 38
religion: Caux Round Table principles and 191–2, 192, **193–4**, 196–7; 'concern for others' in different religions 192, **195**; and holistic approach 76; spirituality and 78
reputation management 160–3, **161**, **162**
research 1, 123–4; and definition of leadership 20–1; into effectiveness of leaders 22–3; treatment of ethics 17–20; *see also* theories of leadership
responsibility: corporate 72–3; definitions 72; leadership theories dealing with 124–5; obstacles to being responsible 79–89; perspectives on 73–9; spiritual basis for 70–2
responsible leadership 1, 3; core dimensions of 34, **35**; definitions of 1–2, 34, 139–40; developing 49; inner path to 149–52; roles of responsible leaders 44–8
rhetoric 108; as the art of leadership 117–19, **118**
rights and interests 64
river blindness, partnership to combat 205–6
Rivlin, A. 103
Rockefeller, Stephen 90
Roddick, Dame Anita 47–8, 88–9
Rost, Joseph 20, 40, 109
Royal Dutch Shell 160–1; *see also* Shell
rules, modified 140–1

Sarbanes-Oxley Act 105, 123
SD *see* sustainable development
self-discipline 44
self-governance 99
self-interest 25–7, 86
self-knowledge 44, 149–50
self-regulation, industry 164–5
servant leadership 29–30, 45, 110, 111
shareholders 87, 143–4; dilemma of internal organization versus 145–7,

145; values 165–6; versus society
dilemma 147–8, **147**
Shell 243–4; Brent Spar issue 160,
162–3; leadership competences
defined by 228; and sustainable
development (SD) 229–43
Shroff, K.C. 70, 71
Skilling, Jeffrey 33, 34
Soapworks 88
social purpose partnerships: emerging
paradigms 203–4, **204**; leadership
challenges of 209–11; reasons for
202–3; strategic alignment and
fusing core competencies 207–9; as a
transformative force 211; values-
driven collaborations 204–7; *see also*
Ulysses programme
social responsibility 72, 155, 166–7;
and competitive positioning 158–60,
159; Fabio Barbosa on 173;
industry-wide 163–5, **164**; and
reputation management 160–3, **161**,
162; and shareholder values 165–6;
value-based environment 156–8, **156**
society: an external stakeholder 143;
corporations responsibilities to 84–5;
leadership challenges in a
stakeholder society 34–9;
shareholders versus dilemma 147–8,
147; social dimension of integrity
100–1; societal values 37; versus
internal goals dilemma 144–5, **144**
Socrates 56
softwiring 12, 232–234
Solomon, Robert C. 41, 111
spirituality 68–9; spiritual-based
leaders and obstacles to being
responsible 80–9; spiritual-based
perspective on responsibility 76–9,
90–1; two companies and 69–72
stakeholder analysis 59, 67
stakeholder theory of the firm 76
stakeholders 3, 138; multiple
stakeholder dilemmas 142–8, **143**;
pressures from external 84–6;
relationships with 36–7, 39–41;
servant leaders and 45
Starbucks 207–8
stewardship 45–6, 110–11
stories, use of 47–8
strategic management: competitive
positioning 158–60, **159**; industry-
wide 163–5, **164**; reputation
management 160–3, **161**, **162**; and

shareholder values 165–6; and social
purpose partnering 207–9; social
responsibility and 155–6, 166–7;
value-based environment 156–8
studies *see* research
subcultures 128
Suez Lyonnaise des Eaux 147–8
sustainable development (SD) 80–1,
227, 229; assessing SD learning
impact 242–3; banks and 172–3;
benefits of SD-thinking 229–30;
emergence of sustainable
development paradigm 230–3;
leadership for 240–2; role of SD
learning 233–40, **234**, **235–6**; social
purpose undertakings and 202–3,
207–8

Taylor, Frederick 74
teleology and ethics 23
theories of leadership 2, 18, 123–4;
dynamic model of leading
responsibly 124–32, **126**, **129**;
normative 27–30; *see also* research
Timberland 206–7
time: and integrity 100; and
responsibility 80–1
TNC (The Nature Conservancy) 208
transactional leadership 28
transformational leadership 29, 48,
124
transforming leadership 27–9;
collaborations and 211
Transparency International 95
triple bottom line reporting 76
Trompenaars, F. 127, 131
trust: challenge of building 36; ethical
leaders and 111

Ulysses programme, PwC 213, 215–16,
225; background to 214–16; factors
for success 224–5; functions and
objectives 217–18; learning
philosophy 219–20; phases of
programme 220–4
utilitarianism 202

values: challenges to integrity and 102,
102–4; cost–benefit analysis and
63–4; different values and their
implications 37–9, **38**; dilemma
reconciliation and 140–2; end-values
28; integrity and 99–100, 101; of
leaders 1, 42, 125, 187–8; modal 28;

in multiple culture settings 130; religion and 191; and strategic management 158–66; value-based environment 156–8, **156**; value-based leadership 125, 218; values-driven collaborations 204–7; *see also* principles
values: post-materialist, emancipative 157
Varela, Francisco J. 151
virtue 112; Aristotle on 43, 108;

dynamics of 112–17, **116**; ethics 23; integrity and virtues 96–7

wealth: capital accounts and 190; creation cycle 146, **146**; creation and destruction 141; maximization and responsibility 87–9
Weber, Max 192
World Business Council for Sustainable Development (WBCSD) 239, 244
wrongs and harms 64

eBooks – at www.eBookstore.tandf.co.uk

A library at your fingertips!

eBooks are electronic versions of printed books. You can store them on your PC/laptop or browse them online.

They have advantages for anyone needing rapid access to a wide variety of published, copyright information.

eBooks can help your research by enabling you to bookmark chapters, annotate text and use instant searches to find specific words or phrases. Several eBook files would fit on even a small laptop or PDA.

NEW: Save money by eSubscribing: cheap, online access to any eBook for as long as you need it.

Annual subscription packages

We now offer special low-cost bulk subscriptions to packages of eBooks in certain subject areas. These are available to libraries or to individuals.

For more information please contact webmaster.ebooks@tandf.co.uk

We're continually developing the eBook concept, so keep up to date by visiting the website.

www.eBookstore.tandf.co.uk